As a Dog Thinketh

AS A DOG THINKETH

Daily Words of Wisdom for Dog People

MONIQUE ANSTEE

TOUCHWOOD
EDITIONS

The information in this book is true and complete to the best of the author's knowledge,
although it may contain errors, omissions, or inaccuracies. All recommendations in
this book are made without guarantee on the part of the author or the publisher, and
neither the publisher or the author are liable or responsible to any individual or entity
for any loss or damages incurred or alleged based on the information presented herein.

Editing by Claire Philipson
Cover design by Tree Abraham
Interior design by Colin Parks

LIBRARY AND ARCHIVES CANADA CATALOGUING IN PUBLICATION

Anstee, Monique, author
As a dog thinketh / Monique Anstee.
Includes index.

Issued in print and electronic formats.
ISBN 978-1-77151-237-4 (softcover)

1. Dogs—Training. I. Title.

SF431.A57 2017   636.7'0887
C2017-902963-0
C2017-902964-9

We acknowledge the financial support of the Government of Canada through the Canada
Book Fund and the province of British Columbia through the Book Publishing Tax Credit.

Canadä

The interior pages of this book have been printed on 100% post-consumer recycled
paper, processed chlorine free, and printed with vegetable-based inks.

PRINTED IN CANADA AT FRIESENS

22 21 20 19 18   2 3 4 5

ACKNOWLEDGEMENTS

Thirteen years ago I was a good dog trainer. I'd accomplished things with some challenging dogs, and decided to venture into the sport of IPO, formerly called Schutzhund, with my Tervuren, Basil.

Since that time, I've become a wiser person. A kinder person. And I have developed a much greater understanding of both dogs and humans—and of myself—all because of two people.

Almost all of the ideas in this book, and certainly most of the thoughts in my head, are sparked from my many conversations and learnings from these dear people. They gave so generously of their time, knowledge, and friendship to help me and my husband, Brian, learn and grow.

This book wouldn't have been possible without their mentorship. Thank you so much, M and C.

INTRODUCTION

As we all know, there is a big difference between being educated and being a good person. Of course, all parents aim to make sure their children are both educated and good, but people can certainly be educated without being nice or good. And likewise, people can be nice or good without being educated. The same applies to our dogs. They can know the exercises, like sit and down, thus being well-educated, but will happily bite you if you interfere with their agenda, making them not nice.

Obedience training was created to make our dogs nice people, with the added bonus of having obedience at the end. As time passed, training got more sophisticated. Kinder. Smarter. More fun for all involved. People get the end result, kind of, yet still struggle with their dogs.

Right now where I live, dog attacks and bites have majorly increased, and my location is not the only one. Yet people are invested in training their dogs, and there is more information to be shared. So what is happening?

I believe we are no longer using these learning opportunities to create character and teach life skills. We are failing to make our dogs nice and a pleasure to live with. Dogs can sit and stay, but struggle in daily life with a myriad of issues, such as reactivity and anxiety, and this has almost become the norm. There is a gap between getting our obedience exercises and having a well-balanced dog that is not only a good person, but enjoys his days and his life. This book explains the gap and will teach you how to get both. It's like 365 days of parenting tips, but instead of human children, it's for dogs.

As any parent knows, no two children are alike. You cannot parent them the same, talk to them the same, reward them the same, or even have the same expectations of them. Dog owners know this, too. While you might need to be very serious and focused with one dog, for another you might need to loosen the dog up and get him smiling. And what you did to raise your first perfect child, who never got into trouble, might be disastrous for your second. You can't raise two kids the same way, and you can't train two dogs the same way either. But you need to be able to read the dog to tell the difference.

A fearful little Chihuahua cowering at the back of my class is not going to learn the same as the German Shepherd Dog trying to eat through my knuckles to get at some treats. The first is too scared to process my request. Teaching him to sit while terrified is going to make him dread sitting. The second hasn't even heard my request because his brain is processing how to get the cookie out of my hand. This dog needs to learn patience, and to listen to me, to get what he wants. Each dog has unique learning needs, and you must learn to recognize them.

To add another layer of complexity, every dog changes! Training a dog is like peeling the layers of an onion. What you desperately need on week one might be totally wrong in week two. My Chihuahua, mentioned above, needed to get cheekier and naughtier so he could sit on his own. But because the fear is there, if I only build bravery, I will turn him into a little itty-bitty tiger. New confidence on top of deep-rooted doubt creates a bully. This type of guy will learn to take cheap shots at dogs and people once they turn away from him. So yes, he needs bravery. He needs to learn to sit on his own like a big boy. But, in addition to that, he needs to learn to never approach people from behind, and he needs to be told that he is being naughty the first time he tries it. Once he is brave enough, calling him on his naughty thoughts and telling him he was a turd will actually make him stronger. Dogs need some stress in order to grow stronger.

This is stuff that we all know in our human relationships. I know when I can push my friends and give them an encouraging boot, but I also know when I need to give them a hug and tell them it is okay. I know when to gently tell them they were being rude, and I also know when to tell them that they crossed a line. Communication is key. It must be the same with our dogs. Do you know when you can push your dog and demand more effort? And when to back off and reward for just a tiny bit less?

This book explains training methods where no hard and fast rules exist. It's all about relationships. It's about trust, understanding, and being a good coach and role model. And teaching obedience.

ABOUT MY DOGS

You'll notice that I refer to several of my dogs throughout. Each dog teaches me something. Hilda was my darling, scrappy Irish Terrier, in her first dog fight at seven weeks old. While that should have been a warning bell, I took it as a challenge! Sadly, scrappy Hilda recently died at age sixteen. She was a cool dog that helped me work with my reactive clients (dogs, not human!). For someone who was so intolerant of the tiniest slight from another dog, she had the patience of a saint when it came to reteaching a dog social skills.

Basil is mentioned throughout. He is my Tervuren, now fourteen and hanging in there for me. Basil is well-accomplished in the competition world, and took me to Crufts to compete in my very first international adventure. He opened my eyes to things much greater than I had previously dreamed. And he reinforced that nothing is impossible so long as you can think outside of the box, and are willing to work extra hard.

Mandy was my Italian Greyhound. We had many adventures together and I loved her with every cell in my body. The feeling was not mutual and she considered me her servant. She became an Obedience Trial Champion, and also won some impressive competitions. We also failed way more, but being successful with an Italian Greyhound requires one to be forgetful and forgiving. When Mandy left this earth, the grief was overwhelming and was present every single day for a full year. I don't think it went away until Pippa politely wormed her way into my heart.

Pippa is my perfect, darling Border Collie. I know she isn't nearly as perfect as I think she is, but I don't care, nor do I want to be confused by the facts! She is the first sheep-herding dog I've had. And as many challenges as she has given me, every one of them has been enjoyable. She's easy to live with, easy to love, and I'm smitten. She understands me. She's brilliant at helping me with reactive dogs. And I trust her.

Kate, my second Border Collie, is new to my house. She came with a myriad of behaviour problems and, as we later realized, health problems too. She's a different dog now, but she will always be a skank—a much-loved, endearing skank. While Pippa pretends to love me (either to make my husband jealous or get into my pockets when I'm vulnerable and unaware), Kate is so much more genuine. She wears her heart on her sleeve, is clear with how she is feeling, and is this shy, quiet little thing, with perfect manners and her soft little voice, yet she reminds me of Stephen King's *Carrie*! We all know not to mess with Kate and her polite ways, or we must face her evil consequences. This is all fine and good, but sweet little Kate is living in a house full of blind, deaf geriatrics who cannot hear or see her clear rules.

Reggie appears in many of these pages, though I believe he remains unnamed in most. He is my seven-year-old German Shepherd. Reggie is a magnificent dog. He believes in right and wrong. He has a cruel sense of humour, which fortunately is mellowing with age. He's proud and demands to be treated with respect. And he's taken me to two world championships so far. He's introduced me to new mentors, has cemented old ones as dear friends, and has taken me on adventures far and wide. He's taught me to be so much clearer in my requests and not to let the small details slide. He has forced me to think more clearly, and demanded that I learn how to be calm. Next to Mandy, he has taught me more about myself than anyone else in my life. He is my partner. And he knows it.

These are the main characters featured throughout these pages. None of my dogs are perfect, but they are perfect for me. They are my teachers, my mentors, and share my daily journey, the same as I do theirs. I am a dog trainer because of them. They help me every single day in my work. They have made me. And from their lessons, and the people they introduced me to, came this book.

ABOUT THIS BOOK

I live in a small community where businesses are made or broken by word of mouth. Years ago, a few people targeted me because we had different philosophies about dog training. They used social media to spread the word about how awful my training was, so I decided I could do a better job of describing my training methods myself. Thus my daily Facebook posts began. As my keyboard got warmed up, their attacks slowed down.

My honesty and passion showed in my writing, which helped the right type of clients find me. Posting on social media also meant that people from much farther away than my little community could learn how to understand their dogs better. Long after the gossip stopped, I continued writing. I started to tackle more and more obscure concepts and put them into words for my clients to understand in my daily Facebook posts. I've built a wonderful community there—a community for which I'm grateful.

This book is a collection of those daily insights and thoughts, which I shared after working with clients and their dogs, or my own thoughts and reflections as I continue to grow and learn as a trainer. It is the growth I witnessed or experienced working with different dogs with different personalities and different problems, and this is what it looked like as it happened.

JANUARY

January 1

Why dogs misbehave

There could be several reasons why your dog is misbehaving. Here are some of them:

LACK OF UNDERSTANDING

Some of our communication is so unclear that it is a miracle that dogs are able to meet any of our requests! Sometimes our dogs simply have no clue what we want of them. And generally we keep asking the same thing, only with a louder voice and more forceful actions, not realizing that the explanation needs to be delivered in a different way.

LACK OF MOTIVATION

The dog is not motivated to do what you are asking. Lack of motivation can come from a variety of reasons. I like to pick on clients being boring. Some owners are just incredibly dull, and they suppress their dogs from being dogs. They have too many rules. Because of the constant rules, when the dogs finally get a taste of freedom, they will lose all control, as there is no way that you can compare with a running rabbit or great dog game. Please remember that the entire purpose of giving rules is to give freedom.

Your dog may not be motivated because her rewards are predictable and always present. If you ask your dog to come ten times, and each of the ten times she gets a piece of cheese, it won't take her long to realize the food is always there, so skipping an occasion to chase a rabbit won't kill her. But if the food is only sometimes there (variable reinforcement schedule) then she has a reason to find out if maybe this time she will get something. We want to turn our dogs into little gamblers.

In addition to this, our rewards themselves are sometimes dull. Cheese? Every time? Nothing is good every time. How about having boring kibble, some cheese, a few pieces of hot dog, and three meatballs in your pocket? If the first reward is kibble, the second is a meatball, the third nothing, fourth nothing, and the fifth a hot dog—wait and watch the speed of your motivated dog. Keep them guessing!

Now, while this sounds like way too much work, it isn't. All it means is on treat-cutting days, you have seven zip lock bags, and you put some of each in each bag. Toss the bags into your freezer, and grab a bag for each training session.

For all of you diligent treat-preparers, once in a while pull your zip lock out of your freezer, have it on you, and don't dispense one single treat. Teach them that while the food might always be there, it doesn't mean that receiving will always happen.

Feeding treats should not be an expectation your dog has of you. It is a reward given only when deserved. Second commands never get fed. Mediocrity does not get fed. Only brilliance does. And brilliance means they should be ten times better than last training day!

LACK OF RESPECT

Quite simply, your dog does not respect you. Would you take advice from someone you think is an idiot? Well, neither will your dog. Respect is a beautiful thing that will only be given when earned.

Your dog must care what you think before he actually chooses to follow your instructions. So many of the dogs I see are coddled spoiled brats, and the saddest part is that they are unhappy.

Your dog deserves to be happy. He deserves to have rules and boundaries so that he can carry out his responsibilities well. Don't become a Pez dispenser for treats in an attempt to fake respect. When your treats run out, so does your dog's interest in you. This really is not the dog's fault but your own.

RELATIONSHIP PROBLEM

Sure, some dogs come with baggage. But more often, these dogs have handlers who still carry their dog's perceived baggage, even though the dog has long since let it go. Sometimes, for example, your Labrador Retriever puppy is constantly measured against your thirteen-year-old Labrador who just died. It's easy to forget how naughty the thirteen-year-old was when he was ten months old.

To have a healthy relationship with a dog means you must be worthy. Build your dog's strengths, decrease his weaknesses, and become his fearless coach, showing him how life should be lived.

January 2

The reason I train dogs

Whatever endeavour I take on, I usually lose interest once I've mastered the skill. Fortunately for me, when it comes to training dogs, that's impossible.

We can never know it all. And there is nothing simple about dog training.

To get the most out of any individual in a relationship takes thought, work, and then more thought. Recently, after many lengthy conversations with a mentor, followed by work, thought, and some more thought, I worked out something profound about my new puppy.

This is the case with every dog that enters my house. Each one has asked me a question that I have not known the answer to. Then their growth and my growth combined results in us finding that answer together. Training is a relationship where you both learn to understand each other's needs and complexities, and then you work out how you can help them be the best dog they can be.

In the case of my puppy, I had to find out the answer to the question that she wasn't asking, and it took hours to work out what that question was. The answer was simple. She was the kid in class that would never put her hand up to answer a question because she hated to be wrong. She knew the answer, but she'd never take the risk because in her head being wrong was forbidden.

My job was to teach her that being wrong is just fine. But you must have the gumption to commit to an answer—even if it is the wrong one.

I'm sure this is something that all good parents have become masters at. And it is something that all good dog trainers strive to master.

January 3
The secret to being the best

We all want a winning performance, and from watching my teachers I have learned their secrets. Work harder than everyone else. Never give up. Always commit fully. Finally, always question what you are doing to see if there is a better way.

January 4
Through the eyes of a puppy

Having a puppy means there is a whole world to be seen: daisies that need their heads bitten off; tree branches that need to be tasted and swung from; pine cones that must be picked up and played with; logs that must be walked on and fallen off; and shells that need to be picked up, crunched, and treasured.

The best shells and sticks must always be pointed out to distract away from poo, slugs, clumps of mud, and other things that also go down the gullet.

There is a whole world full of people, sensations, and scary distractions that must be seen.

There is nothing more fun than re-exploring the world with a young puppy. Go enjoy our glorious world as it is shown to us by our dogs. When were you last excited to see a pine cone? When did you last point out a crab shell to your dog on a treasure hunt?

Through the eyes of our young puppies (or children), we can find beauty and excitement in all the things we have become blind to. Go get out there, and enjoy their treasure hunt with them.

January 5

Don't be a Pez dispenser

When training with food or toys, always make sure that your dog is working to please *you*, and *then* dispense the reward. You must have that personal connection, and make sure to use your voice to let your dog know how brilliant he is.

Your voice needs to show pride and excitement—please don't shriek loudly with lots of volume. This does not demonstrate pride!

We want to use our voice and build up pride in our dog, so that he is happy with what he did. And he learns to like it when we are happy too. Without doing this seemingly unimportant piece, you can quickly turn yourself into a magical Pez dispenser or ball-shooter that entertains your dog. You don't want a dog who is only working for what he can get for himself. There is nothing worse than a self-absorbed dog.

Take that one moment to connect with them immediately before you reward—this minor difference will transform your training by keeping you in the reward loop, rather than just being a dispensing machine. This will help keep your relationship where it needs to be.

January 6

Dogs give us exams

Every dog you get will give you exams. If you answer the questions wrong, and don't end up passing with that dog, you will be repeating the lesson with your next dog.

It took me about four dogs until I passed the exam on handling dog aggression. Other lessons have included learning to be fun and stupid, learning to expect more and not reward just because they are there, and how to be calm and clear.

Learn to enjoy the exams as they get thrown at you. They are coming whether you want them or not, so you might as well embrace the process and enjoy your mandatory learning.

Just remember, we are not training dogs, we are working on ourselves.

January 7

Double your trouble?

If your first dog has bad habits that come from fear or uncertainly, or that are highly reinforcing, odds are your next dog will learn them from him. If you have a dog with separation anxiety, your new dog will quickly learn it too. Or if your first dog is scared of dogs and overreacts, your second will too.

So, if you struggle managing one dog, managing two will be even harder. Doubling a problem just isn't fun, or sensible.

Make life easier for yourself—address your first dog's issues before you get a second dog.

January 8

In your mind's eye

Performance and self-image are always connected. You will only do as well as you expect to do. What you imagine is what you are going to get. You will never do better than what you expect from yourself, though it is possible to do worse! You hold the key to your success.

You can only have one type of thought at a time—positive thoughts or negative thoughts—and that shapes your consciousness.

Whatever you think is what you will picture, and that is what your body language and energy will get for you. You can imagine your dog coming back perfectly, as he does in training, or you can imagine him completely ignoring you and playing with another dog.

If you imagine the latter, this will show in your voice, your energy, and your body language when you call him back. If you think he won't come back, you are right—he most likely won't. But if you believe he will—at least you are doing your part of the bargain in making that happen.

Take action by controlling what you picture. If you feel a negative thought coming on, shove it away, and picture what you *want* to happen.

January 9

No one likes a nag

Are you a nagging mother with your dog? No one likes to be nagged at, your dog included.

If you've said the same thing more than three times in a row, you might be guilty. It is time to aim for clear communication, so that you are no longer constantly chipping away at your relationship with your dog (which nagging inherently does).

You owe it to your dog to be clear and to quit harping on her. Once she understands what you want, both of you can have fun again.

January 10

From gulping to giving: Retraining resource guarding

As a child, I used to go to the beach and find shells. Or pebbles. Or whatever. When I was successful in my hunt, I would show my prize to my parents, and they always admired it.

I just got a puppy. This little puppy did not have the same experience. Every treasure that she found was taken away from her. What she learned was to be apathetic to her environment because any action would get her into trouble. But if she had something that was worth the risk of taking, she would guard it or gulp it. And she learned: do not trust humans with your treasures. Actually, just don't trust humans, period. Or dogs.

Young babies are so mouldable. She quickly learned that I would go treasure hunting with her and point out "non-killing" items. She ate a variety of chunks of crab shell, disgusting fish bits, pine cones, goose poo, and other equally unappealing items. And in the process, learned that I was her partner in the hunt. I would find it; she would eat it. Eventually the sheer abundance of treasures changed from eating, to carrying. And in the process, she learned to trust me both as a person and with her treasure items.

We then progressed to high-value items, such as chewies, and she learned she was safe with them. No one in this house would take them. There was no need to hide with her treasures. She could eat them in the open.

The second step was to work around food-filled zip lock bags, or bait pouches, that she found. These went in the mouth all the way to the back of her throat, and her eyes went glassy as her mind said,

"Make me give it up." I wiggled a hole into the plastic bag, pulled out a cookie and put it onto the floor for her. She then let go of her prize and I continued to wiggle cookies out of the bag while she supervised me and ate her find. It only took two finds of food bags and she was willingly giving them to me for help.

Another young dude tried to gobble a paper towel. Once he had his item, his eyes said, "I dare you to take it." I tried feeding him bits of it, and he did relax, but then he switched back and got too intense eating his little pieces of towel, so I went to plan B. As he went to grab it, I allowed him to have it all, just as he wished. On my terms. I held his mouth closed, while I kissed his velvety nose and asked how it tasted, then took it out. He grabbed it again, so he got to have it again, all of it jammed in there, with his mouth held closed. This continued until he decided that it really was not fun to grab it on my terms. The paper towel stayed within grabbing distance, and he decided to leave it alone.

Don't fight your dogs on fights you cannot win. In these cases, the dogs learned to be dishonest and to gobble and run before they could get caught. To retrain one, she learned that she was allowed items, and no longer felt the need to behave that way. To retrain the other, who was older and had a more established gobbling habit, he was still allowed to have his items, but in a way that wasn't fun and that I controlled.

Please let your puppies be puppies. Let them go treasure hunting, make daisy chains, and explore the world, just as we did when we were children. If it won't kill them, groan and grimace, and look the other way. They are, after all, dogs.

Allow them to play in mud, eat goose poo, dig holes, find treasures, and gallop in fast crazy circles, just as a puppy should. Let's let our children be children as we teach them how life will be. They have their whole lives to be refined adults.

But also get creative in stopping behaviour that cannot continue. In the case of established behaviours, if your dog is doing something that you don't want him to do, help him to do it on your terms. This idea is not mine, but belongs to the brilliant Sylvia Bishop. It has gotten me through almost all pet dog training and domestics.

And if you don't like the behaviour of puppies, get an adult dog.

January 11
Not all information is right

Training puppies can be so challenging. Keen new owners read as much as they possibly can and absorb so much information, much of it wrong.

Wrong? Why?

I just had a puppy at my house. She was the sweetest, kindest, most lovable soul. Despite her rough beginning, she loved people. She loved all people. It was the sweetest thing to see, and made her one of the nicest puppies I've had in my home in quite some time.

But if her new family were to educate themselves on the internet, they would learn to socialize her and to get strangers to ask her to sit for cookies. For this dog, this is the absolutely wrong thing to do.

Her love for people is already so strong that her new family's job is to teach her that they are the best in the world, and other people are unimportant. If they follow the normal training logic that they are taught on the internet, they will turn her into a dog that will drag them in front of a bus to greet a stranger on the other side of the road. With her, I would be extremely cautious about how many people greet her. Asking her to come when called will be an issue. Walking past people will be an issue. Being examined by a vet will be an issue. She'll just become really annoying, always wanting to run to a new person, never sticking with her family.

Be careful what you read. Make sure it caters to your puppy. All information is good. Sometimes. But when it does not cater to the individual puppy, read with caution and think about how this will benefit or harm your individual puppy.

January 12

Disappear once in a while

When teaching a new dog to be responsible for knowing where I am on walks, I will often hide on them. This involves booking it behind a tree, or running down the opposite path at a T-junction on a hike. If you are in a big open field (especially in the summer), just lie down in the grass when they are distracted. As soon as you are flat, they won't see you.

Make them work to find you, and celebrate when they get there. Today Pippa was just feet away from me and was still unable to find me. I watched her facial expressions as she tried to work out where I was, and trying to keep from laughing was really difficult.

Disappearing will teach your dog to check and see where you are every five to ten seconds (a quick look over their shoulder as they do their thing). It is an invaluable lesson to teach, because it makes keeping an eye on you their job. They need to know where you are, or you might just disappear.

January 13

Failure is an important part of learning

I mountain bike with my dogs over some rather crazy terrain. My mountain biking skills started out as intermediate, and daily, stumble after stumble, they improved.

There are certain challenges on my daily trails that I have yet to master. There is a tree root as I'm going up a hill that I cannot get over with enough momentum to continue on up the hill. I continue to try, but have yet to succeed. On some days, I show improvement; on other days, I suck. On the days I show improvement, I fail better than I failed it the day before. One day I'm going to get it.

It made me realize many of our accomplishments in life are learned from continuous failure. We fail, rethink, try again, then fail with more glamour, rethink, try again. Eventually one day we suddenly find the magic of how to succeed. Or not. But the hope is always there that one day we will find it.

Training dogs is much the same. Yet I see so many who consider their failures their own personal shortcomings, and use this as a measuring stick to determine their own self-worth. The only difference in mountain biking and training dogs is the lack of emotion attached to riding a bike, at least for me. No one cares if I fall each time I try to get my bike up that hill, over that tree root, and continue on. But people might care if my dog lunges at theirs, or grumbles under her breath, or doesn't come back when called—or do they? Maybe only *we* care.

I live my life by Wayne Dyer's words: "Your opinion of me is none of my business." And as I struggle on my mountain bike, or with a dog, I continue to look for improvements, rethink, then try again. Failures are not black marks on my self-worth—at least I try to keep it that way. They are opportunities to rethink, analyze, and try again. Failures test our determination, how bad we really want to achieve our goals, and how much we are willing to put ourselves out there to learn the new skills that we want.

I don't feel the need to apologize to anyone every time I fall off my bike, which is embarrassingly often. But it wouldn't be if I stopped trying to negotiate steep hills filled with tree roots and rocks. I only fail because I push myself to be better. As soon as I master one challenge, I'm determined to get the next one, so my riding is never good enough.

And dog training is the same for me. And this is how I live my life with the things I care about.

Everything that is worthy of achieving is difficult. The process of growth will highlight your failures and shortcomings. And it is how you decide to deal with that failure that helps you to grow, or keeps you stagnant.

January 14
Raising a puppy

The hardest part of raising a puppy is not to stifle them. While we want to tend to their every need and cuddle away every whimper, when we do, we stunt their emotional growth.

Our puppies need to be able to problem-solve and work out their own difficulties. We need to find the balance of when to help them, when to give them a kiss and a nurturing shove forward to work it out on their own, and when to simply protect them and keep them safe.

When raising a puppy, I use what they offer to build their confidence. Right now I am spending lots of time with Wee Willy, an adorable Staffordshire Bull Terrier. Willy, like most little boys, sometimes needs help being confident, and his strength is that he is always smiling and ready for fun. When he was scared of a tarp on the floor, I played "catch me if you can." I ran around it in circles and then slowed down so he could almost get me. Just as he was on my ankles, I took a massive leap right onto the middle of the tarp. He couldn't help it. He dove onto the tarp with me, and I fell down and let him wiggle all over me in the middle of the tarp.

I used his strength of always being ready for fun and turned the situation into a fun one for him. He totally forgot he was scared of the tarp and never even noticed it after that.

Find your puppy's emotional strength and then cater your training situations to appeal to that strength. If your puppy is silly, you can make almost any situation silly and get him to give you his heart and soul. If you have a more earnest puppy that just wants to "obey" you, then you will use your relationship and position yourself so he has to tackle the scary object to get to you. I would step onto the tarp and call him on. If I have a puppy that loves to fight, I might turn the scary thing into something that he can bite and kill. I would use my tarp like a matador and get my puppy to be the bull.

Use the strengths that your puppy naturally brings to the table to help him become a perfectly balanced dog. Training dogs this way is a whole lot of fun, for both you and your dog.

January 15

A leadership mindset

It is not our actions that make us leaders. It is the mental place from which we execute these actions.

Walking through a doorway first doesn't make you a leader. Neither does asking your dog to do something before you scratch him. And depending on your relationship, I frequently see these rules making a relationship mind-numbingly rigid. It loses all flow.

No exercise will make you a person that your dog stares at adoringly. It is only the way that you do this exercise that will get you to the goal you seek.

If you want to exude leadership, think of a strong person in your life and try to *be that person* as you open that doorway, or take your dog for a walk. Vary your posture, thinking, tone of voice, and the amount of feedback that you give your dog, based on that person's character.

If your dog responds right away, correctly, then you have found it. If you find yourself struggling, keeping trying on different masks or personas. Dogs are our merciless teachers, and they teach us how to be better people. The recipes are the method to help us change. They are to help us determine if we have the right level of presence for our dog yet. If you are struggling with your exercises, realize that you may need to try on a different persona, which can help you execute the exercise in the right way.

When you learn that new mental place, the emotion behind your actions will change.

January 16

Expectations versus rewards

When is reward not a reward? When it becomes an expectation.

For eight years in a row when my husband went to Hawaii he bought me back gifts of gold. On year nine he got me a mug. I was pissed. (I lie: he's never gotten me gold, and never gone to Hawaii, but you understand my point.)

Please consider this in your training. If you reward every single sit, once taught, your reward is no longer acting as a reward but an expectation. If you deny your reward it will be perceived as punishment by your dog.

Likewise, if your food rewards always consist of steak and liverwurst, but tonight you train with kibble, don't be surprised when your dog's effort sucks. It's because you gave him "a mug." But if you always train with both high- and low-value foods, the low-value ones are appreciated, and the high-value will have major impact.

Training with rewards is a must. But you must also be aware of any precedents or expectations that you could inadvertently be setting. Quickly move onto an intermittent or variable reinforcement schedule and keep your rewards unpredictable.

January 17

Seven lessons from a working-breed puppy

Even though we know that puppies are a lot of work, nothing can prepare us for just how much work a young puppy really is. They want to learn. They are curious. They are busy. They play hard, then sleep harder. And they have so much to learn! If you aren't exhausted at the end of the day, you might not be giving your puppy enough. Here are a few lessons I've learned from raising a working-breed puppy:

1. Puppies are always learning, even when you are sitting on the couch and not paying attention.
2. Never give your puppy the option of not listening to you, or you will spend the next year trying to get that back.
3. Remember your breed and your individual dog, consider her strengths and weaknesses. Diminish her weaknesses, and build her strengths.
4. Every action should be deliberate, and you should have backup plans just in case. In every moment with my puppy, I'm teaching life skills or work, or coaching her on something. I leave nothing to chance, and hopefully that means I will have very little to "fix" later. For example, if she is greeting a person, I make sure it goes the way I need it to go in order to have a bomb-proof dog later.
5. Dogs that are driven to work come with an inherent suicide wish. We must protect them from themselves. They will over-heat chasing a ball. They will dive off a cliff to get something that shines down below. Driven puppies will die trying to do

things that normal dogs would never consider doing. They must be very carefully supervised so that their cliff jumping, over-heating, and other suicide attempts never become successful.

6. Rock eating and woodchip eating are very dangerous behaviours that need to be changed immediately. If you have a puppy that does this, this is your first priority. Address this before he kills himself or needs stomach surgery.

7. Most important of all: never forget they are puppies. Embrace their too-tired zoomies, their sucking on your neck, their tugging on your pant legs, and their curiosity with every dandelion and daisy. They grow up much too quickly, and puppyhood is a critical stage.

January 18

We learn in layers

As we learn and grow, we often get told the same messages again and again, trainer after trainer. We will be unable to hear those words, however, until we are ready.

Dog training is somewhat like peeling an onion. We learn it layer by layer by layer, and can only comprehend the lessons from one layer deeper than where we are at. If someone starts explaining the lesson three layers deep, we will be unable to comprehend it. Gradually as we evolve, our lessons get closer and closer to the core. Very few people have gotten the whole way there.

Sometimes even though you have heard the words that are a couple of layers deep, and thought that you understood what was being said, it won't entirely click until a new trainer mentions it in a slightly different way that triggers the light bulb to illuminate.

I greatly value all of my teachers from when I first started. Even though I was unable to get some of what they said, I appreciate that they shared the knowledge with me and shared so willingly. As time passed, I remembered their words and understood what they had been trying to share.

January 19

Beyond tricks

I can teach my chickens to stand on one leg, and I've taught them how to come when called. And they eat from my hand. All of these have been taught with positive reinforcement. Come springtime, however, my rooster will attack me. With hormones and the season of breeding, he forgets all of his tricks and what he can get from me, and instead wants to protect his flock of ladies. This is fine with my rooster, as I don't have to live with him. When he is in this mood, I can avoid him or deal with him (depending upon my mood!).

I don't, however, have this luxury with my dogs. I live with them 24-7, and they need to have manners, regardless of what mood they're in.

I have worked with many disrespectful dogs that can sit fabulously, and have some very nice trained behaviours when there is food in the pocket, or the bait pouch is on. I define these as pet tricks. These same dogs will then bite their owners for wiping their feet, taking their toy away, or some other infringement on rules that the owner didn't know she had agreed on.

Make sure you are training a dog who you can live with, and then you can teach her pet tricks, too. Our pet tricks are a much-needed piece, and in no way do I mean to take away from their value or usefulness. We need them. But tricks on their own will not give you a nice dog—the same way my tricks did not give me a nice rooster.

Make your training about creating a dog who is nice to live with, and who is a good person.

January 20

Listen with your eyes

People who talk a lot are blind to body language. The way dogs talk requires us to use our eyes to hear them. However, those chatty people that are always talking never seem to be watching. The more they move their mouth, the less keenly they are able to observe.

If you are a talkative person, take a video of yourself training your dog. Simply playing the video back will give you eyes into your training session, like what a training friend would see. It will give you a chance to watch your dog's body language and see if all is as you think it is. This will allow you to listen with your eyes.

January 21

People in my life

I have many different types of people in my life. My dearest friends tell it as it is, call me on my nonsense, and, in turn, expect to be called out on their own. They are honest to themselves and to all around them. Being around these ladies is easy.

One of my other friends is very sensitive. I must be careful how I say things to her, as she can take them very personally, and take much deeper meaning from spoken words than was ever intended. She appreciates being told of the things that she does right, which are many. And her criticisms need to be gently laid out, sandwiched by compliments.

I have others with whom I must be very firm with my boundaries. I can enjoy them very much, but must be cautious of my limitations and rules. There is one who will often twist words into something that wasn't said. She means well, but will hear what she wants, not what was said. For her, my words and meaning must be very concise.

I have others in my life that I refuse to bend for. I find they take lots of energy from me and are draining, and just demand more and more from me.

I treat all of the people in my life differently. With some I am strict. I protect my boundaries, and probably say "no" more than I say "yes." With others I am open, vulnerable, honest, and would do anything for them. And with others I am guarded and reserved and won't compromise.

Training dogs is exactly the same. In fact, reread all of the above, and switch the word "people" for "dogs" and then you know how I train dogs.

Training dogs isn't just about leadership, rewards, or coaching. It isn't about any one thing. Instead it's about the dynamic relationship and communication between two individuals.

It must bend and flow depending on the dynamic of those two individuals. If one is pushy, demanding, and doesn't take "no" for an answer, you will probably find me very strict, concise, and clear in my feedback. Whereas if I am with someone who is overly critical and takes all feedback as a negative, they will get built up, told about all that they do right, how clever they are, and will leave feeling good about themselves.

Train the dog that you are training. Learn what her personality is like, and then be that person for her as you train her.

January 22

Get your kids involved

Teaching our household dogs to respect children requires work and training, in which your children need to take part. Teach your dogs to give your children space. Teach them not to snatch sandwiches out of hands that are at their eye level. And build the bond between your children and dog, letting them get into great adventures together, even if we might not fully approve of them.

Children are also fantastic little trainers; they are quicker to learn and adapt than most adults. Children also have more free time, and will gladly spend an hour a day teaching your dog tricks.

January 23

Don't deny your puppies exposure to stress

Currently, popular methods of dog training are not teaching dogs to deal with real life and all the unfortunate unavoidable events that go along with it.

I see many dogs who get whatever they want. If they do not want to do something, they do not have to. The majority of these dogs are stressed and unhappy, and they lack the ability to cope in real life moments.

Sure, we might be making their first year more fun, but we are denying them the skills that allow them to deal with change and things they don't like when they are adults. As puppies, they learn the world is a really wonderful place, only to find out as adults that it was all a lie! Bad stuff *will* happen to them. Dogs will bite them, a person may yell at them, and some procedures at the vet will not be pleasant (just as it is for us when we visit the doctor).

My young dogs are methodically taught to tolerate things that they might not like. They learn that giving in to me and accepting will make it stop. I start off with minor challenges, such as mandatory cuddling. The message is: right now I want to cuddle you, and wriggling and writhing are not the solution. Only relaxing will make it end.

As odd as this sounds, this type of stress training teaches puppies two things: first you must mentally "give" to me to get what you want, and, second, if there is a stressful moment, think your way through it rather than panicking.

As my dogs have aged through the years, there comes a point where veterinary examinations can become unpleasant, awkward, and painful. I need my dogs to trust that I will never do them wrong. I need them to be able to deal with the stress of the moment, and I need them to "give" to whatever scenario that I present.

Just like children, we owe it to dogs to teach them life skills, and dealing with stress might be the most important one that you can offer. By giving them a perfect puppyhood, you are denying them a perfect adulthood.

January 24

My rules for dog park etiquette

If a dog is on leash, do not allow your dog to approach him.

Never allow your dog to affect other dogs so that they round their bums and tuck their tails. This is a dog's way of telling you that she's afraid.

Always call your dog back when someone else requests that you call her back.

Be careful playing ball. There is no quicker way to start a dog-fight. Or wreck a dog's body.

Don't forget that the reason you are at the dog park is to enjoy time spent with your dog. Rather than standing still and chatting, walk and chat, exercising yourself as well as your dog. If something is to go wrong, it will happen when you are standing still.

On that note, if you have a challenging dog, be careful when you are picking up poo. It is during that stationary moment that they might misbehave.

January 25

Your dog is your mirror

Some days I help people with their dogs. On other days, I help dogs with their people!

More often than not, we are not training dogs. We are working on ourselves, and dogs are the mirrors that show us our flaws.

January 26

Train to please yourself

If you want to really succeed with your dog, you have to be independent of the approval of others. Your own personal approval of your performance, walk, or experience is critical, and no stranger's approval should carry any weight. Strangers don't know where you have come from, what you know, or what it is like to walk a mile in your shoes with this particular dog; therefore, their assessment cannot be accurate.

Many of us develop a thick skin and learn to ignore comments that are not constructive, but to be independent of approval also means that compliments from outsiders, while nice, do not alter your thoughts or behaviour. Both the good and the bad should not affect your inner judgement. You can critically see your moment for precisely what it was.

By all means, seek out feedback from trusted training friends; it is valuable and should be heeded. This feedback is often both honest and critical, and is always looking out for your best interests (at least mine is!). These people understand your journey and goals, and the shoes in which you have walked.

When you are able to evaluate your dog's behaviour or performance without outside opinions altering what you see, then you know you have mastered independent approval. You are now training to please yourself. There will be moments when you fail a performance, but will be thrilled with your dog because he coped with his challenges so well, and other occasions when you will win yet be unhappy with your performance.

Only once you have reached this place can you know that your motives are always based solely on what you and your dog need. You are basing your training decisions on what you want and what you need as a team, knowing where you have come from and where you need to go—not on what will please that particular judge, friend, or peer.

January 27

How do you hold your leash?

I spend a lot of time at dog parks waiting in my car for clients, and during this time, I have become a masterful observer of human behaviour. By watching how someone holds their leash as they get out of their car and walk their dog, I can define their relationship; including both fears and denial and strengths.

And if that part fails, watching how they talk to their dog will fill in any of the missing blanks.

Start watching how people walk with their leashes. After watching five people, you will know exactly what I am talking about. And hopefully by watching, it will make you more aware of how you are with your own dog when attached by a leash.

January 28

What type of dog owner are you?

There are two types of clients. Those who know their dog's issues and desperately want help, and those who are in denial about their dog's issues, and, instead, want to work on an alternate, unimportant, problem that can't be addressed until they face up to the problem they are denying.

We trainers do what we do because of the first group. Unfortunately, to the second group we are the bearers of bad news, pointing out the carefully hidden skeleton in the closet. While on some level they know they created or are maintaining their dog's issues, they have not yet realized that they *themselves* must change in order to fix the issue. As they get guided in this process it can seem like the trainer is adding salt to an already raw wound.

No behaviour can be changed with the same thinking that created it. If you want to stay in a place of comfort, realize you will be unable to retrain your current dog. To succeed you will be rudely shoved outside of your comfort zone and will find yourself treading water.

Be prepared to do the same amount of growth as you are asking from your dog. We always get the dog that we need. They are here to teach us the lessons that we need to work on in our lives. Each dog teaches me a new thing about myself, and never more than I can bear to learn. The lessons are hard to grasp and understand, but once you "get it" those skills can never be taken away.

January 29
Border Collie brains

I think I could write an entire book on Border Collies and the complexity of their brains.

Right now I have a young whippersnapper Collie here who can be rather scary at times. He is a mere five months and I am his third trainer, which says a lot. He is so sweet . . . until he isn't. Feeding him made the hair on the back of my neck go up. It wasn't that he was overly aggressive in that moment, but his energy was not good.

I began training him. I made headway and three days in I could see a difference. Until I put him into a group class. I'm not entirely sure why he had such a problem in group class. Was it because I was rewarding him with food and his resource guarding crept in? He turned into a monster. He had me shaking my head, wondering if I could turn him around and save his life.

In my despair, I changed things. He moved into my house and became one of my dogs. My two Border Collie girls turned him into their own little pet project and trained him all day long, with set lessons. Pippa and Kate taught him to not guard spaces, to give back objects when they told him, and to stay put, where they suggested. And Kate took great joy in teaching him to move away when she told him to.

Through their repeated lessons, he became a really nice dog. I must admit that I forgot how bad he had been.

And it got me to wondering. Do Border Collies require other Border Collies to raise them right? My girls were able to transform him in days into a normal five-month-old puppy who was happy and relaxed and behaved like a functional Collie.

The next day I trained him again—and undid all of their work. He was back to being a tense, weird jerk. There I was with my rewards, telling him he was clever, and he hated it. I don't know if he hated that I was controlling him, or that I had food, or that I was too nice.

If I were a gambling person, I would go with being too nice. My Border Collies were not nice to him. They were clear and fair, and turned him around in record time.

Right now, I don't know if I can train this dog for what he needs to become: a family pet. But I'm going to keep plodding along, and I am going to copy the only two trainers who have succeeded so far, Pippa and Kate, who have done a great job while all three of us humans have failed.

So maybe Border Collies, at least the challenging ones, really do need older Collies around to raise them right.

January 30

Don't hide from a training opportunity

While there are moments in which we must teach the thousand steps to success while our dog learns a behaviour, there comes a point where we must assume the lesson is learned and move on to teaching a more difficult lesson. Some dogs are happy to stay in kindergarten forever. Don't let them.

Sometimes, often, the challenges will look messy. That is your opportunity to coach your dog through if he shows effort, demand more if he lacks effort, and help if the small challenge was over his head.

Messy, ugly training, coached right, is often where the best learning occurs. Don't hide from it.

January 31

Different handlers in your household

Dogs, like children, know who they must listen to and who they can torment and ignore.

If your spouse is inconsistent with your dog, your dog will reflect that in his behaviour with your spouse. If you are consistent with your dog, your dog will reflect that in his behaviour with you, despite your spouse's inconsistencies.

Leave your spouse be. It will not affect how your dog acts with you, provided you are consistent. In fact, it will make for a much happier household, and it just might keep your marriage intact.

FEBRUARY

February 1

Acquiring dogs who don't trust

Working with a dog who doesn't trust requires time. We must be physically present, yet emotionally distant, and wait until they are ready to communicate.

When we are emotionally distant, it is easier for them. First, it means that we are not throwing ourselves on them, making us a lot less intimidating. And by doing this, we have a quieter way about us, which they appreciate. Gradually as they get to know us, we can get more exuberant, which in turn will start making them a bit more robust.

Don't force your friendship on them. You will push them away longer. Make their choices for freedom few and far between, with you as the obvious choice. This is the perfect moment for chain-link dog runs. Leave them free in there, where they are safe, and go be their rescuer by sitting quietly in a corner once they've had time to assess where they are and realize they are safe. When they come to me, I will feed them. But I will not use food to get them to come to me. There is a big, albeit subtle, difference between the two.

I don't believe in feeding dogs who are uncomfortable going forward. It teaches them to go forward and then retreat, which is what a bite will look like. And for some of them, it will build in them a dread of people; knowing the expectation is that they must go forward to take food from them. However, there are breed exceptions with this. Some breeds benefit from feeding, German Shepherds being one of them. Others don't.

If you get the right start with these untrusting dogs, it is onward and upward. Don't force the relationship—be patient, present, and wait until they are ready. It won't take long. I've had them fall for me in as short a time as four to six hours, and as long as three days for one very serious, broken bitch. The norm is 24 hours.

February 2

What is our greatest asset as trainers?

When I think of what makes the best dog trainers in the world the best, I think of their timing, their emotions, the tools they use. But that is all wrong. What makes the best trainers the very best is simply their imaginations. Their minds can see better results, they can envision how a picture can be altered and improved, made safer, made flashier, made easier to judge. Then they imagine ways to get it. They imagine things that other people are blind to.

They see how an exercise is currently done, but that visual does not block their mind to future possibilities like it does to most of us. They imagine how much better it could be. They are always thinking forward, and thinking of better training methods that can improve the execution of an exercise.

Look at your life with your dog, forget what you know, and simply imagine what you could get. Our ancestors certainly did or we wouldn't have agility, scent work, guide dogs, police dogs, obedience competitions, or any of the pursuits that we train our dogs to do.

February 3

Open-mindedness

Every trainer has something to teach. We all do things differently, or we might even do the same thing, with a slight twist, for an entirely different purpose. But even the worst dog trainer is doing many things right.

While I do not train field trials, I have learned many great things from field trial trainers. While I do not do herding, herding shaped my training of pet dogs more than any other discipline. Agility has made me so aware of my body posture and handling, particularly with reactive dogs. Obedience taught me how to teach. IPO, formerly known as Schutzhund, has taught me about building drive and mental control.

So if you are an avid dog learner, go listen to the masters of every discipline when they are in town giving seminars. They will have a whole lot to teach, even if you do not do that sport. Good dog training is simply good dog training, and what makes a person great in discipline A, will probably also make a person great in discipline B.

February 4
Raise the bar

Just because you attend a dog-training class and your dog behaves in class, it does not mean that your dog is actually trained. Does your dog walk nicely on a leash without anyone from the outside being able to see how you are getting it (meaning your handling is subtle)?

Can you handle your dog, groom your dog, and cut his toenails?

Does he lie down without any hand signals if he's heading away from you? (Meaning that he lies down on command, rather than needing all of your body language to make it happen.)

Does he come back when called, immediately, when distractions are present?

Is your dog a nice person?

These are my minimal requirements for all dogs (though the down can be compromised to a sit for sighthounds, toy dogs, and certain sporting dogs.) If you have these four things, it can get you out of almost any situation.

Raise your criteria on what your picture of a "trained dog" is. If you are not getting this from your training class, start asking lots of questions, and find out how your instructor can give you this.

February 5

Reactivity, or a lack of manners?

I've had a run of working with dogs who have atrocious manners, yet fabulous pet dog obedience. They will rip your shoulder off to pee on a rock, but will sit nicely as you put their dinner bowl down. These dogs have all been trained in obedience, and have some fabulous on-cue behaviours, but the training did not make them "nice people." They never learned manners, so much so that all of them almost got euthanized for their lack of manners. All of them ended up with aggression, which surfaced simply from their lack of manners.

They reminded me of some of the smart, albeit mean, kids in high school. They were straight-A students, but were mean and did as they pleased, only caring about themselves. Interestingly all four of the dogs were strong girls.

It seems that "no" was a dirty word for these dogs, and they were spared from ever having a bad day in their puppyhoods. They were loved, doted on, and people turned a blind eye to their misdemeanors. They were all trained, as they displayed impeccable behaviours when there was the possibility of food. No one ever told them they were rude, and then they were almost killed for it once they started biting.

Stress is a vital part of growing up and it is our jobs to expose our dogs to it in a constructive manner to help them become strong, robust adults. Stress naturally happens if you are stopped from doing something that you want to do. And being told "no" is inevitable and necessary for most teenagers. In addition to making them stronger, it also makes them nicer.

If your dog has been taught good domestic manners, she won't fly though a gate, won't jump up and smash your chin when you reach for her collar, will respect your body, won't bite the vet, and will not rip off your arm when attached by a leash. She doesn't get a cookie or praise for not doing these things. It simply is not allowed.

If dogs' domestics are not in place, they may pay the ultimate price. Sadly, a simple "knock it off" would have done the trick the first time they pulled their pranks.

Domestics make them nice dogs. Domestics will keep them alive— and, as an added bonus, easy to handle and a delight to be with.

February 6
All three drives

All behaviours need to be taught in low, medium, and high drive.

Asking your dog for a sit in the kitchen when there's nothing going on around either one of you (low drive) is quite different than asking your dog for a sit when she is chasing a cookie (medium drive). And both of those are very different from asking your dog for a sit when she is galloping after a rabbit (high drive). A behaviour taught in low-drive will not happen when requested in medium-drive. You need to teach your dog each and every level for her to understand that the requirements are still the same.

February 7
Examine your expectations

I think most dog aggression is caused by our need for our dogs to be friendly and to play with other dogs at the park. If we could change the focus of our walks from us wanting them to make "friends" with rude and often obnoxious strangers to just enjoying each other as human and dog, then the pressure on them to have to be friendly is gone. Shortly thereafter, their aggression will be too.

While playfulness is normal and expected in puppies, as dogs hit puberty, they become more aloof with strangers while still maintaining playfulness with dogs they have relationships with. Dogs pretty much have the same social habits as we do.

However, as they age and mature, our own social expectations of them do not change. We continue to want them to play and approach everyone. It is this urge—which comes from the human's end of the leash—that is creating such reactivity problems in dogs. We want our dogs to go forward. They do as we wish, and then get trapped in an awkward greeting that ends with an outcome that we don't want.

Let's just ask our dogs to all mind their own manners as they tootle on past each other to go and sniff some dog pee, rather than expecting them to all be friends.

Aggressive dogs that go on weekly walks with their dog walker and a pack of dogs demonstrate this. They get along perfectly well with dogs they know, but they have no intention of being nice to in-your-face strangers. I confess I feel somewhat the same with my own species.

We have misunderstood what socialization means. Yes, dogs need to be socialized. That means that dogs need to *see* the world, and learn to handle themselves in it with social grace. We need to teach them the skills and habits necessary for participating within our society. Unfortunately, socialization got misunderstood as just interacting and playing with other dogs.

Maybe we need to allow our dogs the same social habits we allow ourselves. I have no intention of playing with strangers at the park. And I really avoid overly friendly strangers who want to high five me. But give me a bottle of wine, put me together with a few of my girlfriends, and watch me transform.

Dogs and humans have very similar social habits, which is why we get along so well. We must let go of who we think they should be and learn to enjoy who they are.

February 8

Raising puppies

When you have a young puppy in your home, he should rarely hear the word "no." Almost every bad behaviour stems from a lack of management. Reward all of the wonderful things that you see, redirect him before he gets into trouble, and exercise the snot out of him as you show him the world. Enforce naptime, too, so he is not overstimulated. Having a young puppy should be a fun experience that leaves you exhausted from all of your efforts.

February 9

Surround yourself with talent

I prefer to surround myself with trainers who are better than I am. This way I only ever see the right work done the right way. I simply don't see anyone practicing bad habits, and I am able to catch my own bad habits because I'm the only one doing them.

By regularly seeing how things should be done, you will be sufficiently motivated to up your game. Your brain will be seeing and processing how things should look, giving you a goal and destination for your training.

Always try and get into classes or training groups where everyone else is way better than you. Be the least talented person surrounded by great talent—rather than pretending to be a great talent surrounded by novices.

It takes courage to do this and will be hard on your ego, but it is how you will become a whole lot better.

February 10

Train right the first time

It takes the same amount of time to train a dog poorly as it does to train her right. And if you justify inaccurate training by saying you don't want high scores and wins, your dog will be the one to pay when you suddenly realize that if you are putting in all this time, you do indeed want high scores and wins.

Be fair to your dog. Train her right the first time. It takes the same amount of time to train her precisely or sloppily, so do it right. Up your criteria and be consistent in your teaching. Then your dog won't have to pay later when your standards increase.

February 11

Puppy play groups

Puppy classes that make playing a priority are setting up some of those puppies for social issues later on in life. If these guys have a temperament flaw (perhaps they love other dogs way too much, or are really scared of them), these group festivities teach them to be much stronger, or much weaker. And in addition to the strong getting stronger and the weak getting weaker, every single puppy leaves that class with a dog obsession.

For puppies that lack confidence, or are bullies with other puppies, over-socialization is just as bad as no socialization. You will make them dog obsessed, and I bet you that the fearful dog-obsessed puppy will have aggression when he hits puberty, just the same as his over-confident friend.

Instead these groups should focus on short, safe interactions with other puppies, so *every* puppy enjoys it. And keep in mind that your dog should think that you are always a much more fun option to play with than the other dogs. Puppy play should be boring in comparison to playing with you! Teaching your dog that you are the most important person (and the most fun person) in the world is really easy to do, if they have not yet become dog obsessed.

February 12

"Working it out" doesn't work

Recently a stranger's dog charged and attacked a dog I was out with when I was on my bike. As her dog tried to fight mine, and I tried to peel her dog off mine, she told me to let mine off leash so they could work it out.

I wish I were joking, but this is true. While her dog was trying to eat mine—after nearly knocking me off my bike—she told me to leave my dog and walk away. People like this leave me so conflicted.

The reasons this advice is wrong:

- The dog I was walking had serious aggression and would have put her dog in the hospital. She totally misjudged my dog. She confused his training with who he was.
- Not all dogs work it out. Most just learn how to fight better.
- Dogs die in dog fights much more often than you would think. But no one discusses it.
- Always look at the source of advice. This lady let her dog try to attack mine. If I follow her advice, I too will have a dog that behaves like hers (that would run away and attack other dogs).
- Letting a dog act out like this is really letting an ass be an ass, and allowing him to master intimidation.

On the other hand, without people like this, I would be out of a job. Every vulnerable, young dog who is charged like this will become a future client of mine. Every dog like hers who is allowed to charge other dogs like this becomes mentally stronger, and that also keeps me in business. Dog owners like this are giving me an entire generation of new students for my Growl classes!

Without people like this, I would suddenly not be busy. I could organize my office. I could keep my training building sparkling clean and have a spotless parking lot. I could even write my next book with all my spare time!

Not to mention that I missed my moment to crash to the ground off my bike, break my leg, and experience two dogs fighting on top of me. This could have ended up a very lucrative experience for me. But unlike that dog owner, I am not unfair. She is being very unfair to her own dog, and to all the dogs she allows her dog to charge, not to mention those dogs' owners.

Please do not allow dogs to "work it out," especially when you forced your dog onto some unsuspecting person who was happily enjoying their day, until they ran into you.

February 13

The word "reactive" is overused

Certainly not all, but many of the dogs who are labelled reactive are not actually reactive. They are aggressive.

To be "reactive" means you are reacting to something. I can be a reactive driver when someone slams on the brakes in front of me. I can be reactive if someone yells at me unfairly. If I were a dog, I would be reactive to a dog jamming a nose up my bum.

Many dogs labelled reactive are not reacting to a problem; they are causing the problem. The semantics, however, have softened their misdeeds and somehow the other is to blame.

Please be honest with the words you use when you ponder who your dog is. Focus on teaching her to mind her manners—be it sitting nicely or not pulling on your leash. You will have to help them and make it easy to start, but you won't need to for long.

Forget the label, as it often becomes an excuse. Instead help them to be a normal dog, with normal manners and normal training criteria. Drop any labels, which only helps them remain a perpetual victim, and teach them how you want them to be. Your honesty will make your training more effective because you will be seeing things for what they are.

February 14
Don't take it for granted

Never stop guiding and showing your dog what you want. Regardless of someone's current skill level, accomplishments, or titles, everyone needs continuing education to maintain a high level of performance. Your dog is no different.

Also, never stop praising and acknowledging what you like about your dog. Dogs are not robots and they do have feelings. We all need to be told when we have done well, even if it is something as simple as a snappy, fast sit.

February 15
Do now, think later

Bobbie Anderson, a teacher of mine, always used to tell me that training is 80 percent thinking and 20 percent doing. But don't try to combine doing and thinking.

When you are *with* your dog, it is the time to *do*. There is the urgency of getting the information to your dog in a timely manner, which removes time for thought. You simply must *do* in that moment. When you need to make a decision under the pressure of time, it's impossible to weigh out all your options. Simply do, and think later. Fight decision paralysis. Know that the wrong answer, delivered at the right time, can actually be better than the right answer delivered too late.

There is no time for thinking when you are training your dog. It will throw off your timing completely. In the moment, you need to just *do* then reflect on your choice later, when you are back to thinking.

Do your thinking when you are driving, in the shower, lying in bed, or any other time away from your dog. I start thinking when I first wake up, and often it prevents me from going to sleep. My biggest epiphanies have happened when I am lying in bed or taking a shower.

If you find yourself only doing and not thinking, or only thinking and not doing, you've missed the boat.

February 16

We can't help but make it worse

Sometimes when we start retraining issues, we make the issue worse. Our attention and focus on the problem create more of a problem. This is usually because we either cheerlead and rejoice over normal ho-hum behaviour, or we start to bully.

No one ever praised Uncle Jim for not driving drunk, so why are we praising our dogs for not eating Fluffy? This is normal behaviour and should be expected. Sometimes your praise is so unhealthy and out of context that it will actually maintain what you are trying to remove.

What about bullying? Because we have a little bit of control over the problem, as we try to retrain it, we continue to use it, and use it, and use it, and end up backing our dogs into a corner.

Because our dog was good with Fluffy and didn't snap when a nose was jammed up his bum, we force him to get humped by Fluffy, and meet Thor, Bingo, Maggie, and Cujo. And we put him into situations that are completely unfair because we want him "socialized."

As our dog's leaders, we must be fair. Don't cheerlead and rejoice over normalcy, or you have nothing more to strive for. And, the purpose of control is to give them freedom, so once you do have that control, don't keep making them do it again, and again, and again. It is not fair.

If you want your dog to respect you, first you must respect him.

February 17
Value the work

The very best trainers in the world find a way to make their dog's work have its own intrinsic value. While rewards are given, they are of secondary value compared to the work itself. Trainers build joy and emotion into the work, and the rewards are the icing on the cake. This gives value to your praise.

February 18
Puppy training for competition dogs

Training is not about training a behaviour. It is about teaching the right emotion for learning. Teaching with the wrong emotion when a dog is young will end up creating big problems that will be very difficult to fix.

Without the right emotion, things will look great, but will eventually fall apart. These are the dogs that look great up until about ten months old—then you spend forever more trying to build motivation in their work.

So pay attention when training your youngsters. Remember to teach your puppy the joy of learning rather than just focus on the learning.

February 19

Avoid verbal leakage

"He who knows, does not speak. He who speaks, does not know."—Lao Tzu

Apply these words of wisdom to moments in your relationship with your dog when things are going wrong. If you know how to fix the situation, you will probably have a silent calm about you. If you do not know how to fix it, verbal leakage will ooze out of you, which lets your dog know that you do not know. This can either stress them out, or put them into protective mode.

When I'm working with new clients, verbal leakage is one of the first clues that helps me figure out what their struggles are. When clients start chattering a whole lot, I know something has triggered them. If I know it, their dogs know it too.

If you find yourself to be one of these people, the next time you catch yourself chattering away to your dog, force yourself to stop and bite your tongue. Or, if that is much too difficult for you, jam your mouth full of bubblegum so that it is near impossible. Rather than words, alter your posture so that you appear confident. Relax your muscles. And do your job, so that your dog can do his. Be his coach, and lead him through it by demonstrating how it should be done.

Until you can master being silent when you feel the rug pulled out from under you, you are continuing to tell your dog that you are unsure of an impending situation and "do not know."

February 20

Walking a dog is like driving

Walking our reactive dogs has so much in common with driving. It's all about staying focused on our task and being sensitive to our surroundings. If we do that, we can help our dogs do the right thing.

Here are some training tips to help you get over hurdles with your reactive dog. None of these are to replace your current training. Rather, they should enhance your current training.

- Keep your eyes on where you need to go (the road) and not on what you are fearful of (the dog approaching you).
- If you are in a busy area, look a few dogs ahead so that you have reaction time, just like driving on a highway.
- Slow down going into a bend in the road. You can't see what is around it, so be prepared.
- Be careful swerving around things because you could lose control. And if you do choose to swerve, make sure you hit the brake as you do so, or you will lose control. In other words, quit avoiding people, dogs, and if you do need to get around them, GO SLOW.
- Stay in your lane. The other car will stay in theirs (in theory). Don't pull over every time a car is coming toward you. It shows what a nervous driver you are.
- Don't white knuckle the steering wheel, or your dog's leash.
- Forward momentum is much more gratifying than being stopped. Even if I'm going slowly, I feel like I have hope and purpose!
- Wherever your eyes are is where your car (or dog) is going. So keep your energy focused on where you want to go, not on what you are scared of. I always think of hitting ice. Focus on the

centre line, not the lamp post that you are avoiding. You will go where you focus.

- No distracted walking or driving. You need to be aware of your environment so that you can readily respond to changes. Leave your phone at home. Even if you are chatting, make sure you don't forget to pay attention.

With reactive dogs, you don't get to go on autopilot. Stay in the driver's seat.

February 21

Treats should be a surprise

Many people are hesitant to train with treats and toys because they think their dogs will only work when there's a reward. Their fears are not entirely misplaced.

We need to teach with food and toys. However, concepts don't take long to teach, and quickly thereafter treats and toys need to become a reward for a job well done rather than just done, or used for teaching.

Feeding your dog treats for a job well done should continue. But the act itself—if it's just a regular request—should not be rewarded. Always use your voice just before you reward so that your voice has value and meaning for those moments when you don't also reward with a toy or treat. When you decide to reward a good behaviour, make it a surprise rather than an expectation. Only reward the best responses, not every single one. Though I do praise all.

A treat should always be a surprise. If you constantly feed your dog treats for every small thing that he does, your treats will become expected. He will start sniffing and looking at your pockets or hands. If he is looking for a treat, the solution is really simple: he doesn't get one.

February 22

Rethinking resource guarding

Right now I have a board-and-train dog living with me. I sat down to enjoy my dinner, with her carefully watching from a safe distance, and started eating my food. She was lightning fast, and in a single movement she was in possession of my rack of ribs. In that moment I realized I am a resource guarder.

And so did she.

So is resource guarding wrong? After cooking my ribs for an entire day in my slow cooker, there was no way I was going to lose them to her. Nor anyone else.

Resource guarding does exist and can be a massive problem. But frequently human meddling causes it. I can guarantee the next night I knew where Ms. Doberman was as I ate. She taught me not to trust her while I eat. But well-meaning owners frequently teach their dogs the same by meddling with their dinner.

Use prevention protocols sparingly. Once a week is the maximum I suggest, quickly moving to once every two weeks.

If you already have an issue you need to see a dog trainer. Rarely is resource guarding improved with direct retraining. Often, fixing the relationship plus basic domestics will make the problem almost go away. With a tiny touch-up on resource guarding added in at the end, if at all. I find this the scariest form of aggression to retrain—and, in some breeds, once you mess with it, you can accidentally take it from bad to dangerous really quickly.

But you need the eyes of someone with a minimum of ten years of working with dogs. They need to tell you whether the can of worms should be opened or managed. Reading this wrong in a dog could cost your dog their life. Some dogs need permanent management, and do well with it. Sometimes the can of worms needs to stay closed.

If I were a dog, I'd be the can of worms that needs to stay closed. Retraining would get me euthanized. The more you mess with me when I eat, the more suspicious I become, and the more guarded I get. I can't envision a training protocol where I would tolerate someone hovering over me with the threat of touching my rack of ribs, even if it was in exchange for an overenthusiastic wine fill. Piss off. Leave me alone. It would be best to put me somewhere secure and leave me alone to enjoy my dinner.

Some dogs feel the same. Know when to tell the difference.

February 23
Soul Dogs defined

> *"It is said that there are four types of horses: excellent ones, good ones, poor ones, and bad ones. The best horse will run slow and fast, right and left, at the rider's will, before it sees the shadow of the whip; the second best will run as well as the first one does, just before the whip reaches its skin; the third one will run when it feels pain on its body; the fourth will run after the pain penetrates to the marrow of its bones. You can imagine how difficult it is for the fourth one to learn how to run!"*—(Amyuktagama Sutra, volume 33)

Our Soul Dogs are the fourth horse. Nothing is given for free by these teachers. They ruthlessly shove us outside of our comfort zone. We have to commit, dig deep to find the gumption to continue, then learn, communicate, and teach in order to get any level of success, which might be minimal compared to what we are used to.

These characters teach us patience and respect.

Now think of your own difficult dog. As you begin retraining, you are going to experience an intimate relationship that you may never have had before with a dog. You will learn to understand your dog at a level that most owners will not comprehend. You will learn many lessons that you never wanted to learn. You will connect on an intuitive level that only those who have been there will understand. The worst dogs are willing to teach all of this to us—making them the better dogs and teachers for us to have.

The dogs that come to us perfectly mannered do indeed make us look good and are lovely to be with. But they teach us very little and do not contribute to our growth as dog trainers. While success is needed for our self-esteem and egos, and will be given by the easy dogs providing you do the right work, you may never be successful with your difficult dog.

However, what you will get is growth, learning, acceptance, and a profound level of intimacy. It is this deeper connection, taught through all of the challenges they present us, that makes them become our Soul Dogs.

February 24
Train, don't test

Often our dogs do something undesirable and it's hard to believe that they really did it. So we set up the scenario again to see if they will repeat it. And unluckily for us, they do.

Why do we set up scenarios for our dogs to fail? Why do we wave scary flags in their faces to see if they will bolt away? Why do we walk them straight past another dog when we know they will lunge?

Our dogs will inevitably encounter tests, but ideally they will only happen in real life. It shouldn't be us who sets them up. We train so that when life gets hurled in our direction, we have the tools to cope. But don't ruin those tools in the quest to see if you can freak your dog out or get him to misbehave. Of course you can, particularly if you try hard enough.

Instead of waiting and seeing your dog's response, why don't you make the "scary" flag appealing so that he grabs it and wants to play with it instead? Or school him as you walk past another dog so that he behaves beautifully without thinking of lunging.

Every test you do ingrains the bad behaviour you are trying to remove. Don't test; help your dog give you the right answer.

February 25

Not everyone loves your dog

If I were to ask you who you love the most in your household, you would probably have to restrain yourself from saying your dog's name. You love your dog. I love mine, too. I get it.

But somehow we tell our dogs they are the most important being in our home. We have made their needs and desires supersede all others, beyond common sense. They are dogs. Perfect, kissable dogs, but still dogs. While their needs and desires do matter, my dog's needs will never override anyone else's. My dog does not pay taxes or a mortgage. And, ultimately, he is a dog.

I hear this so often: "If you don't like off-leash dogs, don't come to an off-leash beach." Okay. I have a solution: Why don't we just make all beaches on leash and remove this problem?

"If you don't like the sound of dogs barking, you shouldn't live in a pet-friendly apartment." Okay. My solution: Why don't we just make this building dog intolerant?

In my town there is a major housing shortage for people with dogs. But what people haven't realized is that if you have a dog, you had better be cleaner and quieter than any other tenant so that you don't risk this right. Or if you walk your dog off leash, you had better be super considerate to all others out there so that you can maintain this right.

Now, I get it. The best-trained dog will still act like a complete turd once in a while. But think of your 300 brilliant mega-considerate days as karmic points for the one when he is not so great.

As dog owners, we confuse our ridiculous unbalanced love for our dogs with thinking of them as equals, with equal rights. Nope. If we continue to think this way, we will lose everything that previous generations worked hard to gain for us.

We are allowed to own dogs. We are allowed to own dogs, and have them off leash. Now be grateful, and become invisible. People walking past you should be thanking you for how considerate you are. If not, you too are part of the problem.

Let's smarten up, people. Quit being so entitled. Be glad that we have the places to walk that we do, and do your bit to make everyone else's walk enjoyable while you are out there. Train your dogs. Control them. I don't care if they want to say "hi." Unless they pay taxes, their wants don't matter.

As much as you love your dogs, don't expect others to feel the same. They don't.

February 26

Off-leash freedom for youngsters

When running your little teenage punks, the first thirty seconds of your walk will dictate the tone of the entire time you are out. Take the time to make sure that you get off to a good start: your dog should get out of the car nicely without shoving you into traffic; she should patiently allow you to put her leash on, she should demonstrate full leash manners for thirty seconds, and she should acknowledge you are alive *without being under command*. It's not good manners if you have to command it.

And *then* give her freedom. By not negotiating on the basics, and expecting your dog to give them to you without having been asked, you will set the tone for your entire time out. These critical thirty seconds will make the difference between an enjoyable or regrettable walk.

February 27

Is shaping working for your dog?

A group of training friends was recently discussing the shaping game where you are given a task to teach another person without using words, just a clicker. Like the game of hot and cold, you are allowed to click when people get warmer. However, you are not allowed to tell them when they get colder. Only 50 percent of the information is given.

When we were all shaped, we hated it. We found that not knowing when we were wrong made us irritated and angry. However, the amusing part is that we all really enjoyed shaping others! We loved doing, but hated receiving. It might say a lot about our inner need for control, which is why we are all dog trainers in the first place . . . but I digress. We collectively hated being shaped!

This might be something to consider when training your dog. Does your dog enjoy shaping? Or because you enjoy it so much, do you believe that he does? Keep an eye on your dog. If he starts getting frantic and frenetic when being shaped, he might not enjoy the process as much as you wish he did.

I wonder if the dogs who struggle the most with shaping are control freaks too, just like us trainers?

February 28

Dogmanship: Don't blame the tool

A tool is a tool. The quality of the hammer or the drill never matters as much as the skill of the craftsperson.

I can pick up a drill and do a fairly disastrous job of making kitchen cupboards. But hand that drill over to a skilled carpenter and the cupboards will look a whole lot better. Is it the drill that was flawed? Should I buy a different brand?

Dog-training tools are the same. It doesn't matter if you use a Halti, a no-pull harness, a buckle collar, a pinch collar, a clicker, or whatever you want to use to teach your dog to walk nicely on a leash. If your skills are lacking, the end behaviour will be lacking too. Buying bigger and better tools isn't going to help you until you look inward and realize that it is indeed you, yourself, who is lacking the skills. There are some exceptions to this rule, but they truly are exceptions!

This is the fascinating part of dog training. All my clients come to me needing skills, but many are unwilling to work on themselves. They expect the dog to change, transform, while they stay the same. It doesn't work that way. Your relationship with your dog is just that: a relationship. What you do will affect what he does.

But change is difficult for us. It is stressful. It requires us admitting flaws and being vulnerable. If we rise to the occasion in training our partners, we will end up better people. However, it really is much easier to either stuff more food in the dog's face or pound on the dog some more.

Are some people unable to dig deep to improve themselves?

Some days when I look around, I feel that the art of dogmanship is becoming lost. I see my peers, who are veteran dog trainers, and they all possess what I speak of. They might all be different from each other in the tools that they use, but they are craftspeople. They can take the equivalent of an old, rotten piece of wood and, with love and pride, turn it into something beautiful.

So please remember: it isn't the tool, it is you.

Can you calm your mind? Can you loosen and control your muscles and control your breath? Do you have the right feel on the leash for each dog that you work with? If not, it is time to work on your dogmanship.

MARCH

March 1

Our differences divide us

As dog trainers, we pride ourselves on how we train dogs and the methods that we use.

Our different training philosophies have resulted in non-productive arguing that has caused an ever-growing divide among dog trainers. Pointing out our differences and trying to win the debate on "what works better" seems to have become the only communication between the different camps. And these arguments stop us from growing and becoming better technicians.

We have allowed our differences to define us. If we keep celebrating our differences, the gap will only widen. I propose that we start to celebrate and share our similarities; after all, we are all dog trainers and should celebrate training dogs.

We all train dogs. We all aim for success, and we all aim for the kindest way possible to get that success.

No one allows dangerous behaviour from dogs. All camps deal directly with aggression and the like.

We are all incredibly passionate about what we do. All of our spare time and hard-earned money goes into our dogs, our travel, and our education.

We all love our dogs.

Most dog-training veterans just want to talk dogs, and if you listen without judgement, you will learn a lot. They have forgotten more knowledge than the rest of us have learned, and if we will listen with open ears, they will gladly share.

We all want a dog who is a willing partner with no conflict and stress, one who can do its job.

Let's focus on the common ground that we share. If we can do that, we will find that our differences are smaller than we think, and that everyone can learn something from someone else.

March 2

When transformations occur

What do you do when you need to train a strong independent soul who has become hardened by his disappointing interactions with humans?

I was training a dog, and as I began to request something of him, I could feel him brace against my request. Generally, when you feel a dog brace against your request, you can almost guarantee he won't do as you asked.

At this point you (a) need to make sure they know how to give you what you are asking. Then (b) quickly decide if this is a battle you want to fight, and if it is not, (c) find an alternate route. In the case of this dog, I went with option c.

Why? The dog barely knew me. He knew I wasn't a doormat, but we were fresh acquaintances. He had no reason to trust me. But I still had to train him and control him, and we didn't have the time for dinner dates before we started. So, going back to my original question, how do you train this type of dog, one who braces when he feels you might want something from him?

When a dog braces, I notice their eyes just glaze over. With this dog, when I saw those eyes, I found a reason to praise him. I tried to become his partner, tackling the world with him beside me. I was calmly cheeky, pointing out the things that he desperately wanted to do, then making him feel proud when he did it.

Praise made him soften, loosen, and his eyes returned to normal. Only once he was physically normal did I request of him. He still didn't do as I asked, but then I could guide him, coach him, show him, make him. I now had a cooperative student who was willing to receive my feedback.

Within days, he went from bracing, to being his own worst critic. He was so angry with himself if he made an error. I didn't point his errors out to him. He's not stupid—he knew. He would run in a panic. Or eat grass like a cow. His next lessons will be teaching him that it is okay to make errors. And to lighten up. Quit being so uptight, and enjoy your job.

This dog has quickly gone from being impossible to control and needing no one to having too much work ethic and being his own biggest critic. I find it fascinating how personalities can be so incredibly different when you just alter the pairing.

March 3

When more training won't help

Succeeding—getting your training right during the moments that count—is the result of creating a particular atmosphere within yourself. Those who can consistently create this climate within themselves will consistently succeed.

If you feel yourself continuing to struggle with your dog and certain behaviours, and you know you have done your training, more training won't fix your problem. You need to learn to alter your internal climate. Once you can, you will get the results that you have worked for in the moments and places that you need it.

March 4

Train for the veterinarian

No number of cookies or gradual progressions—small lessons that build on one another—can make your quirky dog enjoy a thermometer up his bum. And no amount of cookies will prepare him to lie flat on an X-ray table to have a painful joint manipulated without anaesthetic (which will happen as your dog ages). It is our job to train them for this while they are young and healthy. This will ensure that they will be able to get the veterinary care they need during their elder-years.

Your dog must learn to accept that not everything is pleasant, but that he can trust you and that you have his best interest at heart, always. All husbandry tasks need to become something that your dog tolerates and allows, even when he doesn't want to. This includes ear cleaning, teeth cleaning, eye drops, toenail cutting, grooming, getting areas shaved for hot spots, going to veterinary exams, and all related procedures.

Start restraints with your puppy right away. Hold them on your lap, belly to the sky, and rock them back and forth. I will kiss them on their precious heads and tickle them. When they struggle and fight I just adjust my hold, moving with them as they wiggle. They learn that struggling and biting gets them nowhere, and if they relax, it feels good. Once they learn this, a down restraint, as would be needed on an X-ray table, is an easy transition. Never do this when you are angry. And teach them right away that this is not a choice but a requirement.

March 5
Crate training

Whether you want to crate your dog in your home or not, being comfortable in a crate is a skill he deserves to learn. When your dog goes to the veterinarian for a procedure or to the groomer, he will be crated. If you have not previously taught him this necessary life skill, he will panic and suffer undue stress—due to your lack of preparation.

You owe it to your dog to crate train him. You also owe it to your groomer and your vet.

March 6

Shopping at Walmart

Taking my dog to a dog park should be like shopping at Walmart. When I go to Walmart, I rarely look strangers in the eye. I might casually sweep my eyes on them and then past them, but I don't stare at anyone. For the most part, other than the occasional nod or smile, I walk around the store like the other shoppers do not even exist.

However, when I was a young child, I sat in my cart and talked to strangers. I looked at everyone, greeted strangers from my boring seat, and more often than not got smiles, waves, and minor greetings in return. Once in a blue moon I also received scowls!

Then there came a time when I was in an awkward age. I was a bit too old to greet boring strangers, but I hadn't yet learned how to be an ignoring adult. My greetings were more boisterous and pushy. Or I was completely shy and awkward and didn't how to behave. Fortunately, this was a short-lived period, and I quickly learned how adults behave in my culture and abandoned my previous greetings and eye contact with everyone.

Dogs are exactly the same. Puppies are learning and greet everyone, regardless of the social cue that was given. Most adult dogs tolerate it, a few scowl and dislike it. Young recipient dogs love every minute of the greeting and the play begins.

Eventually they grow up a bit, and either become boisterous and pushy in their greetings, or shy and awkward, or both. This awkward adolescent stage doesn't last long, and quickly they *should* learn adult behaviour.

Adult behaviour is ignoring most of the other dogs in the park. They casually scan their eyes over approaching dogs and just meander past—the same as my shopping cart and me. There will be moments where they give the canine-handshake equivalent of a bum-sniff to an interesting stranger, then continue on. And once in a blue moon they might even have a rip-roaring game with a complete stranger, though this is an annual event for my dogs.

My dogs never approach a stranger and sniff nose to nose. That is much too fresh; I equate that with walking up to a stranger and grabbing her boob.

Puppies do need to play, and will gradually learn the social rules of adult dogs. Adult dogs will also have rip-roaring games with their established dog friends.

On your next visits to the dog park, please focus on enjoying your dog. Dog ownership is about them making us laugh, but they can only do that if we actually interact with them. Start playing with your dog on your walks, and enjoying him and the beautiful nature around you. Remove your own obsessive need for him to sniff and greet everyone, and instead focus on playing with him.

If you have an adult dog who you have taught to be dog-obsessed, make sure you walk and don't stop when you pass another dog. The purpose of your walk is to walk! If that dog coming toward you is a friend, ask that person to walk with you. Forward movement alone can stop numerous potential squabbles, so keep your dogs moving.

If you don't know the dog, keep walking, and your dog will too. He will learn to float his eyes past other dogs, then walk on past with minimal interest—just the same as you would when you are shopping at Walmart and you pass a complete stranger.

March 7

Dogs show who we really are

Your dog's perfect behaviour will not make you a better person. But how you react to his imperfect behaviour and weaknesses will show exactly what kind of person you are.

Let's try and remove our own egos when we evaluate our dogs. They don't do things to make us look bad. However, your response to his imperfections and flaws will dictate what kind of person you are. When confronted with a big issue, will you:

- Think your dog is out to spite you?
- Dig deep and get him what he needs?
- Blame the messenger?
- Accept and do nothing?
- Create powerful excuses?
- Put your head in the sand?
- Avoid having to do anything by moving to an apartment that doesn't allow dogs and rehoming yours?

Dogs don't do things to make us look good or bad. They simply present the opportunity and we ourselves show who we are. They give us opportunities to grow, learn, become better people, and meet great people. It is our response to these moments that exposes our hand and reveals who we really are.

Hopefully when your dog presents your next test, you will show that you are tenacious, resourceful, determined, and willing to learn.

March 8

When did "no" become a bad word?

The word "no" is one of the most important words you'll ever use with your dog. In my books, it's necessary, and must be used (properly and fairly) for a dog to develop normally

I'm not quite sure how it happened, but somewhere, somehow, people decided it was wrong to tell their dogs "no." Not everything is allowed. And some things are forbidden simply because they would have dire consequences.

By never saying "no" we are denying our dogs the chance to learn several important lessons. Be honest with your dog. Communicate fairly and honestly when he does something that you don't want to see again.

March 9

Put in the time

We all have high hopes for our dogs. Yet only a few manage to do the work that allows those hopes to come to fruition. Most are too lazy and impatient to put the time in and prefer to put their time into complaining instead of training.

Get off your keyboards, revamp your goals, decide how you can find an extra *hour* a day to help you get to where you need to go, and put the necessary time, love, passion, and energy in.

Finding an extra hour a day is fairly easy (providing you don't have multiple young children). Give up social media, a favourite television show, or wake up an hour earlier.

The best in the world all have one key secret to success—they put in more time and effort than everyone else. Your dreams can become reality if you are willing to do the same.

March 10

Redirecting the bite

When you have a young puppy who is new in your home, he is going to fly at you and bite you, sometimes *hard*. I really try not to let them know they have done badly. I will have toys stuffed all over my body, there is almost always one jammed down the back of my pants, and instantly redirect them to a toy.

The reason? Our puppies are choosing to play with us. They are coming to us for fun and entertainment, but because of their age and lack of education they are playing with us like we are dogs. Most of us got dogs because we want them to engage with us, play with us. Yet, if every time they come we squeal because we are feigning pain, or we holler at them because it hurt, we aren't exactly fun. It won't take them long to realize that stealing your shoe and eating it in the corner on their own is actually more fun than being with you and all of your annoying rules.

Build a relationship with your puppy before you start putting the rules on. But don't be a pincushion—always have toys on you so you can redirect your puppy quickly.

Once they have determined that you are indeed the best person in the entire world, then teach them about mouth inhibition and how hard they can bite down on you. But build your relationship first.

March 11

Active or passive?

Please ponder the difference between an active and a passive reward, and an active and a passive correction. "Active" is going to elicit movement from your dog and bring out energy. "Passive" is going to get her calm.

If what you are doing with your dog is simply not working, it could be that you are activating when you should be pacifying, or the reverse.

Sometimes a simple food reward can be used to do either. If you hand it to them calmly from your hand, it is a passive reward. If you toss is at them, or toward them, it will activate them.

There is a time and a place for both, and it is up to you to know and process what is needed, and when.

March 12

Dominant dogs

In a world where people call dogs "puppies" regardless of their age, the consensus seems to be that dominance is no more.

So, I checked. The word "dominance" is in the *Merriam-Webster* dictionary, and it's defined as "overlooking and commanding from a superior position." And the word "lead" is defined as "having charge." The meanings of these two words are so intertwined, if not related. Yet, I'm told dominance no longer exists. However, leadership naturally exists in people, dogs, and even sheep. Some dogs do assert control in dealing with others, but it's not the dogs that you think.

However, the word was so incorrectly used for so many years that I'm not surprised we tried to get rid of it. If a dog misbehaved, he was being dominant, when really, he just misbehaved.

So, yes, it has probably been the most misused word and belief when it comes to dog training. It was used in comparing dogs to wolves, which they are not. But even though we've come to realize that we've used the word *dominant* incorrectly, we don't have to avoid using it now—we just need to learn to use it right.

I very rarely run into a dominant dog, but they do exist. One of my favourites is the most magnificent Alaskan Malamute. He has so much presence, pride, and confidence, in his quiet, gentle way, that all the weak girls in Socialization Class used to flock to him. We dubbed him "The King"—and that he was.

Another is a Chow Chow, who was born knowing how to get what he wants. Both his veterinarian and I told his first-time dog owner that she would be euthanizing him before ten months if she didn't rise to the occasion. She did rise, and he is another magnificent dog. But you cannot "make" him do anything. We don't "tell" him what we want. We ask. Nicely. With an ego stroke. His owner has managed to get him to do amazing things and be a great partner—providing he is asked nicely.

Now, please don't use what I just said to justify your own dog's crappy behaviour and think I just gave you an excuse not to retrain. Dominant dogs are not common. In fact, most of you have probably never met one, and probably never will. You need help with your dog. And if perchance your dog is one that I am talking about, you need help even more, from someone who knows what they are doing.

The thing that has been misunderstood about dominance is these guys are not the young punks with something to prove. These dogs have nothing to prove; they know they are the best in the room. They are quiet, calm dogs that seem bigger than their size. They have presence. They are magnificent. They can make the hair on the back of your neck go up. You know not to fuck with them.

Your eye will always be drawn to them. It is impossible not to notice and admire them. They are not looking for trouble but if they feel wronged, they will have no problem firmly disciplining the wrongdoer. One Akita I knew of, who was older with nary a problem, accidentally got stepped on one day. If memory serves me right, his mistress needed something like twenty-seven stitches in her face.

So, know this: the bratty, pubescent punks you see misbehaving at the dog park or on their walks are not being dominant. Most are lacking confidence, and trying to push boundaries to find their place.

Certain breeds are going to produce more of these characters than others. And not all of them can live with us in harmony. Some won't accept any rules from even the best of handlers.

But some, if you pair them with the right owner, become dogs that we can all admire and look upon as canine royalty—because they are.

March 13

Don't make excuses

Dogs are amazing. My scared little Kate was like a ghost with a small side of evil bitch. Now she's an unsure but trusting little love.

Tonight I asked her to participate in the flapping tarp game during puppy class. It was as if I was asking her to walk through fire, and she behaved as one would expect in such dangerous circumstances: very unwillingly. However, she did it, she did not die, and she got her reward. She turned her back and refused to watch all the other puppies do the exercise. Watching was almost as painful as doing it herself.

Then her turn came again, and she did as she was asked. Again, she did not die. Then, as all of the other puppies went, she got away from me, and went back into the fire on her own. She knew it made me happy, and so she kept doing it. That is what I find fascinating. She found the exercise so unpleasant, yet she realized she was safe. She knew I wanted her to do it, so she continued to do it—for no reward, just because.

Or maybe this had nothing to do with me. Maybe her inner tiger, which certainly does exist, pushed her to tackle her fear. I was pulling her off, yet she kept dragging me to go back, to stand awkwardly on the flapping tarp. That to me shows her depth of character. There was no praise, no reward, and I was actually pulling her off as it wasn't her turn, but she kept sneaking away and going back to stand on the waving tarp all on her own.

Dogs are so amazing. If we don't make excuses for them, if we keep them physically exercised, and then treat them like they are normal, they will become that way.

Sometimes we just make things a whole lot harder than they should be, under the guise of training. Don't put up with it. Expect more. Pretend they are normal, but be ready to adapt.

March 14

Be aware of patience thresholds

Patience. We all have a limited supply. Learning to hold your temper is an important skill for both dogs and humans to develop. And so is understanding when gruffness *is* appropriate. Aggression is not always wrong; sometimes our dogs are completely in the right when they show aggression, and we need to let them know as much.

Today a new whippersnapper joined my crew. She's annoying as hell, frantic in her head, never stops moving her feet, or teeth, and well, she requires patience to be around. She's just a child with her adult teeth barely in, but that is hard to tell when she leaps through the air and grabs your arm.

Two of my dogs struggle with losing their tempers, and now they have to deal with this creature. I only make them deal with it on hikes, where they can escape and get distance if they so choose.

But today they got their space invaded at rocket speed, they got their faces frenetically cleaned, they got ankle bites, pinchy bites on their skin that I was unable to prevent in time, and they also learned how to tell someone off without going postal.

I was so impressed with both of them, with their restraint and how clear they were with their communication. They were nothing less than brilliant. And within the course of a brisk hike, they turned the monster child into something slightly more civilized. While I pretended to be dog training, I really went on a beautiful walk and watched these two do my job for me.

We came home, they ate, they slept, then we went back at different training challenges. Both tried for me, but after they aced their challenge, they were done. They were tired and grumpy. And shortly thereafter, each of them snapped in a completely unrelated challenge.

Why?

Self-restraint and patience come in limited supply. Today they gave me all they had. They were physically and mentally tired, and they needed an easy evening after their challenging day. Except the creature is living here, so they had to see her again. Ironically, neither dog lost their temper on the cause of their angst. Both of them lost it about something else—old triggers that they had let go of.

I got the maximum out of both dogs that I could today. And once their maximum was up, they both showed leakage elsewhere.

Tomorrow is a new day. Tomorrow we all wake up with a new supply of patience for The Annoying One. And the creature will be better tomorrow as she had a multitude of teachers today, all telling her that "we don't behave that way here."

Despite the two errors for my grumps, I'm mighty proud of all that they showed today. They showed me what they are capable of, what great teachers they can be, and how far they have come (providing they are not too tired!).

March 15

Honour your old dogs

When you have a puppy come into your house, she requires so much attention. And much of this attention is individual, as she needs to do things on her own and bond with you. If you have other dogs, older dogs, this will break their hearts.

Make sure that you still honour your old dogs during this time. While your hours will be spent with the baby, go for quality time with your older dogs, and soothe their bruised egos. Try and find special things to do with them that are not time exhaustive.

March 16

Has dog training gone insane?

I've worked with several dogs who had long overdue euthanasia appointments, and they have all come from the same trainer. Now, let me quickly defend their trainer. This trainer is great with almost all dogs. But some dogs fall through the cracks and become tigers. This is an experienced, well-respected trainer.

The oddity here is that these dogs arrive with die-hard owners who are doing all they have been told by their trainer. These are not slackers who raised their dog wrong. These are people who have busted their butts following instructions and are doing everything they've been told. Only they were told the wrong thing for that particular dog. They were told that corrections were wrong, and that lessening stimuli and rewarding proper behaviour could fix everything.

Let me clarify: these were not my students.

One of these die-hards went to training with a tiny puppy who is now a teenager. The instructions were, "If he bites you, it is because you pushed him over the threshold. In the moment, back away, then make the training easier." Again, not my advice.

The problem is that she pushed her dog over the threshold just by walking into the kitchen. Her dog lunged across the room and bit her.

Why is it okay for this dog to behave this way to his human? And why, after she had asked multiple times for help from a trainer, was she told to make his training "easier" so that her dog could succeed when she is walking into her room? There *is* no making it easier for her dog to help him succeed. It is her house and she should be able to walk into any room without fear of being attacked.

I know what my dad would have done if I ran at him with a kitchen knife and tried to stab him because he walked into the kitchen. I know what my mum would have done, too. And it certainly wouldn't have been backing away and then making my training easier.

Walking into her kitchen landed her in hospital. Maybe next week her grandiose offense might be walking into the closet. I hope she is good at mind reading, because the next offense might put her into critical care, or worse. She had better be mighty vigilant because if he loses his temper it is her fault for pushing him beyond the threshold. Seriously?

I don't know about you folks, but in my mind this is an abusive relationship. She has to tiptoe around her dog, and be careful not to anger him. It's like giving him beer to make his life easier so that he doesn't hurt her.

There are thousands of occasions where we need to reward the right. And, yes, we need to be respectful of one another's quirks. But there are also lines that should not be crossed.

Easier training and more rewards will not fix this dog. She's been using that tactic his entire life and now he is dangerous. So, can we be honest? Corrections are needed to keep certain dogs alive.

Somewhere we became too stuck on the process of feeling good, and forgot about the result we need. Coaching, parenting, and training don't always feel good. But we still need to do our job.

March 17

The tipping point: Adding a dog

Everyone who has several dogs has probably experienced the "tipping point." It's when you get *one more dog*. You know, you go from a life full of harmony to a life with, well, none. Normally this moment occurs around the five-dog mark, heading to six, but I have seen different owners struggle at lower numbers.

Recently one of my very talented clients got a new dog. She is a teenaged punk bitch who is fearful, rude, and, as a result of the two combined, a bit of a bully.

I saw the difference this dog made on that harmonious family. They went from two happy dogs and two happy people, to one dog struggling with her confidence, one dog saying, "fuck it" and running away to do her own thing, and one very frazzled owner. And perhaps more telling, one very smart absentee owner.

I offered to take the dog for a few days, and then added her to my wonderful training dog group, and shortly thereafter to my own household. It was then that I realized it isn't always the number increase that changes the tipping point. In this case the dog herself was the tipping point.

She turned my glorious training dogs into problems. Given my job, this was a benefit because we got to work on things that I'm sure the owners struggle with, but I had never seen before.

But then there came my own household. The normal harmonious house of geriatrics turned into barking, demanding fools. If I went outside they barked. If I went inside they barked. No matter what, my dogs demanded and pushed until I felt my blood boil and wanted to run away from home.

I had never before thought of a personality as being a tipping point. But this dog's personality certainly is. Her energy and presence make all others around her change. They go to their default, whatever that might be. Dogs who once struggled being scared are more fearful when she is around. Dogs who are pushy and bold are ruder when she is around.

As fearful as this tipping point dog is due to her life circumstances, she is not truly fearful. I do believe her influence and effect on others speaks to her inner strength and determination. She was born strong and made weak by her circumstances. She truly is a wolf in sheep's clothing; only she believes that she is a sheep. Once she realizes who she really is, and her place in the world, she won't be such a negative influence on others.

March 18

Unflappable dogs

I have a new dog here who had me torn for the entire first day. I didn't know if loved him or hated him. He's funny but not too clever or honest. He's cute. Rather endearing, yet rude. And he's rather willing to bite. He's got heart, sass, and can hold his own—all traits that I greatly admire. Yet . . . my dogs hate him. They want nothing to do with him. Maybe they hate him because he is rude and has a temper. If he wants something, he thinks that using his teeth is how to get it.

My friend summed him up beautifully: He's the kid who no one ever took the time to tell that it is not okay to smack other children. Unfortunately, he has spent so much time smacking kids and enjoying how it makes others unsure of him that now it is taking some level of persuasion to explain that this is not nice.

And, in addition to that, as soon as our conversation begins, he yells in his loudest voice that I am not allowed to do this and he is phoning the police. Go ahead, son. Go ahead.

None of this fazes me. It is not his fault that people failed to parent him. Deep inside he is the perfect kid's dog, or therapy dog, or autistic dog. You could stab him with a pencil in a fit of fury, and he wouldn't care. You could put hair clips in his ears and he would wear them proudly. He is the perfect dress-up candidate.

But this same solidness of character makes it very challenging to tell him not to smack other children. It is hard to influence the unflappable.

What did faze me was his lack of obedience. He has no clue what "sit" means. Or how to walk nice on a leash. Or anything. Or, so I thought.

Then I happened to have a cookie on me. I got full attention. Perfect sits. And a pleasant dog, until the food was eaten.

He has been taught that if there is no reward, he has a choice. Somehow, through the process of obedience training, his instructors missed the most important part and the entire premise of why we teach obedience: to create nicer people.

Somewhere in this dog's past, one of his many owners took the time to train him. He has attended training classes. He learned his lessons. He was taught to be a what-is-in-it-for-me kind of kid. And his old owners failed to teach him any morals or character lessons. They forgot to teach him to be a nice person. And not to smack other children.

His old owners were failed by the industry. And now his new owners live with a love/hate dog. They deserve an award. Their marriage survived his arrival into their home, so I'm thinking nothing can tear them apart now.

Hopefully in another week he is going to be a whole lot easier to love. And a whole lot easier to live with. He has to be. He cannot stay the way he is.

March 19

Memory recall and adrenaline

James McGauch of the University of California at Irvine discovered that if he gave rats a shot of adrenaline after they learned something, they remembered it better. Adrenaline beforehand didn't work. It only boosted memory when given afterward.

Now think of your dog having a bad experience. The memories gained in that moment will be recalled before a previous memory of happiness in that same situation.

The moral of this story: when something bad happens to your dog, spend the necessary time to get him back to the right emotional place.

March 20

Trust your trainer

We all need help, but we also need to follow our gut. If you do not trust your trainer, find a new one. It isn't going to work if you second-guess every suggestion he gives you. Unless you believe in what he is telling you, you will not be able to execute it correctly, making it ineffective.

If you don't trust your trainer, talk to him about it, and then politely move on. If you discuss more of what type of person or methods you are looking for, most would be happy to help you find that right person.

Don't stay if it doesn't feel right. And if you opt to stay, buy in. But staying, without buying in, is just a giant waste of your money and everyone's time.

March 21

Retraining social issues

Retraining your dog to mind his manners and actually "like" other dogs is the equivalent of doing a 100-piece jigsaw puzzle. There is no one thing that is going to fix it, but your 100 right things, done in the right order, will. When you are retraining temperament issues it is going to take time, so learn to enjoy and embrace the journey.

As you put each piece of the puzzle into place, your dog should improve, but you need to put many pieces into place before you can actually see the fullness of the final picture you're trying to create.

Here are some of the pieces as I see them (and keep in mind they are different for working dogs):

- Learning to feel safe in the same room as other dogs.
- Learning that we will advocate for them, and will prevent them feeling uncomfortable.
- Learning to get up and move around without getting adrenalized.
- Learning to pass by other dogs.
- Learning not to stare at other dogs.
- Learning to walk past an off-leash dog approaching.
- Learning to mind their manners and not lose it.
- Learning how to be off leash with other dogs in a social setting.
- Acquiring a few dog friends.
- Having older socialized dogs present who will assist them as they are given more freedom approaching off-leash dogs out in the real world.
- On-leash pack walks in the real world (not a controlled environment).
- Off-leash pack walks in the real world (not a controlled environment).
- For those who want, learning how to play, or at least learning how to behave, around other dogs.
- For those who don't want to learn how to play, knowing how to calmly walk away.
- Learning appropriate ways to respond when other dogs are inappropriate to them.
- Responding to verbal commands when in high drive.
- Learning to maintain forward momentum going past a dog, without wanting to greet them.

Once they learn a lot of these pieces, these dogs end up becoming the best teachers for other over-reactive dogs.

March 22

A little wiggle room, a bit of control, and a touch of love

We need to allow some dogs to maintain certain bad behaviours that we would never normally allow, because taking it away will make the dog a shadow of his former self. If that "badness" is the only *oomph* the dog has, it needs to stay until more *oomph* is created. Specific badness is sometimes needed to grow confidence. However, you must teach control at the same time so these dogs don't explode on you once your confidence building is a success! And I would only advise doing this under the advice of a veteran, successful trainer.

We must know not to insult a strong dog with gushing, crooning praise, unless it is done at home, in private, where they might secretly love it. We must believe the praise we give to an intelligent dog; otherwise we are lying to him. We must know the give and take when getting a control-freak bitch to cooperate with our own agenda. We must also know how to make that same control-freak bitch love us when she doesn't need us. She must want us, and for that to happen, we must be worthy.

March 23

Veterinary examinations

We owe it to our dogs, and our veterinarians, to train our dogs for veterinary procedures. Our dogs need to learn that a strange humming, vibrating thing might go on all areas of their bodies (clippers), that all parts of their body will be examined, that scary lights might shine in their eyes, and that they will be restrained for blood samples and other scary procedures.

Teaching this takes some time to start, but will make their geriatric days when they need frequent vet care non-stressful—and make it easier for your vet to give your dog the care he needs.

It is not your vet's job to train your dog for examinations. It is yours. You owe it to your dog.

March 24
Honour thy dog

Always make sure you and your dog get what you need. If you are on a walk, a shopping trip, or any kind of outing, don't end up regretting not doing something that your dog needed to help him be a better dog.

Don't allow someone else's expertise to make you doubt what you are doing (providing it is working). And don't allow strangers to bully you into situations that you know your dog cannot master.

Rather, always take that moment to build your mental strength, and continue to do precisely what your dog needs, despite it perhaps being the opposite of what you are being pushed into doing.

Honour your dog. You know what he needs. And you are the one who has to look into his face and know in your heart that you gave him the help, support, or even the training situation that he needed to become a better dog.

March 25
Art or science?

We are repeatedly told that dog training is a science. I disagree. I think it is more of an art.

Each dog is a canvas with some paint already splattered on it. It is up to you to create your perfect dog. We are given a topic, given a base splatter of paint that we must work around, and then the creation is left in our own hands.

There certainly is a scientific component to it: if you do this, you will get that. But first you must envision your canvas so that you know what you want to create, and then use your science to help you get it.

This is the reason that if you present one problem to ten dog trainers, you will get ten answers. All might be right, but each trainer will create a very different canvas, depending upon what they saw.

March 26

Becoming a great trainer

Becoming a brilliant trainer is not about possessing inherent talent, or some genetic skill. It is about being humble, making yourself a vulnerable student, and more importantly than anything else, proper practice done every single day, including the days you don't want to.

Mental discipline and consistency are necessary pieces of the puzzle if you want to be a great trainer.

March 27

Dogs reveal us

Our dogs do not make us look bad. They just expose who we really are and give us the opportunity to make ourselves look bad.

Put your ego aside, put your expectations aside, and enjoy the moment with your dog. Then, in those moments where your ego might get bruised, only your great relationship with your dog will be exposed.

March 28

Consistent training is a must

Your dog will never improve if you don't practice a skill a minimum of four consecutive times a week. And, not only do you have to practice the skill, but practicing it wrong will teach your dog how to do it wrong. You must practice it right, using the tools you were given. If you struggle in your homework, which you will, ask your coach for solutions.

In an ideal situation, certain behaviours would be trained multiple times a day to give continual reminders to help your dog, and help you master the skill. Sometimes it is us, at the human's end of the leash, who need to practice several times a day to remove our old habits and remember how to do something right. If you struggle to change from your old ways, aim to work on mastering a skill for several short moments a day.

March 29

Small, manageable, yet difficult lessons

Sometimes the mother hen in us prevents us from allowing our dogs to solve their own problems, which in turn cripples our dogs from thinking through stress.

Recently I watched two perfect examples. One dog fell off the path that we were walking on and rather than try and climb back up, he just stood like Eeyore, with his head held low, mastering learned helplessness. He patiently waited to be lifted back up. The second dog jumped into water, then when he wanted back out, just stood there and barked his fool head off. Neither dog tried to fix their problem. One just waited patiently to be rescued, while the other demanded help, and now!

I teach my dogs how to problem-solve right from day one. If they need help, of course I provide it. But I also present them with opportunities to show me how brave and clever they are, so they can feel proud of themselves, and I can make sure I tell them they are.

What kinds of lessons? When a puppy does not know how to climb up or down stairs, I carry them almost the whole way up or down, but plop them down where they only have to master one stair. We graduate to two, then three, at which point, they no longer want your stinking help.

I walk along driftwood at the beach. Some of the trees are big cedars. My puppies or my clients' dogs follow along, and inevitably fall off, or cannot jump from one log to another. If there is an easy solution, I don't look back. I continue on and let them work out how to get back to me.

I put their dinner inside a cardboard box. They need to work out how to get in to get to their bowl.

I feed them (their food is in their bowl) inside my bathtub, shower, under a cupboard, or up high, etcetera. For some puppies that need some tenacity and bravery, I might try and hold them back from getting to their dish. Only effort will get them there.

There are many, many scenarios to create a problem-solving opportunity for your dog. Start finding small problems for them to solve, and then make sure you let them know how proud you are of them when they do it.

March 30

Write it down

You cannot succeed if you consistently rehearse your failures in your head. As you beat yourself up or recount your failings, you are reminding yourself of how to fail. This is all that you will remember to do. Be mindful to let go of your errors and instead focus on your successes.

After every training session or walk, write down everything that you did right. It will help you start to change your way of thinking.

March 31

Intuitive dogs

Some dogs are perceptive, intuitive, and we connect with them on a different level than regular dogs. I call these dogs "Intuitive Dogs."

Many people might confuse a trained dog with an Intuitive Dog. A trained dog is technically well schooled. They will hear our requests and cooperate. We compete with these dogs, and succeed in life with these dogs. They are a joy to live with and are easy. If you have not yet had an Intuitive Dog, you will struggle to understand the difference. But ten years from now when you get your first Intuitive Dog, you will suddenly realize what I mean.

The difference between an Intuitive Dog and any other dog is something that can only be described as their inner core, their essence, if you will. If you are looking at a well-trained one, on the outside, they appear to be the same as other well-trained/raised dogs, but there is a difference. These dogs will give their entire selves to you when you ask something of them. You get the physical response in addition to them giving you full mental control. Our connection with them is on a whole different plateau. And generally, they have not been easy at the start.

Trained dogs are responsive through technique with good education and repetition. They respond well to our cues. Many dogs become mentally available with good training. They become in sync with us.

The difference is with our mental control. In a trained dog, they will allow me to control them. They willingly and happily respond. In an

Intuitive Dog that control is effortless on both sides of the team. They respond to a thought, or a cue so slight you are unaware you even gave it. And likewise, you inherently seem to just know when they communicate something back to you.

Not only are they available to us, they are willingly available to us. These dogs are responding to the picture in our mind's eye before we speak it. Our words alone are not the cues for these animals. It is our thoughts, our beliefs, and our conviction in the command we deliver.

The difference comes from the inside of the dog. Our relationship and our requests are a conversation and a way to be, rather than a thing to do. It is effortless. The relationship is a combination of trust, feel, and conviction exchanged between dog and handler and back again. Trust comes from consistency and knowing what to expect. It means the dog can depend on her handler and vice versa. This relationship, once formed, just is. It is how they act as a pair, effortlessly communicating with and understanding each other.

I believe that to have an Intuitive Dog you must be intuitive and open yourself. Most of these guys that I meet are struggling with life, and causing major havoc to the harmony of their households.

Many of my clients struggling with their reactive dogs are experiencing exactly what I am trying to describe, but in this case, the cues have gone wrong. They have not yet found their place of harmony, and while their dog is responding to their slightest cue, it is a cue that the handler never intended to give.

The dogs are doing precisely as they have been told. They don't listen to words. They listen to your breath, your muscles, your fears . . . the cues you wish you were not giving. Once you can learn to control your thoughts and physical body, you will have the dog that will be effortless in those situations.

And likewise, if you are frustrated with these dogs, they will know it every single time you look at them. They hate being wrong and try so hard to please. To succeed with them we must be accountable for all of our thoughts.

Then there are the Intuitive Dogs who really are quite untrained, yet their connection is so deep to their person that it really does not matter. While the dog training itself might suck, both dog and human understand each other and continue bumbling along, having fun in the process.

Intuitive Dogs are outwardly available. They are very perceptive to our cues, intended or not, and will adjust their bodies accordingly. But they are also inwardly available. When we ask requests of them, they don't get mentally hard, resistant, or melt, but rather, they deliver, providing they know how.

We must be able to offer up the best of ourselves in order to get the best from them. The relationship is a two-way street, where you too are expected to be inwardly and outwardly available. I had three rescue puppies who all failed drastically in their good foster homes. Their foster homes, which succeeded with many other dogs, were unable to feel the struggles of these ones. As a result, they all had dangerous behaviours at incredibly young ages.

Within days of being understood, they were different dogs and their issues melted away, one by one.

People who do not feel the command they ask can really mess up a feeling dog, even if they are technically correct. Technical cues and release alone are not enough. These dogs can be heartbreakingly misunderstood. They end up stressed and unhappy, never able to do anything right. Many resort to just doing nothing . . . or being hard as steel.

These dogs are deep souls. They understand us on an unspoken level.

And finally, different sports reveal different types of Intuitive Dogs. A herding Border Collie is going to look very different to an IPO (formerly known as Schutzhund) German Shepherd, or an obedience Golden Retriever, or a reactive pointy-eared bitch.

Thank you to thought-provoking Pippa, Squizzle, Labrador Lewie, Biggy, Skye, Klaus, Rocket German Shepherd Dog, Millie Pit Bull, Finn Australian Cattle Dog, Mojito (my favourite Mexican), and all the other complex souls who have opened up their tormented minds for me to unravel.

APRIL

April 1
She will grow out of it, right?

Dogs who are in the teenage stage don't magically grow out of their behaviour problems.

Unfortunately, only their good qualities disappear as they go through puberty. As for the stuff we don't like, the mental strength of maturity, mixed with all of their rehearsal and success at being inappropriate, actually helps them *grow into* their problems.

In fact, if you're waiting for your dog to grow out of it, you're really just giving her a whole lot of time to rehearse her bad behaviour, and this will just make your problems a whole lot worse. Good training is the only thing that will help.

April 2
Who's training who?

In some of my classes this week, I realized how little the dogs cared about their owners' suggestions. In fact, the dogs did a brilliant job teaching their owners to try harder. Somehow the roles got reversed.

These dogs would come into their game-filled classes with toys and treats and, week after week, began to give less and less effort. Their toys weren't as nice as the toys the other dogs had, and their treats had the wrong texture. The fascinating part is that the less the dogs gave (with the exception of one brilliant handler), the harder the owners worked. Different toys were pulled out, better treats were brought to class, and the owners became more and more animated. Their efforts were rewarded one week, but the following week those same efforts were no longer very well-received by their dogs, so the owners tried even harder. Eventually the dogs were just leaping at the end of the leashes to say hello to one another. They only wanted to play with someone else's toys, and the work they used to love became ho-hum, laborious, and quite pathetic.

You can always tell the dynamic of your relationship by what body part your dog gives you. If he stares at you adoringly, you are worthy of his precious eyes. When he was a puppy, my German Shepherd Reggie stared at me with his cheeky grin, daring me to do something funny. Eyes are a good body part to get. They are giving you their attention, their heart and soul. But if all you get is their bum, they are turning their back on you and that is all they think you are worth. It is a harsh truth, but a truth nonetheless!

We frequently misunderstand our relationship with our dogs. To better understand your dynamic, just imagine if your spouse or child treated you the same way your dog does.

If my husband ever walked out of the room while I was talking to him, I would really question our relationship. I wouldn't try to continue the conversation, and I can assure you I would not pull out a beer and crack it open in the hope that the sound would entice him back.

If my dog walked out of the room while I was talking to him, I would also really question our relationship. And I wouldn't pull out his favourite cookies to entice him back. Yet many people do this with their dogs.

This behaviour indicates that you need to change your relationship. There is no one answer why your dog is doing this. I did exercises all week in every class to see who was training who, and I saw many different reasons why dogs don't want to engage with their owners. Two sad dogs didn't like their dominating owners, one didn't want to share his toys, many dogs were disrespectful teenagers with better things to do than listen to their nagging mothers, many were bored by their ever-trying-harder doormat owners, one was a complicated soul who didn't realize that rules applied to him, some were just desperately bored with their humans, and then I had many that were almost perfect.

Just like in our human lives, relationships with dogs are dynamic and complicated. There is no one fix. You need to learn who your dog is, and realize why you are getting the response that you are. Once you know that, the begging and bribery can stop, and you can think of ways to fix it.

At the end of the day when all the food and toys are gone, who are you to your dog? Are you important, exciting, fun, honest, trustworthy, and his best friend? Perhaps more importantly, do you deserve to be his best friend?

Now go fix your relationship, and make sure that you are his one and only.

April 3

Shoot for the stars

A wise person once suggested that I create a totally unrealistic goal for my dog and I—something that we could only do in our wildest dreams—and then get all excited about it and figure out how to achieve it.

What this will do is make you brainstorm and push you way further to make all the necessary changes in your life and training in order to reach your goal. And while you might never reach the unrealistic one, it has suddenly made your previous goals easy and reachable. But you also stand pretty good odds at getting your new goal, too.

I read this now, preparing to compete with my dog in Holland at a world championship. If you imagine it, you can make it happen.

April 4

Make your dog human-proof

Never underestimate the stupidity of a human. You don't know what unfair thing someone might do to your dog. Train your dog for every possible scenario that your over-imaginative mind can create, which will prepare him for what might happen. You cannot train for every scenario but you can get your dog so desensitized to stupidity that he becomes bomb-proof.

If you continually do ridiculous things to your dog and reward him with really great treats, eventually he will look forward to the next idiotic tortuous thing you do.

If you only train your dog to encounter nice, appropriate people, you are failing your dog. Teach him that people will do ridiculously stupid things to him, and that he can overcome them without the need for teeth. Only do these things to your dog yourself, and always reward with a giant meatball, or an equivalent reward, to make the torture worthwhile.

Go up and give your dog a giant smooch on the nose, then feed him a meatball. Go up behind him and gently pull his tail, and then feed him another meatball. In my lifetime of having dogs, I had one gentleman grab my Malinois by her cheeks, lift her gently, and kiss her on the nose. Both my dog and I were too shocked to respond. On another occasion, a baby took some of his first steps by grabbing my Pit Bull's tail and holding onto it like a towrope.

In the real world, you will do all that you can do to prevent any of this ever happening to your dog. But sometimes it is unavoidable despite your best efforts. When an "accident" happens and an unfair encounter occurs, pray that your torturous preparations will pay off and save your dog from feeling the need to bite.

While we won't test our dog to see his response, we can train our dog's response in case he is ever tested.

If you find that "accidents" and "stupid people" keep happening to your dog, it means that you are putting your dog in unfair situations and not doing your job. You and your dog should be a team, out exploring the world together and watching each other's backs. If events like this happen more than once or twice a decade, you are not watching your dog's back or protecting him sufficiently.

In no way am I suggesting that you should torture your dog for training, nor that you should allow people to be unfair to your dog in public. Make sure your dog is always protected by you. No dog should have to tolerate any rude behaviour from stupid people. We must do everything in our power to protect our dogs from unfair situations.

In the event that a not-so-bright person completely takes you by surprise like they did me, pray that your training will give you two to three seconds before a bite or bad response. With that little bit of time, you can get in there and take control of the situation and protect your dog.

April 5
The discomfort of strong corrections

I got into training dogs because I love dogs, not because I want to be mean to dogs. Yet sometimes being a good coach requires you to be hard, which makes you feel mean.

I'm faced with a dog that is rude with a side of nasty. She is a terrible combination of breeds. She has a terrible, fearful temperament and no boundaries. She was failed by well-meaning people who, probably like me, felt uncomfortable with the boundaries she requires.

But the oddest part of this is that she is not uncomfortable with corrections. She doesn't give a damn and they have no effect on her, meaning she needs stronger ones. We humans are uncomfortable with this fact—so much so that other trainers have suggested euthanasia as a more humane option. They are not wrong. Or are they?

This option protects our souls from the discomfort of her reality. My brain keeps trying to chew this concept, and all I keep coming back to is this: death is not kinder than a strong correction. But, in a way, euthanasia is easier *for me* because then I'm not judged and don't feel mean.

April 6

Relief: The emotion we don't expect

When you have a dog that would bite you, there is a world of hurt attached.

First, you are living with an abusive spouse, only it is not a spouse. If it were a marriage, your friends would all cheer when you left, and there would be resources to help you recover. With a dog, people will assume that you failed or didn't try hard enough. Not only are you not supported but you will be judged. Harshly.

And then there is your own inner grief. You love your dog. You know you can't do it anymore. You are at the end of your rope.

This decision is the most difficult one to make, and while you prepare yourself emotionally for the sadness, loneliness, and grief, the emotion that will kick the snot out of you, and pull your feet out from under you, is relief.

While relief is normally a blessing, in this moment, it will be crippling. The guilt attached will knock the wind right out of you. I was prepared to feel crappy. I was not prepared to feel improved. The conflicted emotions and the guilt attached will be very challenging to work through. Just know you are not alone.

If you have ever had to euthanize a dog for a behaviour problem, my heart goes out to you. It is probably one of the hardest decisions you will ever have to make in your life. And it is not one that I have ever seen a person take lightly.

April 7

Don't punish yourself

You cannot succeed with your dog if you consistently think about failure. To succeed you need to focus and remember your success, and rethink all that you do right.

Forget your errors and focus on your successes. Stop mentally punishing yourself when you make an error. We train our dogs with positive reinforcement, focusing on the success. Why do we fail to use the same successful techniques on ourselves?

Learn to control your mental game. This means letting go of your past errors and only remembering, practicing, and anticipating your successes. Once you are at this point, not only will you have changed your dog, you will have also trained, and changed, yourself.

April 8

My puppy, Pippa, at six months old

This weekend my six-month-old, impressionable puppy went on her first big road trip, and it was all about her and not her big brother. She's been on road trips before, but her big brother was always the celebrity. This time it was her turn.

Taking a young impressionable dog on the road is a challenge. They need to see the world, which will automatically happen on a trip, but you have to keep them from learning bad things, or being affected by scary things. At this age though, I must attempt to let her handle things on her own and push her a wee bit forward: I can't always hold her hand.

On this trip, she spent two days sitting in a chair with me at a seminar, slithering from my chair into my neighbour's when I wasn't paying attention. On the way home I had to do a little bit of damage control to make her realize that not every single person thinks she is as cool as all of her newfound friends do.

This included a ride on a ferry where I let her watch the entire world walk past (we sat next to the bathrooms), but I didn't allow anyone to pet her. At a dog-training seminar it might be cute when the dog next to you jams her tongue down your ear canal, but it isn't so much on the ferry (my apologies to the lady sitting behind us).

She had her first exposure to walking past nasty dogs who growled, barked, or bee-lined toward her as we walked past. She is now old enough that she has the tools to deal with it, and as hard as it was, I let her be as we walked straight past. I was ready to assist if she needed help, but she didn't.

She also got to meet her first cat, and she was certain the cat was after my life. She cautiously watched as I battled my allergies and demonstrated that I wasn't about to be murdered. I ignored her and just played with the cat. She took it all in, watching from her careful distance, then the next day gave him a tentative sniff.

When I arrived home, I had a more confident, cheekier, and much prouder young lady with higher drive.

The hardest part of raising a puppy is knowing when to protect like a mother bear, when to hold their hands, and when to pretend you don't see their inner struggle and let them deal with it on their own (but only when they have the skill set to succeed and you are still prepared to step in as needed).

April 9

Teach your dog to solve problems

Stress is present in every sentient being's life, whether we want to admit it or not. As a dog trainer, I strongly believe that allowing our dogs to avoid stress is a grave error. By avoiding, we fail to teach them how to deal with it. And the process of trying to avoid it becomes stressful in and of itself!

Stress management through problem-solving is taught in every single one of my classes. Recently in my Pet Manners class we saw two dogs who both had no idea how to think when they couldn't get their way.

They were held back from a cookie on the floor, and also told what the right answer was so that they could get the cookie. All they had to do was listen and think and the cookie was theirs. This level of stress is teeny tiny, and also very manageable for all dogs.

One dog chose to have an absolute hissy fit. She started leaping and barking, then gave up all effort and stood with her head hanging low, looking rather like a donkey. We helped her through the process and within seconds she worked out the scenario and was performing with enthusiasm again. She learned to problem-solve in this one moment, and now will need to practice a lot more so that hissy fits are not her first solution. We want her to think her way through puzzles, and in the process, learn to control herself.

The other dog chose this moment to try and bite her owner. This wonderful little princess is quick to use her teeth because it has worked for her. When she couldn't get her cookie, nastiness seemed like a suitable solution. But it wasn't, only listening and thinking was, which she soon worked out. We will continue to give her more and more scenarios, and we can teach her that teeth on human skin is not the answer.

Fortunately, in both cases the owners are fabulously committed to training their dogs, and both dogs are lovely little examples of their breeds, and just need schooling.

We owe it to our dogs to teach them how to cope with teeny tiny, manageable amounts of stress or we are not preparing them for life; they will only be able to cope with their predictable bubble, and any change will blow their minds.

Our lives will change over time. You will find yourself forced to travel for a wedding or funeral, you might have to move due to work, health, or finances. You might have to board your dog or have someone care for her if your health suddenly forces you to have a stint in hospital. You might suddenly find yourself surrounded by children or grandchildren.

All of these scenarios will be stressful for your dog. Teach her how to cope with stress now so that she has the skills to handle life in a healthy, functional way.

April 10

Three key principles

You can never lie to a dog. In order to train them, you must believe in them, respect them, and have good intentions. Hold on to these three principles, which are also the key principles in good relationships.

Feel what they are feeling, and operate from where they are at, without lowering expectations or criteria. Then guide them (or shove them, depending on the dog) into how you need them to behave.

My beliefs (the strengths that I see in the dog) will build the traits that I really like about them. The dog will understand my intentions so that she knows I have her best interest at heart, and "have her back" so to speak. My leadership, based on respect of who the dog currently is, and needs to become, will give her the guidance to become a balanced dog who is comfortable and safe in both her body and the world.

Dog training, to me, is not about teaching an exercise; it is about a relationship with a dog. We must have good and honest intentions and beliefs and give them respectful, fair, and consistent leadership. If we do this, our exercises make them nicer beings.

April 11

Be a good leader

Many of my clients don't enjoy the leadership role. However, you don't have to be militant to be a leader. The time you spend with your dog should be fun, but your dog must also heed your instructions. She must look to you for guidance and advice. I like my dogs to ask for permission, such as, "May I chase the squirrel?"

Leadership is about demonstrating and coaching what is right and never giving up your role, even when you are tired or it is really inconvenient.

Leadership is about respect. You must respect your dog for who she is, who she will become, her genetics, and her ancestry. For me, this includes feeling what my dog is feeling and operating from where she is at. I understand her. And I respect her for what her genetics bring, even when it doesn't fit in with my own social needs.

Leaders, however, don't settle—they are consistent and fair in their expectations. While I understand my dog's genetics, I don't allow them to excuse or lessen my training or expectations. My expectations for her are the same as any other dog, and I expect her to mind her manners. While my execution of helping her is different because I am operating from a place of understanding how she is feeling and the struggles she is having, my expectations do not lessen.

Leadership is gained as you guide your dog through life, giving help where help is needed and acknowledging moments of success. And through your journey, you need to believe in your dog, while understanding her motivations, respecting her struggles, and feeling what she is feeling.

April 12

Behaviour pattern changes

Last night and tonight, my Border Collie Kate woke up from a dead sleep wanting to attack something. I saw blood on the floor, so I wonder if her foot took the brunt of the attack. It was odd. Also, Kate has been rather invisible all this week, which is noteworthy. But what's most unusual is that she's been impeccably behaved. I took note.

My darling Neville recently died. Within the past six months, Neville started to get grumpy with the dogs. He bit a dog for the first time ever. And over the past two months, he had several dog fights with Basil, which was ridiculous because they were both old men, incapable of fighting. Neville had cancer. This week he bled out, and I had to let him go. His temperament change was the cancer brewing.

Gibson the Golden Retriever—my darling, sweet Gibby—also showed a temperament change and gave me a warning sign when he had Hemangiosarcoma. Gibby always slept close to us, but at age eleven, he wanted to sleep away from us. It was his cancer. When he was diagnosed, we put him on medication, and he lived past the expiry date of his ailment.

Which takes me back to Kate. I'll be making a trip to the veterinarian this week. I hope I'm just being paranoid, but I always pay attention when there's a pattern change in my dogs. Hopefully it's simply that she's becoming nicer and easier to live with, with the odd nightmare in the middle of the night. Poor Kate.

April 13

Be careful what you reinforce

In some ways, our dogs are simple creatures. They repeat what has been reinforced.

Sometimes we are unaware of our reinforcing responses. If you respond with a giggle when your dog pulls a naughty prank it can be a huge reinforcer, and you can be sure that you'll see that prank again.

Biting our tongues is sometimes hard to do, but it's oh-so-necessary if you don't want the behaviour repeated. Especially when your dog fancies himself a comedian.

Ask anyone with a Keeshond or a Standard Poodle. Training these dogs requires a poker face, which the successful trainers already know.

April 14

Finding a trainer

Finding a good trainer is not easy. Certifications and accreditations mean less than the paper they are printed on. Affiliation to a group is easy to get, providing you are willing to pay. None of this is proof of talent.

Almost any dog trainer with ten years of experience running a business knows a lot. In ten years, they will have seen things you cannot imagine! Another way to find a good trainer is to go to a winning competitor in the instinct sport of your breed, or in competition obedience. Competitors are realistic about getting results in a respectable time frame, while removing all training aides.

But experience and success are not the only criteria. Once you have found some potential trainers, you need to watch them work with their dogs, which will be more telling. If they have an amazing bond, watching them will give you goosebumps. It is a thing of awe and beauty to see. The dogs will stare at them with adoration, willing to give their heart and soul.

Go and watch the trainers' classes. You need to make sure that what you see feels right to you. And that the dogs in the room are behaving as you would like yours to—and look content doing so. While being a winning competitor makes you a good trainer, it does not necessarily make you a good teacher. You need a successful competitor who also has successful students. Ask for some references.

There are many, many outstanding trainers out there. They are not a rarity but they are hard to find because they are busy training and are rarely inside typing on a keyboard or working on flashy web pages.

While some great trainers will be missed with my selection criteria, this is an easy way to find someone who can help you—someone who actually has the education and experience to pull it off.

April 15

Be honest about breed selection

If you want your dog to love everyone, get a sociable breed from sociable parents. Shop within the sporting breeds.

If you like a dog with a wee bit of an edge who would guard, look at the working/herding breeds and the like. But don't expect them to love everyone! (Even though some can be extremely sociable, you won't know that until your dog is an adult.)

Don't try and turn a genetic police dog into Lassie. And don't try and make Lassie a police dog.

Don't lie to yourself about how much exercise you will do either. If you prefer your couch, don't pick a high-energy breed. Recently a client was looking at high-energy breeds because he walks two miles a day. To him two miles was a lot. To a high-energy breed, two miles is just a warm up.

Be honest about what you want in a dog, and make sure you select a breed that has that temperament and energy match. While some from each breed will be exceptions, know what you are choosing, and make sure it fits into your lifestyle.

April 16

We don't need no stinking approval!

If you want to succeed with your dog, you have to be independent of approval from others. The only approval that matters, whether it's about your performance, your walk, or your experience, is your own. No stranger's approval or opinion should matter. They don't know where you have come from, what you know, or what it is like to walk a mile in your shoes with this dog. Therefore, their assessment cannot be accurate. Develop a thick skin, and learn to ignore comments that are not constructive.

But being truly independent of approval from others also means that compliments from outsiders, while they might be nice, should not alter your thoughts or behaviour.

Neither the positive nor the negative opinions of others should affect your inner judgement of your own moments.

When you're free from approval, you can see your moment for precisely what it was.

April 17

The dog trainer's plea

I love my job. I love my job more than you can even imagine.

But. Some weeks my job is exhausting. Emotionally exhausting more so than anything else.

On a typical day, my people have a problem. They ask me a question. I give them a solution. Then, remarkably often, they ignore my solution. The exhausting part comes from after hours, when I must counsel them through all of their own emotional baggage as we repair the error that resulted from not heeding the advice they paid for.

Why?

When there is a disaster with your dog, the emotional toll on all involved is extreme. The people are now high-strung, devastated. I am exhausted from the heavy communication, and I'm angry thinking of their dogs, their poor dogs, who will always pay for their people's errors.

Their dogs are sad. Depressed. If they are still alive, they know they have behaved badly. They feel the energy at home. Though they probably have no idea why. (In reality, they never were bad. Their owners put them in unfair situations that they could not handle.)

There really is no moral to this story, other than it's been an awful week. Each day, all day long.

But I can say one thing: if you trust your dog trainer, then trust her enough to actually listen. Even when it doesn't fit conveniently into your life. Or, if there are exceptions that you need, run it by your trainer. We are human, and we do know how challenging life can be, and we can help you find solutions that work for you and your dog.

So use us. Run ideas by us. But please, don't ask us for our opinion then choose to ignore it. But, if you do, and you do get into trouble, know that we will be there to help you pick up the pieces. Again and again.

April 18

Bad training habits

I like to reward. It makes me feel good. And my dog likes his rewards.

If a reward is an expectation, it no longer works as a "reward." For example, if I vacuum out your car every week and every week you give me 20 dollars, I will come to expect that amount. If one week you give me five dollars, I probably won't clean your car again (unless I naturally love that type of work, which I don't).

I was doing the same with my dog. Because of the predictability of where I was placing my "rewards," they were expected. If they did not arrive on schedule, my dog's performance was affected. In retrospect, the lack of reward was indicating to him that he hadn't performed to my standards, so he started trying harder.

I must force myself to be unpredictable. Sometimes the reward will be 20 times better than normal, but will only come after 30 good things have been executed. Sometimes I will reward all the tiny details. And sometimes he just gets a "good boy." To be fully educated he must know all possible outcomes.

Being a creature of habit, I am good with being unpredictable for a while, and then fall back into what I am comfortable with.

For my dog to receive the education he needs, regardless of what is in my pockets, I must remember to stay unpredictable.

April 19

Switch up your rewards

Last night Pippa ate her first bit of roasted tongue. Pippa has lived a fairly dull life as far as dog treats go. She mostly gets really boring stuff, and occasionally really good stuff. Why?

She has learned to give me all her effort for boring food. Now I have a whole lot of variety if I want to reward her heavily. The day she got to try Cesar (wet dog food otherwise known as doggie crack), her eyes bugged out of her head. She had no idea food could be that delicious.

If I have a dog with no work ethic, or one who is having challenges, I will use the food that I need to use to get the effort. But quickly, I want to scale it back to the most boring food I can use that will still get the job done as quickly as possible.

If they get the best treats for the easiest and simplest of challenges, what will you give them when they excel with a very challenging exercise?

Be conscious of the treats you give. There is a time for beef heart and other heavenly treats. But if the exceptional treats become your norm, you have set the bar very high for your dog, and she will be disappointed when you pull out a measly piece of kibble! Unless she is a Labrador—then she won't care!

April 20

Training or enabling?

Recently I got to work with an amazing handler. She had done her ten thousand hours of practice, yet still lacked a finished result. She was trying to teach her dog to ignore something, but it indirectly became the very thing that made them both change what they were doing and go into a ritualistic behaviour pattern. This routine was making them both that much more alert and aware of the thing that they were trying to ignore.

He wanted to lunge at dogs. She wanted him to ignore dogs, so she rewarded a myriad of alternate behaviours as soon as she saw a dog, with great skill and timing. What looked like great training from the outside was inadvertently putting focus on the other dog.

I mean, let's be honest. Let's say we are sitting in a restaurant having a casual conversation, and every time you notice the waiter is about to come to our table, you begin firing math questions at me. I'm not stupid. By the third occurrence I'm going to start looking for the waiter when you ask me the math questions.

When the objective is for the dog to ignore, step one must be for *her* to ignore. She is the dog's coach and must demonstrate what she wants. Ignoring means all the praise, eye contact, and acknowledgement must stop and, instead, she must walk along normally like nothing has changed. Both of her arms must swing, and she must look like a normal person, walking a normal dog.

And by golly, when she tried this, he quit lunging. Just like that. After years of lunging, he stopped when she stopped.

Now, if she hadn't done all the foundation work, this would not have worked so perfectly and instantly (and I might not have looked so amazingly brilliant). But fortunately she had done her foundation work to perfection, and she just needed an outside eye to shove her to the next step. This is a lesson I regret not having on video! Sometimes the answers are so easy, yet so incredibly difficult to find when you are trapped in a negative feedback loop.

April 21

Embrace your entire dog

Remember: dogs are whole beings. They are not a fast sit, a sliding down, and a great retrieve. They have their own minds, worlds, and emotions, and we must remember that as we train. They are more than the series of behaviours we program into them.

My puppy, Pippa, has so much that she needs to learn to be the dog that she needs to be. When I look at how far we have to go, and at how little she knows given her age, sometimes I feel a mild panic. But you can only train the dog you have, and for her, more important than learning the series of behaviours is learning the series of behaviours with the right emotion. First, I need her to be "up" and brave.

As she learns what she needs to learn, I have not forgotten "her": her personality, her needs, her sense of humour, her energy, and most importantly, her joy. By taking the time on our foundation building blocks, we will end up saving time, as we will have nothing to fix later. (At least in theory!)

You must embrace and train the entire dog, and not focus only on the things that you ask them to do. By being mindful of their complex little worlds, and making sure they get what they need, you are truly honouring your dogs.

April 22

Our dogs are our teachers

We are not training dogs; we are working on ourselves. This process is uncomfortable at first as you try to find meaning from answers that make no sense to you. As you start to grasp the solutions, your lessons will transform your life, and it will become an enjoyable process.

Our dogs are wonderful teachers when we are willing to be open and become their students.

April 23

Listen to the dogs

Let's be honest: there are good trainers, adequate trainers, and bad trainers.

Regardless of the tools they use, good trainers have dogs who are both happy and trained. Bad trainers have dogs who are either happy or trained. A good trainer is not limited by what is in their pockets or what equipment they use. They have their mind, their presence, their ability to read dogs, and impeccable timing.

They can see what they like, and motivate the dog to give them more of it. They can minimize what they don't like by building an alternate behaviour or emotion, or just by asking that it goes away. They make their dogs into believers; they believe they are the best dog in the world, and their relationship with their person can take them through thick and thin. The weakest dog will look strong beside a good trainer and the strongest dog will look proud and contained.

A good trainer knows when to rush in and help their dogs, and they know when to let their dogs work it out on their own. A good trainer knows when to push for more and when to settle for less. And they know when to call it a night. There are no recipes for training dogs. Nor are there absolute rules. And we must sometimes break our own rules to reach our goals.

Don't be so naïve to judge a trainer by his or her tools. Rather, listen to what the dogs say about how they are being trained. They will tell you the truth. Today one client sounded harsh to his dog, and as he made these very tough commands come out of his mouth, his dog's face went soft and his bum wiggled, giving his soft owner away. I've seen many a kind, ball-toting person whose dog tells a very different, sadder, story. Listen to the dogs; they will tell you.

April 24

Our problematic dogs

Wayne Dyer once said: "How people treat you is their karma; how you react is yours."

People will judge you when you walk your dog. They will judge you for your dog's behaviour, for how you handle your dog, for the breed you chose, for the equipment your dog is wearing, and the list goes on.

My friend recently said the most brilliant thing to me, which stuck: "Your opinion of me is none of my business."

Now apply this to your dog walks. People will have opinions and judgements regardless of what you do. Ignore it. Do what your dog needs you to do.

And smile. Be nice to the judgemental person. Your reaction shows your dog that you are in a happy place and that your critic had no impact on you—and that your critic doesn't need to be disciplined by a dog!

I will leave you with one final Wayne Dyer quote: "If you change the way you look at things, the things you look at change."

April 25
You cannot lie to a dog

Our facial muscles have a mind of their own and will show the emotions that we are feeling, even when we try desperately to hide them. Emotions leak out of us and cannot be fully contained. Even when we try and fake an emotion, we cannot. For instance, a fake smile uses less muscles than a real smile. In our fake smiles we use our mouths. In real smiles we use our mouths, but we also use tighten the muscle around our eyes.

You cannot lie to a dog. They are masters at reading our bodies and faces. They know what you are feeling, regardless of what you choose to tell them, and what you believe you are communicating.

This means it is time to get a grip on your emotions, and make sure that when you say, "good boy," your entire face says the same. Your eyes need to tighten while your mouth smiles to convey your happiness. Learn to feel what you say, and say what you feel.

You cannot lie to a dog. Make sure that you feel and truly convey the emotions that your words are meant to say, otherwise your dog will not believe you.

April 26

Influencing our dogs

There is a big difference in teaching a set behaviour, such as a sit (the act of teaching your dog to put his bum on the ground), and retraining an emotion (from which most behaviour problems stem), such as dog aggression.

With "sit," I am asking a dog to use his body in a particular way while attending to what I am communicating. This is easy to do. It is a simple transaction. If you do this for me, you will get this. The "this" is most often an external thing that you can give to them. This is very easy to teach to anyone, even people with little feel and timing succeed.

If I am working with a behaviour problem, I am teaching a dog to control or change an emotion. There is no set behaviour that I am asking for. Instead, I want him to keep it together and not have an emotional outburst while minding his manners.

For example, if I have a meek dog who is fearful when other dogs ram their faces into hers, she will desire safety first and foremost. I can offer her safety (and make sure these things will never happen when I am with her, and it is me and her against the world). She will always value and want what I can offer. I'm offering a relationship, and it's something I'll always have.

However, this is much harder to teach. Feel and timing is needed, because you we cannot smother her with protection all the time, or she will get weaker and not stronger. You must be able to read when she is beginning to feel scared, so that you can help her deal with it. But if you don't have feel and timing, you might not notice the beginning, or you will notice too late and won't be much use to her.

Dog training is about creating influence on our dogs. How can we influence their behaviour to get what we want? There are many ways, which will depend on if you want a behaviour, an emotional change, or both. A hungry dog will work for food, but a hungry dog in the throes of fear will only seek safety, not food.

Our job as trainers is to influence them to get what we need.

April 27

Greedy dogs

Hungry or greedy dogs are the easiest to influence. However, getting a behaviour consistently when the food is gone can be a lot more challenging. Make sure you always praise *before* you feed, so that your praise develops value. Then when the food is not available, your dog is still getting something from the transaction.

April 28

Know your beginner breeds

Some people believe that all breeds of dogs are the same—they are just dogs. When raised right, they should all look the same.

I believe this sentiment is a dangerous one for dogs. If I believe my Border Collie can be like my German Shepherd, who can be like my Irish Terrier and Golden Retriever, I've completely forgotten breed traits, instinctive abilities in certain breeds, and, in all honesty, respect for the dogs themselves.

Through knowing who they are, what they were bred for, and by being honest about things in the breed that we might not like, we can put the training in place so that it never becomes a problem.

Having good intentions while raising your puppy will not necessarily give you a great dog. Some breeds take ginormous skill to raise successfully, while others are easy. Beginners need beginner breeds, mid-level trainers have a much larger selection to choose from, and

the quirky, high-energy, or very mentally strong breeds should probably stay only with the overachievers or experts.

A few great beginner breeds are Pugs, Golden Retrievers, Smooth
Collies, Whippets, and Cavalier King Charles Spaniels.

When beginners get breeds whose needs are way above their skill
set, failure is almost inevitable.

April 29

Humility for success

I think what I love most about dogmanship is that as soon as you think
you might know a little bit, you get a new dog who reminds you
that you don't! This must be one of the only fields that requires you
to be humble for success—you must be willing to ask for help or
you will fall flat on your face!

As I sit here writing this, I look down on the floor and see Kate,
my new project Border Collie, reminding me of this rule.

April 30

Elements of great dogmanship

When our dog's level of excitement rises, more often than not ours
rises as well. However, we must know when to dial it way back,
which often is a fight against every fibre in our bodies. This requires
discipline from us, not from the dog!

Sometimes we need to go into particular situations with a very
deliberate mindset and energy, which will vary depending on the
dog and the day. But the key to success is not how you go in—it
is knowing that split second when you should become totally and
completely soft, in your mind, your muscles, your energy, and your
thoughts: as soon as the dog shows effort.

Great dogmanship is about feel and timing, which is turning it on, then turning it off, by altering your own internal state. You should be able to control your own energy as quickly, deliberately, and smoothly as you can flip a light switch.

Great dogmanship is having your emotions, energy, and muscles on cue. You can become whoever you need to be at the push of a button, depending on who you are working with. One mentor said it best: it is putting a mask on, becoming that person, for as long as your dog needs it, then knowing precisely when to take it off.

And please remember: it isn't the ability to put the mask on that counts. While useful and necessary, it is knowing when to take it off that will give you greatness.

MAY

May 1

Excitement isn't always bad

I will never forget the time I was talking to a teacher at school in a very happy and excited way, and she responded in a very calming, monotone voice. Not only did she refuse to share my happiness and excitement, she found it problematic and tried to calm me. It angered me immensely. Never did I go back to that teacher again for anything, as she wanted to change who I was.

There are moments when we need our dogs to be calm and controlled, and we must train accordingly. But there are also moments when it is totally right for our dogs to be excited and bubbling over. Don't try and calm them in those moments. Rather, share their joy and enthusiasm, and then give them a request (a simple "sit" will do).

Needing them to be "calm" in set moments is very different than *always* requiring them to be calm. To request that of them is like sucking all their self-esteem out with a straw.

For many dogs who are forced to be calm all the time, their excitement ends up oozing out of them in inappropriate ways.

Don't raise your young dogs as though you live in a library. While library behaviour has a perfect time and place, they also need moments of gym behaviour. There are appropriate moments for energy and excitement, just as there are appropriate moments for calm and thought.

May 2

Respect the breed

I'm witnessing a complete lack of respect, and it is breaking my heart.

When you select a purebred dog from working lines, you are getting with it an ancestry of generations of dogs who were bred to do a certain job. This job is in their core; it is part of who they are, whether or not you choose to teach it.

To select a breed and then decide that you want the dog to be the opposite of what genetics dictate is absolutely disrespectful. While you may achieve your goals and accomplish what you wish, it will be at the cost of the dog. She will not be happy and proud if you are asking her to be the opposite of what she should be.

Please don't be naïve when selecting a breed. Understand who they are and embrace it, and make them the best that they can be. But don't ask them to be the opposite.

I respect my dog's thoughts and feelings. And he should respect mine. This all begins with being honest about who they are and moving forward from there.

May 3

Walk the walk

One of the highlights of my day is watching my dogs be dogs first thing in the morning on their hikes. If I were forced to pick only one thing to do with my dogs, I would give up training and pick hiking. It is my favourite time spent with my dogs.

I am often in awe of how many people *do not* walk their dogs. How can we expect them to be great house pets, or our partners in competition, if we do not take care of their bodies and give them time to mentally clear their heads?

All dogs (with the exception of most English bulldogs) benefit from 75 minutes of exercise in one long hike. If you are struggling with a really busy dog with behaviour problems, commit to one two-hour hike a day for two weeks. You will be amazed at the difference in your dog in this short period of time.

I consider my dogs to be athletes and, as such, I take the time to condition their bodies, which also clears their minds. Walk your dog. Not only will your dog be much happier, it will make you happier and healthier too.

May 4

Freedom for reactive dogs

Freedom is a relative term, especially when we are describing dogs that have never had any. An extra inch of leash for a reactive dog who must always be reined in can be a big bonus. A foot of additional leash can be a huge reward for some of these dogs, and full freedom on a flexi leash (providing you know how to use it) can be heaven to them.

With many of our difficult characters, the more we attempt to rein them in on their walks, the more they want to bust out. Sometimes it feels like you are walking a coiled spring ready to explode! You must graduate to giving carefully controlled freedom so that they can start to be the dogs they need to be.

Your rewards for good behaviour will be freedom, with loss of freedom as a consequence for inappropriate behaviour. You will be surprised and relieved at how quickly your dog comprehends the new rules and manages his own behaviour a whole lot better. Because, let's be honest, freedom is a whole lot more valuable than a cookie.

Freedom holds more value than a food reward. It fulfills a dog's inherent need to explore. And our weaker aggressive dogs need freedom even more, so that they can learn to stand on their own four feet.

As your training advances, switch your reward from food to the gain or loss of freedom. It is this piece of advice that will give you a "normal" dog.

May 5

Socialization for teenagers

Most people are really good about showing their young puppies the world. Ideally, your puppy will witness every scenario that she will ever need to encounter by the age of 13 weeks.

However, this socializing must continue. Perhaps the most important age to get your dog out and regularly seeing the world is between seven and ten months. This is the age that many dogs become weird or fearful and never bounce back.

Make sure they are seeing the world, going into shops, sitting at your feet while you have coffee and beers on outside patios, going to petting zoos, walking around busy downtown parks, etc., every single week, until they are at least 13 months old. At that time, you can back off and just enjoy your normal daily walks and routines with your dog, with perhaps monthly outings.

The seven-to-ten-month-old stage might be the most important one of all.

May 6

Our bodies give us away

When we are feeling scared or vulnerable, our bodies will naturally seek out the fetal position. Obviously we don't drop to the ground on the trail when we feel uncomfortable, but our bodies will still seek that position. If we're standing, we'll bring our shoulders forward and push our bums out.

Focusing on this alone will totally change your dog's response to all of the things that make your heart flutter.

When presented with a challenge fight the urge to drop forward and stick your bum out. To prevent yourself bending at your torso, thrust your pelvis forward. Then to stand taller, imagine a string on your head pulling you up to the sky. As this happens, you will naturally straighten out your spine. Then stick your chest out and bring your shoulder blades back. You have now opened up your airways, and have shown a confident posture for your dog.

Think of your posture as you pass things that make you uncomfortable. If you can maintain a confident posture, soften your muscles, walk your path, slow down just a tiny bit, and act like you own that entire pathway, your dog will turn into a marshmallow beside you.

Our dogs long for us to take control. It is hard to persuade them of that when our body is seeking the fetal position! So stand tall, and do your job. Your dog will thank you for it.

And, as an added life benefit, the body language you learn to communicate and lead with will become your source of confidence in future group activities in your professional life. We are not training dogs; we are really working on ourselves through our dogs.

May 7

Train before bed

Dogs live in the moment. We all know that. What we don't know is that they also sit around thinking about what they have done.

We all know the concept of latent learning is a powerful tool when training your dog. If you have a difficult lesson that you need to teach, teach it right before bedtime, and you will be amazed at how much greater your dog's understanding is in the morning when she wakes up.

Latent learning is a powerful force. Sometimes teaching your dog a lesson and then putting her away to think about it is more useful than continuing on. Learning and then going to bed cements an idea in her head, making our job of teaching so much easier.

May 8

Signs of a good breeder

I love breeders. I love great rescue organizations too, but this is about knowing if you have the right breeder. And I'm talking about avid supporters of a breed or sport who have made bettering dogs a lifetime quest. A good breeder differs from backyard breeders and puppy producers in many ways. Here are some signs that you've found a good breeder:

- Every friend they have on Facebook has the same dog in their profile picture, or participates in the same sport.
- They spend their holidays travelling the world looking for better bloodlines, or scouring the internet doing the same.
- Their way of life revolves around their breed, and their next major dog event.
- Every tote bag, T-shirt, and sweatshirt they own has a picture of their breed on it.
- When you ask about a bloodline's heritage, they will be able to tell you every dog in the pedigree and why they are there. It is a great fix for insomnia.
- They can tell you the strengths and weaknesses of all dogs in their bloodline and what they've done to protect and improve this litter. This includes official traceable health ratings specific to their breed, and they have the certificates and numbers to prove it, such as OFA and Cerf (for eyes), just to name a few.
- They know where their National Specialty, or Nationals, was for their sport for the past five years.
- Many have to supplement breeding with another income. It is hard to make money when the sire is from some faraway land and the bitch only has four or five puppies!

- When their puppies are ready to go, not a day before 49 days, you can barely pry them out of their hands, and they'll always have new stipulations and expectations for you. Hang in there. Given the love that has gone into your dog, you can forgive cold feet prior to parting.
- People who get one of their dogs keep going back, dog after dog, or if their needs change, they will still consult them for bloodline advice.
- The cost of your dog, unless it is a breed that has tiny litters, will be cheaper than pet stores or puppy mill dogs. There are no add-ons to the price. Parti-colours do not cost more than solid colours. Papers are included. I have yet to know a breeder who can actually show a profit on her income taxes. They must exist, but I don't think I know one!
- They will know solutions for behaviour or health problems, or the right person that can help you with their type of dog. Your puppy will have already been to a vet prior to you getting him, with documented details of what was done and what needs to be done next.
- If your life changes and you are forced to let go of your dog, it is a contractual obligation that he gets returned to his breeder.
- Getting a dog from the right breeder comes with an encyclopedia of knowledge attached, free for the lifetime of your dog. Use it. In some cases it also comes with bargain grooming prices and rock-bottom boarding costs!
- And finally, a great breeder knows when to call it quits. This might mean switching from breeding Great Danes to Papillons, or from German Shepherds to Himalayan cats. But regardless, they know when they are too old to honour their breed, or to take back returned puppies, and hand over the towel to a keen young student of their breed.

I love my breeders. They have all taught me so much. We couldn't have the great dogs we have without them.

May 9

Take time to think

Dog training is a thinking-person's sport. When I'm "doing" it I get ideas, and sometimes I can easily work out the solution. But nine times out of ten, after a really thought-provoking training session, the solution will come to me when I am lying in bed, when I cannot turn my brain off.

This week alone, there have been two occasions where I went to bed tired, then my brain started to churn up solutions or analogies that kept me awake for hours as I pondered all angles.

Make sure that you keep a balance between thinking and doing: 20 percent doing to 80 percent thinking. Not reading. Not discussing. But straight, flat-out thinking. Your solutions will come to you when you are walking in the forest, having a shower, or other moments when your mind is completely clear.

For me, it is my morning walks that give me almost all of my solutions—they are the best thing for my improvement.

May 10

The balance of want versus accuracy in training

There is a very fine line between building "desire," otherwise known as "want," and getting accuracy when training your dog. The more want you have in your dog, the messier your exercises will be. Having a happy, wild partner is a joy, but not when things constantly get knocked over and broken in your house.

However, accuracy with no want is not enjoyable for you or your dog. Try and find the delicate balance between want and accuracy, and when forced to choose between the two, always choose more want.

May 11

Your yes-to-no ratio

Have you ever counted how many times you nag your dog with "uh-uh" and "no"? We are often unaware of how negative we can be. While the word "no" is important, don't abuse it.

When you are teaching your dog new concepts, or when you're training difficult things, make the wrong thing hard, and the right thing easy. We learn more from what we do right than from what we do wrong. Therefore, set up your lessons so that the right way is easy for your dog to choose, and the wrong way takes more effort.

I have some clients who are *tsk-tsk*ing at their dogs every ten seconds, but don't realize it. I challenge you to put a handful of dollar bills in your pocket (or a roll of loonies if you're Canadian!), and for every negative, nagging sound that you make to your dog, give a dollar away to someone.

"No" is a necessary word, but your dog shouldn't think it is his name. Let your yes-to-no ratio be high. I aim to say, "yes," 99 percent of the time, and, "no," just one percent of the time. Your dog should not be hearing "no" daily, and probably not even weekly. But when they do hear it, you need to mean it and follow through without an apology attached.

A young dog or a dog who is new to you should only be hearing "no" once or twice a day for serious infractions. If you are using it more than that, it means they have too much freedom with which to get into trouble, or way too little exercise.

Don't chip away at their self-esteem all day long by nagging at them. Alter your training so that you can praise them for their brilliance instead. Rather than ruin your relationship, improve your management or exercise them more. A tired dog is a good dog.

May 12

Too much dog?

We would never put a green rider on a green horse. Yet unskilled novice dog owners often get dogs from breeds that are way above their skill level. Luckily, sometimes it works out. But there are many situations where it does not. Some dogs simply require more skill than their people possess.

If you find yourself smashing your head against a wall and never making the progress that you feel you need to make, consider board-and-train, or a day program where a trainer is training your dog for you.

While you will still have training to do, and will still need to improve your personal skill set, these programs will get you over the hump so that you can be successful.

May 13

Puppy training 101

Training a new dog or puppy is not just about teaching "sit" and "down" or walking on a loose leash. You will inhibit and confine your dog's growth if this is all you do.

What you should be working on, first and foremost, is creating a desire in your dog to want to be with you. Your puppy should want to work for you, should be happy when she pleases you, should listen when you speak, and should generally think that you are the coolest person in the whole world. We must teach puppies to not lose their tempers, be nice to others, share their toys, be handled, be left in a crate, follow us around, play with us, cuddle with us, and handle themselves in public.

My rescue puppy is working on all of these things every single day, but my actual obedience training with her has been very limited. But it won't matter. If I can teach her all of the above, she will be such a keen and willing student that she will pick up on all of her lessons quickly.

These fundamentals will make teaching the other things a piece of cake. That is what dog training is all about, but this is also the piece that seems to get forgotten. Training is giving a dog the tools to be a "nice person."

May 14

How you see your dog

If you believe your dog will succeed, he will, and you can acknowledge it. Or, if he fails, you can gently guide him to succeed, and then you can acknowledge it.

If you expect he will fail, he will, and you can correct him with disappointment foremost in your mind. Your mental energy will be very different, because your dog let you down, again.

The eyes through which you see your dog will dictate how your training session of that day goes. Be fair to your dog always, even when you are irritated with him.

May 15

Look for the good

When working with a fearful dog, I want to coach strength and bravery into her, and this is the direction that my chin will be set as we head out on our adventures.

I still believe that my dog is brave despite the damage done or the behaviours I see. Because I have told myself this, my mind will be looking for teeny moments of bravery, which I will see, register, and remember.

Don't look for the flaw that you are trying to remedy.

Look for moments of brilliance and remember and believe them. You will get what you see. So make sure you see all of the good.

May 16

The voices of their ancestors are louder than ours

I once worked with a fabulous specimen of a dog from a breed and a bloodline that is intended to bite. And they do—well.

This dog was selected for a job where the animal is required to be gentle and kind to people. This dog was given great training, mastered the complex tasks of the work, and yet was unable to be kind and gentle to people. Genetics took over, and bites were given instead of kisses.

I was asked to assess if we could make the dog sweet and gentle, rather than wanting to bite. My answer was, "Yes, however, one day when the environment is more stimulating, his ancestors will speak louder to him than you do, and he will listen to them, not you. They will have a more influential voice when guiding him, and he will bite." The dog might be fine for 300 consecutive jobs, but on the 301st, his ancestors might guide him.

This dog was euthanized. A completely healthy dog was euthanized because he did what he was bred for. This case still haunts me.

If you want Cujo, get Cujo. If you want Lassie, get Lassie. But don't be naïve and think you can turn Cujo into Lassie. You might be able to nine out of ten times, but the one time he does what his ancestors tell him to do, he will be a dead dog.

A fabulous, young, healthy spirit was destroyed for being a perfect specimen of his breed.

Humans can be so unfair to dogs.

May 17

Suppression: Dogs under constant command

Suppression is blind obedience; dogs are always under command and micromanaged and rarely allowed mental freedom, if at all. This is very stifling for them.

If you have only ever been told what you can do, you are unable to think beyond that. Making an appropriate choice is not something that you have exposure to. So when freedom is given, the odds are heavy that the choice made will be a wrong one.

These dogs often behave while in close proximity of their owner, but as soon as they get out of reach, they do not listen at all. If you find this is your dog, start commanding way less frequently, but demand perfection when you do.

To have a dog who will listen when he's away from you, start out by giving him mental freedom for large amounts of time, where he is not under command. Once you give mental freedom and then teach control, you will find that you rarely have to use it in life.

May 18

Get your own puppy

People thought I was an ogre when I wouldn't let every single person pet my adorable puppy, Pippa. How could it be beneficial to her if every single person stops, bends over top of her, and pats her on the top of her tiny head? At that point, her self-worth was low, and she didn't need every single person confirming it by bending over her as she submissively peed on their feet. Few considered her needs, but I will always put her needs first. If you feel an overwhelming need to pet my puppy, perhaps you should get your own.

I spent a hundred hours teaching Pippa to do a "tuck-sit" for my sports. But random strangers offer cookies and expect her to be lured into a rock-back sit. Why should she have to obey their requests?

. I taught her to jump up when she went to get her cookies because that is what she needed to grow into the confident, proud, cheeky bitch that I wanted her to become. And she did become one. She pretends to love all people, and in part she does, but really, she likes to control people to get food from their pockets and has mastered how to make people pet her, even when they don't want to. I think her love of people is more of a Border Collie manipulation game to clean out their pockets.

Did I always let her jump up into adulthood? As a three-year-old, she now believes that jumping is correct, but if I don't want her to mob a client, I tell her, "off," or, "lie down." She will still jump up on her friends when allowed to greet.

In dog training, there are no rules. Just train the dog you are training. I continue to do that with Pippa, despite what others might think! Each puppy has unique needs. This wee introvert needed to learn the value of listening to select people, not everyone.

May 19

How much time do you have?

If you have all day, it will only take five minutes to achieve. But if you have only five minutes it will take all day. Never tackle an issue when you are rushed.

May 20

Make every day different

Will your dog live for twelve years? Or will he live one year twelve times?

Make sure your dog's life is varied, interesting, and full of fun experiences. Don't fall into the same ho-hum routine every day for his entire life. He should go to new places, have new experiences, and enjoy his days, with every one being slightly different.

While I normally walk in set places, today I went somewhere totally random and took my geriatrics swimming. Keep their days varied, so that every single one is worth living for.

We are blessed to have them in our lives. Let's treat them as they deserve.

May 21

Domestic leash skills

Dogmanship and good handling are becoming a thing of the past, and are not something frequently taught, or even pondered, by many. Many people have no clue how to use a leash, and use it more as a tow rope than an aide for communication.

Leash handling is actually based on the concept of reward and punishment, but not many people think of it this way. Your reward for a job well done should be muscle release, whereas tension is a consequence. Or we can use it as negative reinforcement where tension is removed when they do as we suggest. When they do well, we need to have an absolute softness about us. Or if we plan on them doing well, we need to have that softness in advance. Tightness will trigger badness, be it reactivity or pulling.

When you walk your dog, her leash should sit in your open, relaxed hand while both of your arms swing. Many people are rewarding their dogs with treats while their muscles are tense, but no one wants to be held rigidly or controlled like that. Save the hot dog, and instead be respectful with your hands and muscles.

We cannot lie to dogs. They know that if they did well we would relax. So if they tried, and you did not relax, in their hearts they will know they failed.

Ponder this! This is the most important and valuable piece of domestic training that I can share. As a trainer, you are only as good as your hands.

May 22

How to get the right dog from the right rescue

Many rescue organizations are amazing, but some are not. Just like puppy mills, some people who operate rescues can be in it for the money. They might pick up a dog from one location and drive it to the next for a chunk of money. There are a few key things to look out for when you're choosing a rescue organization.

The application process for a dog should be slightly painful, and it should include a house check. Photos should not cut it. We can all send photos of our neighbour's beautiful fence, so why even bother? If you love your dogs as much as you claim, at least make the effort to check me out in person to see if I am worthy.

Never adopt a dog fresh off a plane or car. You have no idea what you are getting, nor does the organization. Rescue dogs need to live with a foster, in the foster's home. A foster who is also an experienced trainer will know who that dog is right away, while normal fosters might need to live with that dog for a minimum of a month before they know.

Find out if the dog is okay with other dogs. The way a dog acts with other dogs in a foster home is *not the same* as the way it acts walking past a strange dog on the street. Make sure you take any potential dog on a walk and go past another dog. Too much interest could be the beginning of dog aggression and may be easy to remedy, but if you see lunging, the road to rehab will be long, if it's even possible.

If the dog was returned to the rescue from a previous adopter, ask questions. It could indicate a behaviour problem, and you need to be honest with yourself about your own training skills. This would be a good moment to hire a trainer to assess the dog for you.

Beware of the drama. If you hear something like, "This dog will die if you don't rescue him," or if you hear a tragic tale about how the dog was starved and beaten by a herd of donkeys before dragging himself across eight highways, where he was run over four times, to someone's front doorstep . . . it's not in your best interest.

Extreme veterinary care is a turn-off. Treatments for lumps, bumps, abscesses, skin issue, and teeth problems and any other surgeries may seem admirable, but if it leaves the dog with a life of maintenance, rehab, and future concerns, I question the benefit. Was it done from the rescuer's giant heart, or is sheer marketing genius meant to tug at people's heartstrings? It should always be for the benefit of the dog. Large dogs with three legs or major joint surgeries constantly struggle with movement (at least all of the ones I've seen do), and this will affect their temperament, mood, and lifestyle. Keeping these dogs at their best will require regular swimming.

If you are determined that this three-legged dog with half a jaw and a rewired nasal cavity must be yours, be sure you have money *and* time to spare, in addition to all your love.

Regular veterinary work, however, is a turn-on. Dogs should be checked by a local vet, and should be healthy, spayed or neutered (unless unique circumstances are involved), and all the regular maintenance procedures should be completed. Even if a veterinarian in another country saw the dog you want to adopt, make sure he is also seen by a local vet.

Dental work can be a giant expense with a rescue dog. Your rescue needs to have either warned you of the condition of your dog's teeth and the money involved in having them fixed, or done it for you in advance. Always check teeth pre-adoption. If you have no clue what you are looking at, ask the rescue for permission to talk to a local vet who has seen the dog. The vet will give you a very clear picture so you can budget accordingly, or make an educated decision about whether you can honour this dog's needs.

It is true that good rescues are always running out of money because rescuing dogs is expensive work, but beware of a "Donate Now" button on their website. Take the time to talk to people who have adopted dogs through this rescue, and find out how the rescue honours their dogs once they have your money. While it could be a genuine and genius rescue, verify.

Adopters will always go back to a good rescue for their next dog. Good rescues *always* take their dogs back when needed. No exceptions. Good rescues will advise you of the pros and cons of your dog.

Make a decision with your brain, not your heart. You cannot help this dog if you feel sorry for him. You must respect him, and see his strength and determination in order to be able to help him. If you find yourself feeling sorry for him—*do not pick that dog*. You will end up creating behavioural problems.

And my own personal bias: adopt locally, unless you are applying to a rescue that specializes in a certain breed. Some breeds are so unique that few people want them, and a larger geographical area is needed to find them their rightful homes.

May 23

The demise of Perfect Pippa:
How my sweet dog became an asshole

I walk my dogs every morning. We run into people and dogs. We even run into some people with bad dogs, but my guys are robust enough that they can act like responsible citizens and suck it up. And I confess, some days my dogs are the bad dogs, but that is why we train. We train so that when everything goes wrong, I still have their ears.

Until the day I didn't. And Perfect Pippa turned into an asshole.

I'd been bumping into a lady and her out-of-control reactive dogs, one of whom was scary. She thought that because her scary dog has never attacked anyone it never will. But it will. And hopefully, it won't be my dog.

But in the meantime, her dogs have gotten to practice charging my dogs. I protected my dogs, and thought we left these encounters unscathed, but I was wrong. The next day when I was walking, we met a saintly man with his nicely behaved dogs, and mine turned into assholes. I had barking, lunging dogs. After just five instances of her dogs barking at mine, mine now looked the same as hers.

So how do sweet dogs transition into reactive dogs? They find out that other dogs are scary, get their confidence shattered, and learn that we cannot protect them. Dogs need to be robust enough to endure bad moments and recover. It was the repeated bad moments that shattered Pippa's confidence.

For the moment, I have reactive dogs. I have been handed the power to create dog reactivity in other people's dogs. It only takes a couple of scary encounters of my dogs charging and barking, and then I can pass the burden on to someone else. No bites need to take place. We only need to damage your dog's confidence.

And saying, "they are friendly," seems to absolve all responsibility, letting me off the hook for how my dog might ruin yours.

I now have reactivity in my dogs. There is no quick fix here, no magic loophole that can make this right. Nothing but time, training, and more time is going to fix this. Time that I must find.

In the meantime, I'm not going to yell, "She is friendly," as Pippa charges strange dogs on the trails. I will admit, sadly, that my dog is now an asshole. And more importantly, I won't need to yell it because I will not give her freedom again, until I can trust her to give me her ears, including the times when she does not want to.

"She is friendly." I dare someone to put that in my eulogy.

May 24

Maintain non-negotiable rules

I recently confessed my dog was an asshole, and someone cautioned me to only retrain with positive reinforcement.

Why?

I teach with positive reinforcement. I advance with positive reinforcement. But the day my dog says, "no," the "no" has to be dealt with. I'm not going to wait until she says, "yes," so that I can reward her.

You cannot reward a lack of effort. You cannot reward an unwilling student. To keep things simple, I've chosen to ignore the reason why she is an unwilling student. I'll deal with that once she cares what I think.

There are certain non-negotiable rules at my house.

1. You will not rip my arm off with a leash.
2. You will "down" no matter what.
3. You cannot eat your veterinarian, and you must allow me to handle you.
4. You can hate strangers, but you must mind your manners.

In this scenario, to rehab my young lady, we have begun with reminders on rules 1 and 2. She knows them inside and out, but somehow felt they were negotiable if a strange dog was present. Nope. The rules never changed, my little friend. These rules are absolutes and never allowed to slide.

Naturally swinging my arm as I walk fixed rule 1. And rule 2 required a pop-on leash, then a pop-on flexi leash.

Today the fun retraining began with my dogs as a group. We were back to our normal level of control, but the first time I asked for a down they all stood up tall, looking to see who was out there, and why I was asking. Then I got my training discs that make a sound when thrown and threw them in front of my dogs. Down means down. It does not mean, "look around and decide if you want to."

The next time I asked for it, they hit the dust. For that, they got positive reinforcement—and kibble chucked at their chests.

Sometimes I think we have made dog training so incredibly difficult. Yes, my dog became reactive. But at no point did that mean that she no longer has to walk nicely on a leash, or can ignore my request to lie down. Just because she had her confidence knocked doesn't mean she's leaving grade 12 and getting put back into kindergarten.

There is a time and a place for communication that addresses how they were wrong. Why have people become so scared to tell dogs that what they did was crap?

If my dogs want to hike with me every day in the wilderness, they need to listen. They need to let me call them off, or control them around a bear, deer, cougar, and even more importantly, someone's pet dog. And no, I'm not dumbing down a non-negotiable just because my dog had a bad experience.

Rule 4 is still a work in progress, but with the reminders of rules 1 and 2, rule 4 is starting to right itself.

May 25

The dog within

> *"A Native American Elder once described his own inner strug-*
> *gles in this manner: 'Inside of me there are two dogs. One of*
> *the dogs is mean and evil. The other dog is good. The mean*
> *dog fights the good dog all the time.' When asked which dog*
> *wins, he reflected for a moment and replied, 'The one I feed the*
> *most.'"*—**Experiencing the Soul: Before Birth, During Life,**
> **After Death** *by Eliot Rosen and Ellen Burstyn (1997)*

Make sure you acknowledge and attend to the behaviours that you
want more of—both in your dog and yourself.

May 26

Emotions are contagious

Just like yawns, emotions are contagious. If you see someone smiling,
you will almost always smile back, even if it is a micro smile that is
over in less than a third of a second. Our emotions get passed on to
others and affect others.

Some people are defined as "senders." Senders are physiologically
different and have an enormous amount of influence over other's
emotions. They are very good at expressing their emotions, and as a
result, have a much greater impact on those around them.

As I look at the people I view to be exceptional dog trainers, I think
they are all senders. Their emotional state does affect others around
them, including their dogs. When they are happy, we all smile with
them. And when they are unhappy, we try very hard to get them
happy again!

Please consider your emotions when you are around your dog. If
you are training and a training partner irritates you, your dog will

be affected by your new mood. If you are walking your dog and a dog rushes you, your dog will be affected by your emotions. Learn to control your emotions in such moments.

On the flip side, use the right emotions in such moments to alter your outcome with your dog. Learn to block out the irritant of the training partner, or learn to say something nice (and normal) to all people that you walk past, even when their dog just rushed you. Your emotions will in part school your dog about how you want him to behave.

Learning ironclad mental control for your dog is the biggest gift your dog can give you. You will learn to be in control of your own mental climate, and that truly is a blessing.

May 27

Distance erodes control

Distance will always erode your control—the farther your dog is from you, the less control you have over him. And drive will decrease your dog's hearing. Train for it.

May 28

Raising a puppy is an art

From day one, we must have a picture in our heads of who we want our dogs to become. Once we have that vision, it will direct how we raise them.

For me it is not as simple as certain things being allowed and certain things being forbidden. While I know what I allow and don't allow, raising a puppy is about compromise, which depends on the puppy. My end goal of who I want is in my mind, and I will compromise on what is allowed and what is forbidden to get them to be the dog who I need them to be. Even though some of the things being allowed are totally undesirable, sometimes they are needed to create pieces of the puzzle that are otherwise lacking.

We can only take the drives and strengths that our dogs bring to the table. If you are not seeing what you want to see, you might need to allow and work with an undesirable trait, and mould and nurture it into a strength.

This is the part of training dogs that is not a science—it's an art.

May 29

To shape or not to shape for competition obedience

Shaping, a training method where you break down one behaviour into numerous successive little steps, is not always a good thing for competition-obedience dogs because they learn that if they get no feedback, they need to try something else. We create popcorn dogs who learn that silence means they need to offer something. And they learn that when there is no click, or no feedback, they've done something wrong.

Given that our sport is a silent one, and we have to compete in silence, we should be very careful of communicating that silence means you did it wrong. Or, we have taught that competition means you did it wrong.

We've all had someone give us the "silent treatment." According to them, everything is "fine," but meanwhile you have to guess which possible sin you've committed, and figure out how to make it right without ever being told what you've done. This is extremely frustrating. When you are with these people, you feel like you are walking on eggshells and are never quite sure what's expected of you.

Be mindful with clicker games so that you don't allow the silence to become stressful for your dog. While there are many dogs who do not respond this way, there are still many shaped dogs who really suffer from undue stress when put in the obedience or rally ring.

Make sure the tool is right for your dog. And make sure that you never ever teach your dog that silence means she is wrong.

May 30

Read between the lines

Every breed comes with a breed description and standard; it's written down and it sounds glamorous. Your job as a new potential owner of said breed is to understand what this description really means. Learn the art of reading between the lines.

Here are some examples from an old breed book, which is slightly more honest than many current books. I will give my interpretation; see if you can guess the breeds:

1. The purpose of the dog was to chase game until it became exhausted, and until the sportsman could come up with it and dispatch it. *Translation:* Will chase moving objects. Might bite moving objects. Will not come back when called, only when exhausted.

2. The breed has a distinct personality marked by direct and fearless, but not hostile, expression, self-confidence, and a certain aloofness that does not lend itself to immediate and indiscriminate friendships. *Translation:* Dogs will look at you and weigh you up to see if you are worthy. They won't be friendly with you until (a) they know you and (b) they decide you are worthy.

3. This rugged stout-hearted dog will guard his master, his mistress, and children with utter contempt for danger or hurt. *Translation:* Will attack anything if he feels it is necessary, and might get a Darwin Award in the process.

4. Dogs move quickly behind the cattle, give a sharp nip and escape before the resultant kick could reach them. *Translation:* Bite and run, from behind. Movement makes them want to chase, so watch out for bicycles, joggers, and diaper-clad children. They have enough courage to go forward, and enough fear to know when to get out of dodge.

5. His temperament, as with most of the large dogs, is that of a gentle giant. He has no vice, is absolutely friendly, and is one of the most faithful of all dogs. As a guard, he is supreme, as the instinct to look after his own territory and that of his owner is deeply imbedded in him. *Translation:* Darling, loyal, lug of a dog. But don't mess with his home or family. The voice of his ancestors will always put him in conflict with any training that says otherwise. When push comes to shove, it is a gamble whose voice will be louder, *so get a fence.*

1. Afghan   2. German Shepherd   3. Irish Terrier   4. Pembroke Corgi   5. Mastiff

May 31

Ageing dogs

One of my old guys is having one hell of a time. He has not been blessed with ageing gracefully. He is a sensitive soul, and very connected to me.

His first health struggle was with sciatica. He became terrified of a certain spot in the house because that's where he was when he first experienced pain. As his pain continued, he connected it to the entire downstairs floor of my home. He considered it a danger zone and refused to come out of his crate. We got through that stage. The pain is gone, and so is his fear. But it really can throw you for a loop when you see such behaviour problems suddenly appear, from seemingly nowhere.

Then he became really sad. Sad and distant. I couldn't work out why, until I realized he thought no one was talking to him anymore— he had lost his hearing. He seemed to associate the silence with us ignoring him. Poor treasure.

Then yesterday he become clingy and worried. He would whine until I would rescue him. And for the last two nights, he has needed me to go and sit with him. He was hesitant to move. A tiny bit of investigation, and we realized he had lost his vision.

During these times, he needs me. He needs me to sit up with him during the night. To help him down the stairs. To guide him around the yard. To let him know that he continues to be safe.

Hopefully the fear of this new stage will pass and he can go back to enjoying his days again. Or we need to make a decision.

While I'm eternally grateful that my dogs all live to a ripe old age, nothing about this part gets easier. For all of the times that he has been there for me, now it is my time to be there for him.

Their journey, I suppose, has the same turmoil attached as it does with humans. While I have always wished to wake up in the morning to find they have quietly passed in their sleep, it has yet to happen. Yet I fear that if it did, the shock might add more devastation to the loss I have to deal with.

JUNE

June 1

Train the dog you are training

I have been asked what training method I use, so here it is: training is about getting into your dog's head and understanding what motivates him, what makes him smile, and what concerns him. Once you have this, you have *it*—a relationship with your dog. Treats cannot buy this. Something this precious and this complex cannot be purchased with a cookie.

You should be able to laugh at your dog for his silly antics. You should be able to differentiate between when he is trying but has misunderstood your words, and when he is completely blowing you off because you are not as important as whatever else is going on.

When your dog is stressed by his environment, you must know how to distinguish when he needs more help from you and when he needs to be told to grow up and act like an adult.

You need to be aware when something completely strange is going on—is he sitting really slowly because he hurt himself? You should understand him so well that you can think for him—know his struggles in advance and adjust his mood as needed—and help him learn what he needs to learn to be the best dog that he can be.

So, what method do I use? I train the dog I am training. There is no one thing I can do to create the beautiful relationship that I have with my dogs. I respect dogs for who they are, I believe in their potential, I aim to build on their strengths and chip away at their weaknesses. I build a relationship with them so that they care what I think and try really hard to please me.

There are no rules for this process. What is necessary for one dog in one moment might be detrimental for another dog in another moment. When I teach puppy class, I might immediately stop one puppy from dragging his owner, and I might request another owner to allow her puppy to drag her for two more weeks before we stop it. There are no absolute rules when it comes to training dogs.

Each dog has to be trained according to his own criteria, and we must work with what that dog brings to the table. We may have the same goals and directions for every dog, but we might get there fifty different ways, depending on the learning ability, emotional need, and intelligence of the dog. And we must always consider the handling abilities and personality of the handler. This is a relationship between one dog and one human, and rules might need to be gently bent and swayed, depending on the individuals.

Dog training is not science. It is art. Each puppy is a blank canvas, and it is our creation to build, alter, discourage, or deny. Each of our canvases will look different when our dogs are a year old, depending on our feel and timing, our dreams and vision, our denial, our work ethic, our own self-belief and the belief our immediate circle has of us, and, of course, the dogs that we choose.

How can you define this training method with one set of limiting rules determined by a method? You can't. Or the results will be limited.

June 2

Right and wrong

Our dogs do not understand right or wrong. They only know what we allow them to do.

If your communication has been unclear, or if you haven't prevented your dog from breaking the rules, your dog believes his behaviour is allowed. The longer he is allowed to practice bad behaviour, the more ingrained that habit will become. Be consistent in what you allow, and you can prevent any bad behaviours from becoming ingrained habits.

June 3

It's not just the dog who has to change

When I can't get something with my dog and I continue to struggle, my body will start to tense up in scenarios where I have previously failed. My dog feels that tension. Only if I let go of that tension will I succeed.

When we desperately want something and we try too hard, we end up forcing it. When we want it the most, we are incapable of performing well, and we are not the handlers that our dogs need us to be.

Success happens when you create a particular atmosphere within yourself. Those who can consistently create this inner climate will consistently succeed. If you feel yourself continuing to struggle with your dog to get certain behaviours—and you know you have done your training—look inward.

Think your way through, and slow your brain down. Generally, our mind moves at the same speed as our feet. Slowing your feet will help you. Really slow your feet if you need to.

Loosen your muscles, slow your thoughts, and slowly inhale. Once you can let go of the tension that inhibits you and your dog, you can see where your training has actually gotten you.

June 4

Train in public

Training at home is fake training. It is a false illusion that will make you disappointed in your dog later, when he does not perform the same way in public.

Force yourself to train in public. Though it will be more challenging with real-life distractions luring him away, *that* is the whole purpose of training. You need those life distractions, as they are exactly what you are training for.

So don't teach recall in an isolated fenced backyard. Do it every day on your walks, when you need it. Don't practice loose-leash walking in a deserted parking lot. Teach it as you walk your dog on a leash.

Training at home is much too easy due to the lack of distractions. It won't help you when you need it to. So rather than waste those training hours, shift that energy to training whenever you are out with your dog. Your dog is always learning. It is up to you to always be teaching.

June 5

Intrinsic motivation

Trainers from the instinct sports—such as herding for Sheepdogs, hunting for Labradors, upland game for pointers, and any other sports that dogs were specifically bred for—all know something that others do not: the value of intrinsic motivation.

While we need to teach with food and toys and praise, they need to be considered teaching tools. Your teaching tools are there to help you clarify the concept that you are trying to communicate, but in no way should they be keeping your dog engaged and with you. Your dog needs to be enjoying working with you, and should not be working for his food. While this almost looks the same, there is an enormous difference.

If you are confused by what I mean, go take all the leashes and training equipment off your dog, empty your pockets, and go and stand still. Is your dog pestering you to do something with her? If yes, all is good. If all you see is a tail and a bum, then when you get her food she is suddenly ever-present, you have some work to do.

I do not want my dogs thinking, "If I do this, I get that." That won't hold when I need them the most.

What we need to instill into our dogs is an inner joy for their work. If they love their work, the work itself becomes the reward.

Rewards quickly steal the play from play and turn it into work. Alternately, focusing on the learning of the work can turn it into play. If you don't believe me, ask some young kids to help you wash your car and observe how they enjoy the sponges and the bubbles, and their finished product. Then the next time pay them five dollars for washing your car. Do that twice, and see the difference in their enjoyment as they do it. Rewards stop inherent enjoyment, and instead get us focused on the reward at the end, not the job at hand.

However, there are exceptions. Sometimes, "If I do this, then I get that," rewards are needed. They have a place when it comes to dull, mundane practice, which is necessary for any repeated drill-like fronts and finishes, but has no purpose to the dog. Evan Graham, an old-time respected field dog trainer, always says, "Leave something in it for the dog." If the work itself gives the dog nothing, then we need to add it.

Intrinsic motivation is complex, and it will take a while for you to wrap your brain around it. Rewards do have a time and place, but the difficulty arises when they are expected. The focus and enjoyment on the challenges of the work lose their value and enjoyment, and rather become a roadblock to the reward. We need to create joyful work, and joyful moments, and find the right balance. Allow work to become enjoyable work (with a reward at the end), rather than focusing on the reward at the end.

June 6

Habits for success

What do successful trainers do to get what they need? They value their time, and know how to say "no" when something threatens to remove that valuable time from them and their dog.

How do you fill the hours in your day? Many of us just waste hours, or spend time helping others rather than focusing on our own dogs and ourselves (this is especially important for fellow instructors).

We must commit time every day to only focus on our dogs. For me, this time is as important as any other commitment in my day. It might make me sound selfish, but really, I owe it to my dogs.

Email, phone, and social media are likely our next biggest time wasters. Prioritize your day so that you honour your dog's needs before you waste time. To get better with our dogs, we need to manage our time better.

Get up an hour earlier. Read more and watch less television. Find an athletic outlet and, even better, do one that can include your dog. To keep yourself motivated to stick to a healthier lifestyle, constantly remind yourself what your goals are and what you are trying to achieve.

Most of us have the time to commit to our dogs and our goals. It's just a matter of prioritizing.

June 7

The ten-moments rule

Sometimes when we are struggling with our dogs, our relationship can turn bitter. When you find yourself in this place, take action to fix the negativity before your relationship gets destroyed.

No matter how naughty your dog is, and regardless of the behaviours that you are struggling with, you need to create a minimum of ten moments a day when you can truly praise your dog with pride.

It is up to you to create a minimum of ten wonderful moments— do not wait for your dog to give them to you. Once you start enjoying each other for those brief moments, multiple times a day, some of your other training struggles will become a little easier to resolve.

When Kate is in a foul mood, it is almost always because her feelings got hurt. Maybe I left her home while I went to teach group class, or one of my other dogs got to be the special dog for the day. When she's in this mood she makes it hard to be nice to her. But the easiest way is to close a door to keep all the other dogs away, and do something stupid with her. In about two minutes she can get herself out of her sulk, and by the third minute she has forgotten all about it.

While many dog trainers might criticize me for this, I must first remind you all that I too am a woman. I get Kate. I get her hurt feelings. I even understand her need to lash out at others when she feels forgotten. And in three minutes I can undo all the hurt and negativity rather than having to manage her mood and be careful of her around other dogs until her wounded feelings are better.

I'll take the three minutes. Fix the negativity.

Dogs have feelings too!

June 8

The dog trainer's dilemma

What is our responsibility as dog trainers when our client gets a dog that will never be safe? I know the answer, but it gets complicated when the dog is young—and stunningly cute—and the clients have no idea what they have gotten themselves into.

I have one right now in class. Just over six months old, cute as a button, and recently acquired, the dog makes the hair on the back of my neck stand up. There has been nothing obvious that the owners would see, and nor will there be before the first bite, but to an experienced eye there is plenty to see.

I wish I was more naïve and didn't see it. But I am not naïve and I do, and I know where it is going. The dilemma is always this: if the dog has not done anything bad, the smitten owners will never believe you when you tell them their dog will hurt a person, and they will not come back to class because you "do not like their dog." Then you cannot help them.

And if you say nothing, when it does happen, you always feel you could have prevented it.

It is an age-old dilemma. Even after more than thirty years of training dogs, I still have not found the right solution to handle the problem.

June 9

Keep them guessing

There is nothing funnier than doing something completely unexpected to a snotty control freak who cannot believe you had the audacity to just do that.

Games are so much fun, especially when your dog believes she knows what the outcome will be and you surprise her with something she never thought was a possibility.

When I get out of the shower, I take the towel off my head and throw it on top of Pippa, my Border Collie. If I'm in the kitchen, I snap the towel on her bum and take off running (expecting to be bitten). I will wait in the closet and jump out at her and yell, "Boo!" I might be happily vacuuming and then I'll turn and chase her with the vacuum. She has learned to keep an eye on me no matter what I am doing, because anything is possible.

The look you get before she enacts her revenge is priceless. Don't be dull and predictable with your dogs. Do things that make them laugh, and always keep them guessing. Have new cards up your sleeve, and be worthy of keeping their attention.

But the more fearful and shy they pretend to be—sorry, Kate!—the more you should do it. The first time I jumped out of the closet at her and yelled, "Boo!" she almost let her anal glands go. The second time she was ready for me. Through stupid pranks we can make them stronger. I don't think I've jumped out at Kate a third time. Now I'm going to have to.

Dogs are so much fun. How lucky are we that we get to play with dogs?

June 10

Make yourself relevant

Often there is talk of science-based training—what people are referring to as positive reinforcement, but applied in the laboratory. There, it must be a measurable and repeatable phenomenon. In other words, a learned behaviour, like a "sit," becomes a reliable and repeatable result regardless of who or what executes the command. Training can essentially be turned into a transaction: when you hear the bell, peck the button and get some corn. On the signal, swim through the hoop and get a fish. On the "sit," sit and get a cookie.

Notice the absence of personal interaction. A pigeon keeps on pecking if a machine gives it corn. As a consequence of using this method where people are unimportant for the results, dog owners have removed their relationship from the learning process.

We have created countless dogs who do things only because they want something in return. We have a what's-in-it-for-me generation of dogs. Dogs need to get paid for their work, and their food rewards are their pay cheque. Would these dogs continue to listen to our requests if they won the lottery, so to speak?

While the method of training has many benefits, we now need to teach our dogs to love their work, not love their reward. The solution is so simple that it is laughable: the relationship needs to be added back to the transaction.

Luckily, it is easy to insert yourself back into the equation. When my dog does as I asked, I let him know. "Good." My "good" is delivered at a moderate level of praise. He did not cure cancer, nor find an alternative to fossil fuels. Most people lie to their dogs through excessive and inappropriate praise, and tell their dogs that something acceptable was worthy of diamonds. Your praise needs to come in gradually escalating levels. If mediocre work gets full levels of praise, your dog will never try harder.

I teach my dogs that the only way to get their reward is to make me happy. If I say "good," then I am pleased by what you did. Put some more effort into that last behaviour and you might make me even more pleased. If you put everything you've got into your effort, I will be really, really happy and I will reward you. It pays to make me happy.

A "sit" does not equal a cookie. But the perfect sit *will* make me happy, and when I am happy I will want to reward you. Happy Mummy equals rewards. And the only way to get Mummy happy is to try really, really hard.

Making mummy happy will in itself become a conditioned reward. Dogs quickly learn that a happy mummy is always followed by something that the dog really wants: food or toys. We have created a dog with work ethic who actually cares about what his person thinks, as her happiness is required to get what he wants. Just like a clicker (a monotone, audible cue), making me happy can be conditioned to be a secondary reinforcer. Then when I need to remove my rewards for moments in time, my praise alone will make my dog happy and feel good about what he did.

When I am praising my dog, my tone and emotions indicate if my dog is on the right path or not. They give him hope in his efforts, and keep him trying harder to please me. It's a bit like a game of hot and cold. I give feedback about whether he is on the right track or not. My first praise indicates to my dog, "You are on the right path." The second praise indicates, "I really like this." And the final is, "That was exceptional. I'm so pleased. Have this reward."

Dogs quickly learn to keep trying harder, to get your praise more enthusiastic, knowing that means the reward is close. Low and medium levels of praise indicate he is on the right track and that you are happy with him, but more effort is needed for a reward. Once you do this, your dog will be working to please you, rather than working for the cookie in your pocket. While the difference is very subtle, you will appreciate this detail when you find yourself needing a dog who still listens even though you only have yourself and your voice.

If you're not using escalating praise when your dog is making an effort for you, you're missing a very large and important piece of your training. Teach your dog that only maximum effort gets maximum praise. And only maximum praise gives rewards.

June 11

Your body doesn't lie

As people, we tend to listen to words first and body language second. Words tend to override what we see. Dogs, however, speak with their bodies, and they will listen to your body first and then your words. And your body speaks volumes. In fact, what you really think and feel oozes out of you without you even knowing it. Even though your words contradict what you are already "saying."

Dogs always respond to a person's emotions, which are delivered through body language. You cannot lie to them by using words and by pretending to feel something else. Your goal is to get your body language in sync with your words. Once your body and words are saying the same thing, your dog training will quickly advance.

June 12

Let's get honest

I've been having run-ins with a woman and her two out-of-control dogs. Both of her dogs are reactive, and one is downright dangerous. Dog trainers and the current world of dog training have failed this woman and many others.

How? She has been told, and believes, that she can retrain her aggressive rescue dog, of a fighting breed, who darn near outweighs her, all without corrections. She cannot. Her dog much prefers fighting to eating.

Instead, she has a dog—well, two dogs—that she cannot control, or walk on leash. She physically cannot hold onto their leashes. They drag her toward their victims.

No one has taught this woman about corrective equipment that can help her get control. It isn't politically correct, so dog trainers skip those conversations. Instead, I'm sure her mentors are watching, waiting for her to euthanize her dangerous dog. Because euthanizing is easier than putting on a pinch collar and risking being bad-mouthed by your peers in this small town.

Her solution thus far, rather than looking like a water skier behind a boat, is to unclip the less-dangerous one. Can we fault her? No. Her no-pull harness was not designed for her lunging gladiator. And no meatball or roasted liver treat outweighs the reward of a freshly caught Border Collie.

It's time for people in the rescue world and dog trainers to get honest again. If we want to adopt this type of dog out, we need to admit that the training methods we suggest for your perfect but unruly Golden Retriever, or Cocker Spaniel, or Bernese Mountain dog, and all regular pet dogs, will not be suitable for a dog bred to protect at no cost, who outweighs you, and who comes with past baggage.

June 13

The puppy socialization bucket list

Dogs need to be socialized. That means that dogs need to *see* the world and handle it with social grace. We need to teach them the skills and habits necessary for participating within our society.

Unfortunately, socialization is now commonly misunderstood and misinterpreted to mean just interacting and playing with other dogs. While puppies do need to play with other puppies, this is a teeny-tiny piece of their education, but somehow it's become the only piece that many people focus on.

Here is a list of excellent activities you can do with your puppy to properly socialize him or her. I call it my puppy socialization bucket list, and it's one of my most sought-after pieces of writing.

- Give your puppy a ride in a wheelbarrow, but keep a hand on his collar so he doesn't leap out.
- Walk over many, many bridges of different surfaces, widths, and heights, with variations in the gaps in between planks.
- Climb driftwood at the beach for footing, balance, and learning how to use her body.
- Climb rocks at the beach.
- Take your puppy to dog-friendly stores.
- Take your puppy to the pet store, but be careful of overly friendly strangers who may not leave your dog alone.
- Take your puppy on a busy path alongside a road where you'll encounter heavy traffic, the odd pedestrian bridge, people, bikes, dogs, joggers, etc.
- Expose your puppy to many types of floor surfaces.
- You may want to bring your puppy to the dog park, but make sure to hold her in your arms as you pass by other dogs, and if

there are dogs that you know to be very safe and kind, you can allow them to meet on the ground.

- Take a walk with a trusted friend and his or her dog, if you know the dog to be kind and calm.
- Expose your dog to children by sitting outside playgrounds.
- Hang out with chickens, ducks, and goats. When my puppy thought the goats were really scary, I protected her on my lap.
- Toss your dog into a giant box stuffed full of teddy bears. When she's covered, have her crawl her way out.
- Throw towels over top of your puppy's head, and graduate to entire sheets; she has to find her way out.
- Hold your puppy for cuddling and kisses every night.
- Handle and or trim your puppy's toenails weekly.
- Cuddle and kiss your puppy as she chews on her bones, sometimes. Certainly not always.
- Walk to a new place every single day. Try not to repeat your walks.
- Crate your puppy every single day for varying lengths of times.
- Make sure your puppy has travelled in different vehicles, in different types of crates or seating arrangements.
- Take your puppy to a greenhouse or nursery, and make friends with all the staff inside.
- If your puppy is really friendly, teach her the art of walking past people without always saying hello. Walk past at least four out of five people without greeting, otherwise her friendliness will be annoying when she is big and strong.
- Maybe one of the most important things: she can pee and poop on grass, gravel, asphalt, or cement, on a leash or free. This makes travelling very simple.
- Every day she is presented with small problems that she must solve: how to get the ball that rolled under the couch, how to

get the marrow out of her bone, how to stay on a bridge without falling off, how to climb over a downed tree that is higher than she thinks she can climb. I help her but *never* do I do it for her. And I only help enough so that she has the confidence to do the rest. If she puts in no effort, I will not help her.

- Teach your puppy to come running back fast at the sound of her name, no matter the distraction. Make sure "come" means that she chases you.
- Have play dates with trusted dog friends.
- Walk on all types of stairs.
- Take your puppy in a boat or a kayak; let her jump in and out.
- Go swimming with a slow steady introduction to water.
- Take your puppy to the petting zoo to meet all the animals, and more importantly, all the children.
- Watch an adult herding sheep. My puppy's eyes almost popped out of her head.
- Swing with your puppy in a hammock.
- Take your puppy to a playground. Sit on a swing with your puppy, and go down the slide with your puppy in your lap.
- Play soccer with your puppy, and tackle the ball from her when she has a hold of it in her paws.
- Take your puppy on vacation with you and stay in hotels and other people's houses.
- Take your puppy in an elevator and go through automatic doors.
- Expose your puppy to someone who smells of cigarette smoke. Many dogs are sensitive to different odours on people.
- Walk past a person in a wheelchair.
- Hang out at the vet's and get cookies!

Socialization is about teaching life skills to your puppy. I exposed my puppy to every possible skill that she might need to be a functional adult. With all of the exposure and success comes a level of confidence and bravery; they will get to the point where they believe they are invincible. Even when she gets into trouble, she knows I am right there behind her to help her with her difficulties.

When puppies feel overwhelmed or scared, hold them in your arms, rather than leaving them on the floor. They can watch from up high, and then they'll start wriggling like a mad thing wanting to get down and do it themselves. Rather than asking them to try it, by taking that option away and making them feel safe they have to then demand they be allowed to try it. This is a difference between feeling forced into an experience and choosing an experience. And when they choose the experience, they will be braver.

My last puppy never did have one "bad" experience. Unfortunately, it will happen, and when it does, they know that I am there to protect and help them. As they go on their adventures in the world, both good and bad, we are a team, and I have their back.

June 14

My definition of puppy socialization

Dogs need to be socialized. This means a number of things, both specific and general. Yes, they need to be able to handle a variety of floor surfaces, but they really need to be able to think their way through stress. They must be presented with problems they can solve, and stressful situations they can master and feel good about. For a specific list of things you can do with your puppy, see my Puppy Socialization Bucket List above for June 13.

But, more generally, your puppies must learn how to learn. They must learn to be calm and clear in their minds. For those of us who have dogs with ample piss and vinegar, we need to teach them an off-switch so that we can enjoy living with them.

If they are working dogs, they must be exposed to the work they will do. They need to learn to work closely with you, and yet also far away from you. Many sports require dogs to make their own decisions, at great distance from you, and this concept needs to be taught early (or rather training must be altered so that this is not squashed out of them).

They must learn to use their noses for scent discrimination, their bodies so they are nimble and don't get hurt, and they need to have the freeness within themselves to have the right emotions for their work. And they need to be biddable and take instruction.

Their instincts must be allowed to be free and explored, and then have rules put on them (if you are using them for your work).

They need to be able to see any situation, and even if it causes stress, they need to learn to cope with it, recover from it, and then bounce back from it.

They need to learn to switch rewards from toy to food, back to toy, and then back to food.

They need to learn to bring toys back to you. To follow you. To come when called. To always keep half an eye and half an ear on where you are around the house and on walks. And your opinion needs to matter to them.

They must believe that you are the best and coolest person in the entire world and follow you adoringly wherever you go. And you must be that person because you cannot lie to a dog.

They must allow you, your vet, and your groomer to handle them and manipulate them.

And they need to trust you so much that no matter where they go in this world, nothing scares them or worries them, because ultimately you have their back.

June 15

Quit following recipes

When you train your dog, you must always remember you are training an emotional, thinking being. By not addressing the emotions and personality of the dog, you really are failing in the training process. It is time to quit following recipes, and instead "feel" your dog. Use "feel" to figure out what your dog needs in order to learn the lesson.

Don't alter your goals. Do start training your dog from where he is at.

June 16

What do you allow?

What you allow is what you will get. Nothing more. Though maybe a bit less.

June 17

How to become a dog trainer

"If the only tool you have is a hammer you tend to see every problem as a nail."—Abraham Maslow

A short course, a certificate, and the title "professional" do not make a dog trainer. In fact, they might do the opposite.

Learning to train dogs as a profession through a quick course often teaches that every problem is created by either dominance (although the word is used incorrectly) or fear and anxiety. Every solution to every problem has to be the same because there is no time to teach more complex methods. The solution is either a correction, or a click and a cookie. If the first does not work, repeat, but with more. These trainers leave their training as hammers, and they see every problem as a nail. In the limited time available, these students could only learn one tool for their toolbox and are far from being dog trainers.

I have many students in my weekly classes who have met all of my criteria for becoming a dog trainer. A dog trainer has feel, timing, and experience. Most of my long-standing students have mastered feel and timing, and are only lacking hands on additional dogs (experience). The only way to develop better feel and timing is through experience. Most of us are happy just training the dogs we own, and through the course of each new dog, we get our experience. Some dogs require minimal feel and timing and make us look brilliant. Others require the utmost feel and timing to make us look almost adequate. However, it's with these dogs that we get a lot of experience.

Teaching a dog to sit and stay is normally incredibly easy. However, certain breeds, or dogs from certain walks of life, make this task extremely challenging and they need feel and timing in order to succeed. It is these types of experiences that we need in order to know what tool and trick to use to get them to cooperate willingly.

As a dog trainer, we learn to have a variety of tools in our toolbox. The difficulty comes, however, when you are required to pull out a certain tool for a certain type of dog. Using that same solution for a different dog might be disastrous, but for the current dog it's perfect. For example, to teach resistant dogs to down, letting them chase a cookie in your hand back and forth before the lure "down" often removes all of the pressure for them. Then we get dogs like my baby Reggie where that movement would put him over the top and make him too pushy. He would need to be stationary for his down lure so that he could think and understand what I wanted of him.

Dog trainers are required to think, and to be able to evaluate the feel of the dog they are working with and understand how a tool will affect them. Experience also fills our toolbox with many, many tools for different situations and dogs, as the need arises. Ultimately, respect for the dog is our ultimate goal. Every single thing we do must be out of respect for the dog.

Dogs are not dumb. They notice everything, including our touch, breathing patterns, posture, the way we walk, the way we talk. Not only do our dogs take in all of this information, they also reiterate it. If they misbehave for the first time after month of success, you need to alter something in yourself. Change your walk, your talk, your touch, and be aware of your posture. The taller you stand, the less pushy they become. While I can point out all of these things to my human students, ultimately the dogs are the teachers because they will respond based on how the information they are receiving tells them to behave.

I'm realizing that many newbies coming into my profession are looking for quick recipes to fix situations, without a desire to learn how to "speak dog." Simply put, training does not work that way. We do not go to dog school and learn to be a dog trainer. Rather, after dog school, and through the course of hundreds of hours and thousands of dogs, through sweat, doubt, humility, and even tears, we learn how to train dogs. Our quest is never reached because the more we know, the more we realize how much more there is to learn. The quick course is just the beginning. Then you need to mentor under someone worthy.

I have many students who have stuck with me with their once-problematic dogs, and somewhere along the way, have developed outstanding feel and timing. Learning to communicate with and understand your dog is an exhilarating feeling. Just recently a famous trainer was at my place and remarked on the beautiful feel and timing of several of my students, and how soft their hands were. It is a beautiful thing to watch the relationship between handler and dog when done correctly.

Becoming a dog trainer means developing your feel and your timing through experience, and has nothing to do with a certificate on a wall. Many of my clientele have turned into dog trainers. They possess feel, timing, and experience. As I look through my client lists I find it exciting to see how many of my students have achieved these abilities.

There is nothing more wonderful (to me, anyways) than being able to train my own dogs. Nothing this wonderful is going to come without great effort.

June 18

The timeline of Kate

Kate, my darling project Border Collie, has now lived with us for ten months.

Very quickly—and I mean day two and five—she learned that biting me was not clever. And also realized I went postal if she bit my other dogs. Now instead of biting, she has become a stealth wolf, but in slow motion; she walks at the speed of a sloth. This means when she wants to bite, we have six minutes of warning as she approaches very, very slowly.

On day two she learned the crates belonged to me, and she was not allowed to guard them.

Within a week or two, her resource guarding was at a manageable level. I could call her off a decaying carcass. And while she continues to steal my things (like my socks), she doesn't threaten my life if I try to reclaim them.

At about two weeks, she decided that not only are all Border Collies okay, but all male German Shepherds are wonderful too. Watching her with my clients' German Shepherds is embarrassing—she weaves in between their legs, rubbing herself all over them.

After about a month, her sound sensitivity was mostly gone. She became happy and was loving her new life. Around this time, she also learned to monitor her own mental health by removing herself from a situation when she was grumpy. When she's in a bad mood, I can usually find her in my closet upstairs.

It was around this time that she decided to love me fully. She held nothing back and expected the same of me. However, this positive change came with a myriad of problems. Because she's such a moody girl it would hurt her feelings when I would do mundane things like taking Pippa on a quick errand while leaving Kate at home. I have since learned to be very aware of her feelings and to make my slights right when I get home. She too has learned to forgive me for cheating on her.

After two months, she stopped reacting to people on the trails when she was off leash.

It was about three months before she would mind her manners and not react to strange dogs in the real world. After about six months she would ignore most dogs when she was off leash. With dogs that could potentially be an issue, she will wait patiently beside me for them to pass. Just recently a Kuvask attacked Pippa. Kate stuck by me the entire time and allowed me to do what I needed to do without interfering. Then, while I checked Pippa for injuries, Kate sat with her back against me, touching me, watching to see if the offender would return.

It took about six months before she was comfortable with all the noise and chaos inside my training building while I taught classes.

Now, after ten months, when she steals a sock, we can pick her up and make it a game; her mental tension is quickly disappearing. Rather than being grumpy when I reclaim my sock, she will bounce back, barking and wanting to play.

She is still terrible in confined spaces with many bodies. My minivan with the other dogs is a problem, or if someone comes into the house and is greeted by all the dogs. I manage the van by making sure she always has her own spot. And with guests and such, it is all about knowing her needs and teaching her to leave before she feels the need to discipline the other dogs.

She still guards my minivan, and if I put her outside, more often than not she hides underneath it, like a kitten ready to pounce. If another dog meanders over, she turns into that sloth-like stealth wolf again, walking slowly toward them, making it very clear that their lives are in grave danger. Reggie refuses to play this game.

She welcomes visiting puppies and Border Collies into our home, but she forbids all other dogs. We both have agreed this is tolerable behaviour I can work around.

I now know that when Kate is exhausted, all of her past behaviours come flooding back. She cannot think when she is tired, and she becomes evil. It's been many months since I've seen her in a situation like this, but I do not believe it has changed. I still need to know when she is mentally fatigued, and remove her to avoid any problems.

She still holds a grudge. Once a dog has committed an offense toward her, which happens frequently in a household of blind, deaf geriatrics, she makes them her training project for the next week or two. She creates games to control them, which presents in ways like not letting them walk in a straight line. Or, if they are standing still, at slug speed she approaches with all teeth bared, snarling, until they move away. Then she races around to their head to make them turn again. Or, if they walk around a corner, there she is, waiting, telling them to turn back. While none of this is allowed, it has taken me time to learn her twenty-five games. She's currently creating her twenty-sixth.

I expect that some of these ongoing problems will ease within the next two years, and some will stay just as they are. And that's okay. For the most part, we all live in harmony and fully enjoy one another's company and quirks.

June 19

Let your body do the talking

When a dog is being a jerk at the dog park, he stands tall and still and is very quiet before he makes his move.

If my dog is acting like a jerk, I too stand tall and still and quiet. The more he pushes me, the taller I stretch, imagining that the top of my head has a string pulling me up toward the sky. My shoulder blades go way back, pushing out my chest, and I find an inner calm and talk very softly and quietly. Even if I am walking forward, my upper body and my mind go still.

If we listen to dogs, they will tell us how we should behave in situations. It works well for my pushy boy dogs and for all of my clients' aggressive dogs when I am tall, still, and silent. Mirroring a dog's own body language makes communication a whole lot clearer.

I do feel that for the sake of honesty I must clarify that when I stand my tallest, stretching to the sky, I am five feet two! Height has nothing to do with it. It is all in your presence, your mind, and knowing how to use what you have.

June 20

Change yourself, change your dog

Your dog won't change until you start making your own changes. We owners are really, really good at self-deception (lying to ourselves so that we do not have to face the truth about what we have created).

We are also masters at playing the victim and blaming others for our dogs' flaws. Our dogs' errors are often the fault of our groomer, our breeder, the vet, the dog trainer, or that rude dog at the park. But never, ever us.

However, to transform your dog, you must first develop some awareness. Once you stop blaming others, or making excuses, you will take back the power to make dramatic changes in both yourself and your dog.

Wake up and see who your dog is. Drop the excuses and reasons, accept them for who they are today, and then train so that you can help them be the best that they can be.

Once you believe this, you will be in a beautiful position to train with new eyes, which will deliver all-new results. But first, first we must open our eyes and allow ourselves to see, honestly.

June 21

A good puppy class

A good puppy class should focus on three things: temperament building, obedience and relationship building blocks, and socializing with rules.

Every week we have a temperament lesson: something that will help make the dogs become better, braver, and more robust. In addition to this they learn the building blocks for obedience, such as down and coming back when called, even under high distraction, and they learn to be around other puppies while still having half an ear for their owners.

Puppy class should be a balance of all three things. We need to be building their temperaments, giving some obedience building blocks, working on the human/dog relationship, and developing some socializing by exposing them to other puppies, children, and people—with rules (you must still come when I call you even if another puppy's head is in your mouth).

June 22

Stay aware

Just because they never have does not mean they never will. Don't get complacent and forget they are dogs.

June 23

The dog will always pay

I've developed a theory based on my experience and it may come off as cynical, so please forgive me, but a dog will always pay for her owners' extended tolerance. The more tolerant the owners are of their dog's monstrous ways and the more "loving" they are, the sooner the day will come when suddenly she *must* find a new home.

It is the most loving, tolerant, and kind owners who, one day, can tolerate their monsters no more.

So I ask, please, please look at your dog. Honestly see what you are creating and if you are raising a baby monster, please go to training classes and do your homework.

The people who often end up in this place are the ones who cannot bear to tell their dogs they are wrong. So instead, after allowing their dogs to live a self-indulgent life where they have been void of all stress, the dogs end up rehomed, and retrained if they are lucky. If they are unlucky, they end up like the little man staring at me right now. Rehomed a multiplicity of times, then living in foster homes for years, and, finally, medicated. This little dog has been a piece of cake to turn around. Step one was teaching leash manners. Step two was telling him that biting my dogs is not allowed. And hopefully step three will be finding him his own family, once again. Only this time a family that will be fair and communicate when he is right *and* when he is wrong.

Please don't make your dog pay for your lack of guidelines and tolerance. You owe him training now, before you emotionally disengage from him.

June 24

Accepting your dog's best

On occasion, we must accept our dog's best effort even though it is not perfect. In the quest of seeking perfection, by asking for a teeny bit more, we will destroy all that we had.

Sometimes that little bit more is impossible for your dog to give. Know when you should ask for a bit more, and know when to make the most out of what you have.

June 25

Abandon micromanaging

Learning to *not* do our dogs' work for them is one of the hardest lessons to grasp. We never want them to be wrong, so we fiercely deny them any opportunity to learn. Just as they are about to achieve something, we do it for them, taking away any opportunity for learning, or feeling good about what they accomplished. We want them to be responsible, yet we never give them responsibility. We want them to be brave, yet we never allow them to push through something scary.

We constantly demonstrate that our dogs are unable to do most things by always doing it for them, and then we wonder why they have no confidence. Stop doing all of the work for your dog. Don't deny her the opportunity to show you how brilliant she is.

June 26

Dogs resemble their handlers

Frantic handlers have frantic dogs. Boring handlers have boring or bored dogs. Fun handlers have fun dogs. Calm handlers have calm dogs. Do you see a trend? Decide what type of dog you want and in what situations, and become that handler for your dog.

June 27

Develop "feel" in your hands

Do you have hard or soft hands when training your dog?

Aim for the softest hands possible. The more aroused your dog is, the softer you must go, and the calmer you must be. When his arousal is increased, it is like the dial on all of his senses got turned up to loud. He will be hyper-aware of what your hands are saying. If you say something too loudly, you will get an extreme reaction.

We tend to do the opposite. When we are adrenalized we get hard pokey fingers that hurt. We lose our fine motor skills and develop hard hands.

Be aware of your fingers and your touch, and be aware of what effect your hands and fingers have on your dog.

When in doubt, less is more. Softer, gentler hands will find you the goal that you seek. Let your muscles go soft, and be mega-aware that you handle your leash with micro-cues.

In moments of high arousal when your dog feels that the universe is yelling at him, make sure that your hands whisper.

June 28

Look at the dog

When judging another trainer or handler with their dog, don't look at what they do, what equipment they have on, or how full their pockets are. Look at the dog.

Is the dog happy? Does his skin slide loosely over his body showing no tension? Is the dog proud? And more importantly, is he well trained? If you answered yes to the above questions, the dog is being trained perfectly.

June 29

It's in his kiss

You can tell the strength of a dog by the strength of his kiss. Kisses hide nothing.

June 30

Make the wrong thing hard and the right thing easy

Make the wrong thing hard and right thing easy. But don't make the wrong thing impossible and deny the chance for learning.

If you have a dog who is acting out because of way too much energy, tire him out. It is hard for him to misbehave when he is tired.

If you have a dog who takes everything in and acts out, refocus his attention to help him stop acting out. Put some stimuli on him that will keep his mind busy. You can clip keys onto his collar, put a backpack on his back, or even bells on his feet. For the dog who gets over-aroused with a leaf blowing or a car going past, this will help him keep his mind focused inward. It will make your walk much more enjoyable. You have helped him to make the right choice, but he still has the freedom to make the wrong choice.

If you want them to go over a jump, make going around the jump much more work. Put blocks in place so the only easy route is over and not around.

Whenever you are struggling with communicating with your dog, find a way to make what you want to get easier, and what you don't want harder. But always remember, harder is not the same as impossible. Never deny them the chance to learn!

JULY

July 1

Look normal with your reactive dog

If you look and act normal and relaxed when you walk past another dog, very often your dog will become normal and relaxed, too. I know that sounds a lot easier than it is, especially with a reactive dog. Here's how to do it:

- When going past another dog, make sure your muscles relax. One muscle tensing can be enough to trigger an explosion. Loosen your hand, forearm, and shoulder, and walk through with purposeful determination. And breathe.
- Imagine in your head exactly how you want your dog to look as you pass by the oncoming dog. As you visualize it in advance, also have plan B ready in case your dog has another plan in mind.
- Walk your line and claim your path—no more deking into ditches and hiding behind trees. Your body language should look like a normal person casually walking her normal dog.
- Loose leash walking seems to be a lost art. Just by keeping your hand open on your leash, with only your thumb closed in to lightly hold it, you'll see your dog respond differently. Think horse riding and reins; you offer suggestions through your leash that your schooled dog will take.

As we start to master our challenges and feel great about ourselves, we still get stuck when we see a dog that scares us. When approaching these dogs, recite your mental checklist of your handlings skills: (a) walk your path and don't avoid, (b) open your hand, (c) swing your arm, and (d) slow down.

Your dogs will get safety in a group (a pack walk). This is a great step, but you still need to go walking on your own. Go walking alone right after so that you remember to do everything on your checklist.

After every walk (at least to start) calculate the percentage that you did your mental game right, the percentage that you did your technical game right, and then list every technique and moment that you did right. This will help you to remember it, and make it firmer in your memory.

With many dogs, we must go softer, not harder, as they start to learn what we want. Your cues must be way less, your movements slower and softer, or you will actually trigger them to respond to the other dogs.

Never go past a dog while your own dog is misbehaving. You need good behaviour before you pass your challenge, so go slow enough so that you can get it. Keep your forward momentum, but go at a snail's pace if needed. You need to master each and every pass by. Going slow calms you down, and it calms your dog down. As soon as you are past the other dog you can pick up your speed again.

Standing still is the hardest step, and some dogs might never get to this point. Always watch carefully when you are stopped, and help your dog.

Go hunting for victims. It is much more fun than trying to hide in the bushes and avoid dogs. Take the challenges head on, and pretend it is your idea.

Don't be as reactive as your dog. People will be rude to you, often with the best of intentions. Smile sweetly and, in your mind, thank them for donating this training moment.

The ruder the person who judges you, the bigger you must smile. Imagine in your head what dog they will end up with next. Karma is a bitch.

If your dog is off leash, teach him a verbal cue to get him moving forward as you pass by another dog. You can always manufacture this momentum by throwing food forward. However, be aware of the presence of other dogs when doing this, and don't do it if your own wants to guard food.

July 2

Respect is a two-way street

There is always talk of whether or not your dog respects you, but respect is a two-way street. Are you worthy of it? Do you respect your dog?

July 3

Be safe

If your dog has social issues, cutting him loose at the dog park to help him socialize is *not* okay.

In certain breeds (in fact, many breeds), one fight is all they need to develop dog reactivity. If you are letting your dog with social issues off leash and he is randomly scrapping with other dogs, you might be leaving an entire trail of dogs behind you who will need hundreds of hours of retraining to fix the damage that your dog did. I am not talking savage fights here; I am talking about moments where your dog made a psychological impact on another dog, even though the impact will not be seen in that initial moment.

Either walk your antisocial dog in places with few dogs and always call him back when you go past another dog (and if you do not have that control, do not let him off in the first place), or, if it is a large, unfenced park, walk him on leash. However, if your dog has gotten into trouble, make sure that you have the right equipment on your dog (whether it's a head collar so you can close his mouth, or a muzzle) so that he cannot hurt anyone else. You don't need some innocent, albeit untrained, dog getting injured for running over and grovelling at your dog's feet.

And if you are in an unfenced off-leash park, with an on-leash dog, don't get angry when dogs approach you. Granted, their owners should be calling them back, but the reality is that most won't. Rather than getting upset, use it as a teachable moment to get your dog to behave in an acceptable manner.

July 4

Control your mindset

When training your dog, the most offensive and violent weapon can be your mindset. If your intentions are not pure, and if you only see things in your dog that you do not like, you can do ample damage.

Make sure you see and note things in your dog that you like. And on days when you are in a crabby mood, don't do training that is going to irritate you. Instead, go for a hike in the forest. Enjoy your dog without any expectations, meaning he can't disappoint you.

July 5

Pack dynamics when dealing with a loss

When sweet Rita the Pit Bull died she left a hole in our household. Ironically, Rita's best friend, our Greyhound, Mandy, came back to life once Rita died. Even months later, she still had that new zest for life. We had not realized how Rita's decline had affected her best friend.

It wasn't until about a week later that I started to notice another shift in my household. In my house, all of my dogs have unique relationships with one another. With Rita gone, there was a void. She was the old matriarch peacekeeper in my house.

The dog who noticed her absence the most was, strangely, Basil. This was strange because Basil was not particularly smitten with Rita (only with himself and me!). However, her absence allowed my young German Shepherd male to exert his manliness, which caused Basil to struggle.

To help Basil, I started to do a lot more special stuff with him on his own. He became my errand dog, and was given other privileges to make him feel special and strong again.

Remember, in a pack everything is connected. You are not the only one who will be grieving the loss of a dog. Nor will you be the only one affected by the change.

July 6

There's no single right way

Recently I had the opportunity to watch a trainer who has a different toolbox than I do, and yet he holds the same philosophy.

We both isolate the fundamental skills lacking in many dogs, then create exercises through obedience that help these dogs build the personality traits that need strengthening.

And really, this is what training is all about. We see the temperament involved, then add concrete exercises that help dogs learn the emotion they need to be happy, adjusted, and nice.

When we are teaching an exercise, remember that we are using these training moments to make our dogs a nicer person. They need this, and we owe it to them so that they can live harmoniously in our world.

It goes to show that there's never just one right way. The options are endless.

July 7

We are all equal

When it comes to training dogs, there's one thing we all need the most, and we all have it: time. We all have 24 hours in our day, and we all have commitments that we must do within those 24 hours. We all know that it takes 10,000 hours to develop mastery.

The most committed and determined of trainers will find ways to use their 24 hours creatively to get the training time they need. As a result, they continue to log in way more training hours every single day than the majority.

This means that they always know, down to the minute detail, what they need to work on each session, because their rehearsal is still fresh in their memories from a few hours before. Sometimes five-minute sessions multiple times a day are easy to add into your packed schedule, and will still benefit you. But will you prioritize and adjust your schedule to make that happen? The choice is yours.

When it comes to the most important ingredient for training dogs, we are all equal. How we organize our calendars and schedule our days is up to us. Your success is in your own hands.

July 8

Etiquette for dog owners

These things really shouldn't need to be said, but they do. Here are my rules of etiquette to keep our dogs living in harmony with everyone else:

- Be considerate in public.
- I love my dogs. But I am aware that everyone else might not, nor should they have to. My dogs are mine, and I keep them to myself.
- If a dog walking toward you is on leash, please leash yours out of respect as you pass.
- Always rein your dog in going past children. Be considerate of who you are passing. Make sure your dog in no way bothers them.

- Don't allow lots of barking at home. Just because you love your dogs it doesn't mean your neighbours should have to listen to them.
- Don't feed someone else's dog unless you ask.
- Be considerate where you potty your dog.
- Don't allow your dog to pee on buildings, doorways, or on the fences of carefully manicured yards. Remember, where the first dog pees, the next one hundred will also pee, quickly burning lawns and trees.
- Don't let your dog pee on benches, children's play equipment, or mailboxes. In general, don't let your dog pee on anything that people need to touch.
- If your dog is coughing or really sick, let your vet know before you go into the office.
- If your dog is coughing, do not let her drink out of community water bowls, or interact with others. The same applies for sneezing and puppy warts, or anything else contagious.

July 9

Don't treat your dog like a tiger

If you treat your dog like a tiger, he will become one.

What I mean by this is that if you are fearful that he will eat the mail carrier, your body language and handling will tell him that you are scared of the mail carrier, and you will inadvertently cue him to do exactly what you fear.

Instead, treat your dog like a normal dog, but be ready if he decides to be naughty. Have a plan B in mind, but you must introduce your dog to the situation as if he is already the dog you wish him to be.

July 10

Lead the way

If my dogs ever show worry or concern, I go before them and demon-strate how it is done. This means my two hip bones and two shoulders need to be aligned with my target, whatever that might be. This tip is universal for almost every scenario in life when your dog balks.

Walking onto a bridge, I go forward and continue facing forward in the direction I want my dog to go. I pause for a moment to get used to the footing, then go. Keep shoulders and hip bones forward, which means don't look back.

If he is nervous of a nice dog, I might go and feed that dog a cookie (if allowed), and then leave. I won't ask my dog to greet them. I just demonstrate that there is nothing to worry about. I keep my hip bones and shoulders on the dog I'm greeting and never look back to my own.

If my dog is scared of a statue, I might go touch it and talk to it, keeping all my focus on the statue (not my dog) then confidently walk away.

If my dog is scared of a benign animal, I will go and pet it and move it. If my dog is scared of a mean animal, I will make the mean animal move away.

This simple thing will give your fearful dog confidence, and your dog will believe in you.

July 11

A lesson in humility

We are all perfect dog trainers—until we get a dog who tells us otherwise.

Until you have owned a "difficult" dog, it is hard to imagine how humbling it can be. Not only do you realize that you know nothing but it is challenging, exhausting, embarrassing, depressing, and filled with judgement from all the owners with perfect dogs.

Your dog will give you a very thick skin. You will learn to ignore comments, to train your dog regardless of the challenge being presented to you, and to have gigantic celebrations about the dumbest things, such as your uptight, fearful bitch peeing in public for the first time ever!

Please realize that during these very lonely times, you are far from alone. Many of today's great trainers all started where you are. So enjoy the lessons given to you by your dog. You will eventually learn to love them.

July 12

Heat tolerance

It's so bizarre that people are more likely to run their dog on a treadmill than they are to take their dog hiking on a hot day because of fear about heat tolerance. One local dog trainer just announced that dogs should not be walked in 68°F (20°C). That means that our dogs should stay home here in the Pacific Northwest from April to October! That's insane.

When dogs are no longer going outside in warm temperatures, or being asked to do anything in warm temperatures, we are going to breed out all heart and work ethic in our dogs. And, even more importantly, without realizing it, we are going to breed out dogs that can tolerate the heat.

Unless we consider the heat and get our dogs out, our dogs will literally melt when faced with it. We have gotten soft, and we are no longer asking them to work in it, and more importantly, we are not building their tolerance to it.

My dogs compete in sports that are performed outside. That means I am out training in snow, wind, rain, hail, and even the sun. Likewise, I am out exercising them in snow, wind, rain, hail, and even sun. In the summer, I spend time acclimating them to the heat, so that they get used to it. That also means getting them in running shape, in the sun. If I don't, how can I expect them to perform in it?

Learn how to look at a tongue that is showing heat. Know how to cool a dog down. We must take care of our athletes, to keep them in prime shape for their sports.

I live in the Pacific Northwest where we have moderate temperatures almost all year. I realize that in Florida things are different. We must never give our dogs heat exhaustion; once they get it, they never fully recover. But there is a flip side. In our quest to be careful with our dogs, the pendulum has swung way too far to the other side, where we have forgotten common sense.

Get your dogs out in the moderate heat. Enjoy them in the summer. Just don't be foolish. (For my thoughts on dogs in cars on hot days, see July 15.)

July 13

Teach your dog to swim

Summer is the time for you and your dog to hit the water. Swimming is such a fun thing to do with your dog. And swimming is also a necessary skill for your dog to learn.

Some dogs will be in the water very quickly, while others will take an afternoon of patience before they are confident enough. I always start teaching them with Charlee Bear brand dog treats because they float and are easy to see. Royal Canin German Shepherd Dog Food also floats, but it's darker in colour and harder for dogs to see.

I toss my first cookie about six inches into the water. My dog will go out for it. If that was easy, I will throw the next cookie farther. But, if it was too far, I'll throw the next cookie closer to make it easier. Once you have found the right starting point for your dog, ask a little bit more for the next three throws. By more, I mean about an inch farther into the water. Then go right back to your starting point for three throws, to build success and confidence. Then make it harder again. If your dog is successful, your first three will consecutively end up one inch further out in the water. Then your next three will be back at shore, as easy, confidence-building cookie grabs.

If you take your time to start with your swimming lessons, your dog will be out in the water before you know it. If you keep pushing them and pushing them, it will take longer to get them out there.

July 14

Raise your expectations

My dogs are not trained purely positively. I tell them no. I correct them if they are rude. I reward them when they do right. Funnily enough, my husband hasn't been trained purely positively either. I correct him when he is rude. I thank him when he does kind things. And he isn't aggressive (despite the study out there saying he must be because corrections cause aggression)—and neither are my dogs.

Positive reinforcement training fits all of our own emotional criteria to be kinder and not cause stress or discomfort, yet we don't always practice it with our families and loved ones. We have been told that we can remove all obnoxious habits in our dogs with positive reinforcement alone. I wish it were this simple. If we have a dog who chases rabbits and deer when off-leash, positive reinforcement will not fix it. Corrections will, but positive reinforcement alone will not. If we have a dog rudely leaping on people, positive reinforcement won't fix it. Granted, never say never. There are brilliant positive reinforcement trainers who will be able to achieve this. But most won't.

And this partly explains why we are losing our dog privileges. We've put aside common sense when it comes to telling our dogs when they are being rude and intolerable. Instead, we have become so kind and tolerant, with endless worry about doing no harm or causing stress. We want to reward all badness away.

My dogs are raised with the same guidelines that I have in all the other relationships in my life. We communicate. There is give and take. There is a whole lot of fun, but there are also consequences if you cross the line. Our life is in harmony, in balance, and so is our training.

I once read this little saying: "Humans are like tea bags. You do not know how strong they are until you steep them in hot water." I believe this to be true. And I do not worry about causing stress as I know that dealing with it will make my dog more well-rounded. Stress is not to be avoided. It is to be embraced.

I expect my dogs to behave. And they do. Expect the same of your own. Here is permission to give your dog clear boundaries again, even though they may cause stress. A fair correction on his leash for being rude won't make him aggressive, I promise. And if he is so out of control that he wants to discipline you for that, then consider that your invite to discuss "teeth are forbidden to touch human skin."

We would never allow family members to be as rude as we allow our dogs to be. Nor do we give them rewards once they are nicer. Start applying those same principles to your dog. Keep your rewards for when your dog is learning or when rewards are deserved. Add in corrections for lack of effort or rudeness. The same as you do in your human relationships.

Dog training is not as complex as we've made it. Just be clear. And always fair. Honour your dog by not raising him to be a self-indulgent jerk who falls apart when he encounters change because he never learned how to handle stress.

July 15

Dogs in cars

It's starting again. What is with shaming people who leave dogs in cars? Who gave license to anyone with a camera to start trolling parking lots, to get proof to humiliate and shame people for taking their dogs on an outing on a cool summer's day?

Here in the Pacific Northwest people have been taking their dogs to work since the beginning of time with nary a problem, yet after one local tragedy where several dogs left unattended were killed in a vehicle, owners have been continually harassed. I was once questioned at 8 p.m. for having a dog in my van. My car had full airflow, including a natural breeze, a fan, and a window shade, and I was parked under a tree. I was wearing a sweater.

My concern is how the power has shifted to allow citizens to stop people with no cause, question them, and then publicly harass them via social media. If our police did this we would be up in arms, yet we support it when it is done on Facebook. How did we give our neighbours more rights than our police officers?

If it is stinking hot out, windows aren't open, and the dog is in distress, then yes, please act.

Act: do something to help the dog, which does not include being passive aggressive via social media. Actual help makes you a hero—you saved a dog. Trolling a parking lot and taking photos of happy dogs in cars on an average summer day does not make you a hero.

If you want to help dogs, go and volunteer at any shelter, they will be happy to have you. There, every dog's outcome is in danger, and many a dog is truly in distress.

So how do we leave dogs in our cars safely? Quite easily actually:

- A nifty gadget called a "vent lock" leaves your car open, but locked. Your dog gets air, yet your vehicle is safe. (Visit cleanrun.com)
- Reflective shade cloths will reduce the temperature in your car by as much as fourteen degrees. (Also found at cleanrun.com)
- Rechargeable portable fans, such as the one made by Ryobi from Home Hardware, keep the air moving through your vehicle. They make summer easy. (Found at homedepot.com)
- For the die-hards, get permanent metal bars in your windows, so that windows can stay down and your car remains secure.
- For additional security, get a thermometer in your car, and get it connected to your phone so that you know if the heat goes up.
- On really hot days, think like any mature decision-making adult, and if it is unsafe, leave your dog at home. Common sense says that if you can't handle it, neither can your dog.

My fear is that if we do not break this current trend of having the right to stop and question a stranger with no grounds other than a social media-induced paranoia, what is next?

We will see photos of irresponsible owners who let their dogs off leash, risking being hit by a car. Or owners who tie a dog up outside a store where they could get stolen. Or owners who feed bones to their dogs, whose teeth could break. Or owners who walk their dogs on sidewalks from May to October, when their feet could burn. Or short-haired dogs with no coat being walked in the rain. The list is endless. I would never tie a dog up. But that doesn't necessarily mean people who choose to should be shamed for doing it.

The frenzied fear that is being created by social media is going to leave cities full of dogs that don't go anywhere, to avoid the risk of their owners being questioned and judged by random strangers. Bored, unsocialized, unhappy dogs who will live their lives watching out the window, rather than going out with us.

Take the power back. Live with your dog as you always have, providing you are not an idiot (and your friends agree).

July 16
Dig deep

Dog training books, videos, and forums are all great places to learn tools and techniques. Yet not a training book out there discusses the most important skill of all—digging deep. This is by far the most necessary piece when you are working with your dog.

Many of us can do well when everything is going right. But who can think on their feet when everything is going wrong and turn it around? And will you willingly go back out again, with some great ideas for solutions, when you know everything's falling apart?

Remember to think of these moments as you progress in your training. When you master it, you get to jump forward a level. So dig deep, find your inner determination, and go and learn your lessons with your dog.

Everyone who has that inner grit manages to overcome their hurdles and accomplish their goals. Those who prefer to stay in a place of comfort only move forward in minimal increments. And those who fail to prioritize their goals are always waiting until tomorrow to start.

The disciplined trainer is the one who will get to the goal, even if she is unskilled at the start. What differentiates us the most as trainers is our ability to dig deep.

July 17

Believe in your dog

You've got to believe in your dog and believe that she can do it for you—"it" being the impending challenge, whatever that may be. If you don't believe in her, she will not find it within herself to deliver "it" to you.

But belief doesn't mean to pray or hope. Belief means to *know* that she can, and then school her so that she is able.

Though nothing is this simple. Sometimes the task is easy, but today, for some reason, your dog chooses not to do it. You must be more tenacious than she is; don't leave without getting what you asked for.

July 18

Direct with your body

Agility trainers understand the art of directing a dog with their bodies. Even if you are running forward, your energy can go in another direction, and you can send your dog there.

Now think of retraining your reactive dog, and apply the same. Imagine you and your dog are walking past a dog. If you can keep your body and momentum going forward, in the direction of where you want your dog to go, you will most likely succeed in going past it.

But if you choose to orient your hips and shoulders toward the "victim" dog you are approaching, you are telling your dog to go there. You are actually directing your dog toward that dog.

Always remember to drive your dog forward, past the dog. Don't get stuck in that moment—keep your energy going forward beyond the challenge instead.

July 19

Self-improvement

Good dog trainers regularly seek to upgrade their skills and general techniques. They spend time, money, and humility in the ongoing quest for self-improvement.

They recognize good training when they see it, and seek to surround themselves with those who will not only help them improve their dog skills, but also their mental game: encourage them, inspire them, and make them realize their own potential. Great training partners not only make you a better trainer but also help you improve on a more personal and inspirational level as well.

Through the course of training our dogs, we learn personal skills that make us much better people.

July 20

Don't marry a method—marry a result

There are two criteria for judging the effectiveness of a training method. Did the dog learn the lesson? Is the dog happy after he learned the lesson?

A good trainer will create a confident animal whose skin slides loosely over his ribcage, who is open with his ears and other body language, and is self-assured. And a good trainer will have a beautiful relationship with her dog, regardless of the dog's temperament. A good trainer can create this with almost all dogs, regardless of what tools they do or do not have.

After these questions have been answered, we should look at the method. We all love our dogs and want to make them feel good; however, results must come first. Be as kind as possible, yet as firm as necessary. When results are compromised so your dog feels better, dogs end up on Prozac, or euthanized for bad behaviour. Do not compromise the result.

Start to evaluate training methods by looking at the dog in front of you. The dog will tell you more than what training tools are being used; he will tell you what he likes and doesn't like, and what works and what does not. If you listen to the dog, you will probably not get the answers back that you are expecting.

Conversations about training tools have a way of sparking such raw emotions that all constructive dialogue stops, regardless of how happy or unhappy the dog looks, or how he behaves. Don't buy into this nonsense. Let the dog tell you. Did he learn the lesson? Is he confident and loose? Evaluation really is that simple.

If the answer is "yes," then the method was right for that dog. If you answered "no," then you need to try a new method for that dog. We must start judging results, not training methods.

July 21

Dog ownership can be so heart-rending

When I got Kate, I knew she wasn't as robust as my other dogs. I also knew that Kate feels things more deeply than others. She's emotional, and driven by her emotions. She feels more happiness, more love, more joy, but also more anger, and more worry.

Recently I had to go away. Every time Kate experiences something new in my house she struggles. The first time I went away she had a seizure. The second time I left she was fine because she knew I'd be back in a week. The third time I left she was great for the first week, but struggled the second week. She didn't know two weeks were possible.

When I got home I had a dog who was spending many hours in the quiet closet upstairs. I didn't think too much of it, and we still had fun moments every single day. I hadn't realized that poor Kate worried so much that she triggered an autoimmune disease where the flesh of her nose area literally falls off.

How can a little creature feel so deeply that they can trigger a disease this serious?

This fragile soul breaks my heart. Her health has made me responsible for all of my actions that affect her. Now that I know this, I must find a solution where changes are not a form of torture for her. And I must make her believe she's staying in this home, in sickness and in health, and in happy days and evil days. If she knew how loved and safe she is, her mental and emotional angst would be gone. My job is to make her know this through clearer communication and medical means.

July 22

The value of genetics

Right now, I'm blessed to be spending lots of time with three Border Collie babies. Based on this limited sample of three, I have decided that Border Collies don't learn quite the same way as other dogs. They learn many things with just *one* repetition, so if you don't respond in that first moment, you now have a behaviour that you get to live with for a lifetime.

I remember when I had five-week-old Siberian Huskies and plopped them on the ground and watched them scatter far and wide, with zero care in the world for me. Almost all other breeds at that age seek out humans and stick with you. Not these guys!

And I remember my Pit Bull, Sybil, who was in her second intense dogfight with two of her littermates at *seven weeks old*. Thank goodness they only had their milk teeth. This was extreme behaviour for any breed—and a foreshadowing.

I knew a ten-week-old guarding breed puppy that had already been fired from two other dog trainers for resource guarding. Resource guarding is not uncommon, nor problematic, in working, guarding Terrier or herding breed puppies, or any breed with some push. It is supposed to be there. However, seeing this same behaviour in a Golden Retriever puppy is a worry, as a Golden should not be acting this way.

Few puppies are crazier than sighthound babies. They have two speeds: not moving and galloping. I think they get all of their naughtiness out in their first year, so they can spend the rest of their lives sleeping and being perfect.

Then there are the Shelties who come out of the womb barking and the Malinois babies who explore the world with their mouths. And many Cattle Dog puppies who have great fun scheming their next naughty prank. There are herding breeds who herd and control or respond to movement and pressure at their first ability. And there are scent hounds who come into this world with their noses on the ground. Or pointing breeds, who see something and won't move.

I am always in awe of how different breeds can be. Their instincts and bloodlines play such a vital role in shaping who they are. We are given these puppies that all look different, think different, move different, and feel different. And it is our job as handlers to try and steer them in the direction of functionality so that their lives will be long and happy and always lived out in our homes.

A big part of their success is in how we raise them, but breed and genetics play a big part. If you want a dog who is kind and loving to everyone, human or dog, including your pet rabbit, then don't shop within the group that was bred to kill things. That would be the Terriers, the flock guardian breeds, and the guard dogs.

Don't get one of these characters determined to make yours the exception. Honour the breed and accept them with all of the traits they come with.

July 23

Sometimes dog training logic isn't logical

This week I struggled with something with my dog. I was making it easier to help him succeed, and my problem went from being minor to major. A wise mentor suggested that I ask for way more by making it way harder for him to succeed, and also removing almost all rewards.

After doing this, my dog suddenly worked as he should. Which got me scratching my head. I tried to help him succeed and, in the process, all I did was remove his effort.

I suppose I'm the same way. If I have a real challenge in front of me, I focus on it completely. If I have a mindless challenge in front of me, I do not.

By making his work so easy, and offering so many rewards, I made his work a mindless challenge, and he worked accordingly. The saddest part in all of this is I know this about my dog. But, I'm forgetful. And I like to reward. And I like him to succeed. So I forget that he likes a challenge, and instead I sabotage his effort by making it mindlessly easy.

One day I will be as smart as my dog.

And while I have momentarily upped my game (until I forget again next year), I am seeing so many of my clients make the same error. So many help their dogs through the most minor "achievements," and then offer praise when their dog really put forth no effort. Silence and raised expectations would have been much more appropriate.

Thanking a university student for printing their name nicely on the top of the page is degrading (though in kindergarten this would be totally acceptable). Yet we do this to our dogs.

We do need to help our dogs. We do need to acknowledge what they do right. But we need to give problems they deem worthy of solving, at their education level, to prevent us from creating apathetic workers.

So, this is a thank you to all the great training friends and mentors who call us on our enabling!

July 24

Coming back when called

Coming back when called is probably the most important thing to teach your dog. And probably one of the hardest things to teach.

Right now, in my advanced puppy class, we are working on calling the dogs, off leash, out of a puppy play group, and most of the puppies are actually coming when called. We have a classroom of puppies who would rather spend time with their owners than with the other dogs. But how on earth are the owners going to maintain this?

On walks, when your dogs are off leash, be spontaneous, and do things they might not expect. Run away and hide behind a tree. Take off and lie down in long grass. Sneak behind a barrier. Take off, running away from them when they are not paying attention. Have a game when they get back to you. Make yourself more exciting, which will in turn make it entertaining for your dog to keep an eye on you.

The hardest part about teaching a dog to come back is teaching the owners that it is the dog's responsibility, and not theirs. Your dog should be checking in with you, rather than you continually trying to make them check in. What I mean is that as my dogs are running, every ten seconds or so, they look over their heads to see where I am. Your dog should be doing that to you.

The other part about dogs coming back when called is their ultimate reward: leaving again. Don't make them come back and stay with you to be petted and hugged. In this moment, in the real world, they do not want it. They want their freedom. There might be one or two dogs who are an exception, but for the most part, they want to go. So let them. The sooner they come back, the sooner they can go.

July 25

Take your dog swimming

Today and yesterday at the end of Competition Obedience class, the dogs all went swimming.

Dogs who have never "liked" each other behaved well with one another. They all had a blast, and they were all focused on swimming. The next time the dogs meet they will have more of a fondness for each other because of sharing such a fun experience (they loved swimming!).

So if your dog doesn't like other dogs, get them doing their favourite activity when others are present. For challenging dogs, their first off-leash time should be at the beach, or an equivalent fun place. Very few want to fight at the beach. Most would rather run, play, and eat dead sea things.

Obviously keep it safe so nothing bad can happen, but do pair their favourite things with another dog so they build some nice associations.

Keep it safe. And go have fun.

July 26

When corrections are the most fair

I have a wonderful little Rottweiler puppy living with me right now. He tries so hard to please. We've been working on following, getting him to realize that temper tantrums are not the right solution to a problem, sharing his prized possessions, receiving cookies when he has his toenails trimmed, walking past people, following me past a variety of my crazy animals, not leaping into my dinner plate, car rides, all the other normal daily events that happen in my household, and of course, crate training.

What I find bizarre is that people nowadays are so unwilling to make strict rules for their puppies (like crate training them, or anything else that the puppy does not want to do). He needs them as much as—if not more than—the fun stuff, like earning cookies for following and greeting the world appropriately.

Likewise, a correction the first time any dangerous behaviour is shown will make that behaviour go away, forever. If my puppy was guarding under the couch and dove out to bite someone who came too close, I would not go to a resource guarding protocol, which is really months-long management. Instead, I would let him jump out, catch him in the act, and tell him that was wrong.

If my puppy bites me with intent over food, I will correct him. If my puppy tries to chase a car, bites a jogger, or lunges at a dog with evil intent, I will correct him. By doing it once, I will never have to address the issue again. What is fairer: one correction to remove a serious, life-threatening behaviour in return for a lifetime of freedom and off-leash fun, or constant management and monitoring for a lifetime?

As I say that, this little guy hasn't gotten a single correction or even heard "uh-uh" or "no." He has been guided, reinforced, and coached through life. But that doesn't mean there isn't a time and place for corrections because there is. And one day in his little Rottweiler life, he will need to be told "no." Just not today.

What I find odd about people who struggle to put rules on their babies and see them uncomfortable in crates is that it seems they would rather correct and nag at them all day long for trivial, unimportant things. This will do much more sinister damage.

I wish for a world where people could read dogs and see the consequences of their actions.

This is puppy training broken down:

- Quit nagging at your dogs. Count how many times you say, "no," and all other forms of indicating that he did wrong. I have had this little guy here for four days, and he has yet to hear it.
- Reward and help way, way more. When they are this tiny, they are willing little nerds who beg for praise. If you show them, they will do it.
- Don't ever allow life-threatening behaviours, such as biting with the intent to hurt.
- Make sure you introduce your puppies to stressful moments, so they can learn to become strong, independent dogs who can think through it. As hard as it is to hear them cry, it is your job to give them fair rules.
- Show them the world, but don't pressure them to interact with it.

If we all did this, we could have almost an entire generation of dogs who would not need Prozac; they would be able to handle the stresses of life because they would be taught how in small, successive increments.

July 27

Don't be a doormat

No dog wants to follow a doormat. Quit being their cheerleader and become a coach. Cooing to an adult, regardless of reasons, is so disrespectful. Your good wishes are keeping them weak, or alienated from you.

These are not tiny children who need our mummy voices. Often these are mature adults who you are degrading. You wouldn't talk to your spouse like that. At least you wouldn't if you are still married. Nor would you talk to a respected peer at work in that degrading voice.

So stand up tall, help them, and treat them like you would a co-worker who needs some strength and a helping hand.

Once you respect your dog, you will find that their ears will open to you. Because they will care what you think.

July 28
Retraining fearful dogs

Many fail when it comes to retraining fearful dogs. They are trying to retrain fear with food, but if you are drowning, you need a flotation device, not a cookie. If you are about to get hit by a bus, you need to be pulled off the road, not offered a cookie. Offering your dog food when he fears for his safety is an odd response. It shows that you lack compassion for your dog's struggle. When we feel scared, uncomfortable, or vulnerable, we need compassion and safety, not a snack.

However, when I retrain fearful dogs, I still use food, but I pair it with a soft, slow rubbing touch that makes dogs feel really good deep inside. This happy, safe emotion will now be associated with this ritual of rubbing/touching and food. Now I can offer the good feeling of safety and comfort as I offer food.

Food is only useful to a fearful dog if the process of eating it provides a feeling of comfort and safety. The food itself is not the solution—what's useful is the *feeling* that comes along with the food.

Now please, I beg, don't feed your dog and then start a cheerleading dance. If I am drowning and you start cheering, I will think that you are happy for my discomfort. Or that you have a social disorder. In any case, I will know that you don't understand my angst.

And don't use a whiny or sucky voice. Kissing and cuddling belong at home in private. It will not help your dog become strong in public.

And offering food alone will turn some dogs off food when it's being offered in places where they could feel unsafe. They will start to associate the offering of treats with the feeling of being in danger. This will only teach them to be suspicious when they take treats. (And we wonder why there's an increase in anxiety in dogs.)

July 29

What kind of trainer are you?

Trainers are judged on the methods they use, and then lumped into categories like "force-free," "balanced," and "corrective."

Somehow the label has become the focus. Shouldn't we be more focused on the results? Our goal as a trainer must be for a well-trained, happy dog for our clients in a reasonable amount of time. While I can gladly wait two years for the perfect sit, I cannot expect the same of my clients. I get twelve weeks to train their dog, and I had better do a good job or that dog might be out of a home.

Trainers evolve over time, and experiences change the methods we use. Some dogs force us to change. We learn more. And our methods evolve. Experienced trainers have probably belonged in two or three categories in their time, switching with education and then switching again when dogs demanded it.

I have personally struggled to figure out what slot I belong in, but none of them seem to fit. That's because they don't. My friend defined it for me. He said, "I'm a dog trainer," and that about sums it up.

There is no category for me to fit into. There is no label. Every dog is different, and every dog defines how she is taught. I aim for efficient results. I train each and every dog, aiming to be as kind as possible yet as firm as necessary. And I adapt and change as the dog requires.

I don't have a singular method or slot but rather use all of them as required. I am a dog trainer, and I train the dog I am training.

July 30

Train puppies in the right emotion

When you get a puppy, you are given a lifetime of endless possibilities and potential. But these perfect creatures go through odd moments. During these stages, make sure you always remember to pay attention to their emotional state during your formal training, more so than the behaviours they are performing.

With my own puppy, I want her with me with her tail up. Until her tail is up, I won't be teaching her any formal work. I do not want her learning her formal job in a wrong mindset, because this will become her default mode in the future.

It is important to always remember attitude more than anything else. If the attitude is not right, don't train heeling. If the attitude is not right, don't train anything that you need good attitude for. If they are uncomfortable in a park, don't teach your formal work until they think the park is the coolest place in the world. And for me, I will know when that day is here because I will see her tail up. And she will be able to play with me there, uninhibited.

Of course, you can still teach domestics and other puppy learning. But formal work, such as things we get judged on in our sports, should be put on pause.

Puppies all go through odd stages with periods of fear. If your puppy struggles during these moments, put formal work on the backburner and show her how much fun the world is. Explore it with her. If she is really concerned, silently carry her until she is busting to get out of your arms to go and explore.

I'm lucky to have older confident dogs who are happy to show babies how bold, balanced dogs behave in different situations. They are such great coaches, demonstrating how it all should be done. With their coaching, and with me building up my puppy's drive, this stage will soon be a distant memory, and one that will never affect her work because she isn't working while she is in it!

July 31
Know how to read your dog

There are two parts to training a dog. The first is teaching the lesson and the second is working with the temperament and personality. The first part is easy, it is the recipe following that we all do. There are many recipes for each and every thing that we teach dogs, which will require varying levels of skill to execute. These methods are just following consecutive steps.

The success, fairness, and humanity of the method all come from the second part of training: working with the temperament and personality.

The kindest method can be very unkind if you are not adjusting it to the dog, and if you are not aware of external factors involved and how they are affecting your student. Regardless of attempting to be kind, you need to actually pay attention to what your dog says!

Some trainers are more successful than others because of their ability to read the dog. By looking and being able to see the dog, they know where he is at. When you know where your dog is coming from—where his effort is, how his ego and self-esteem are affecting his performance—you will know what recipe to give and how to adjust it.

Pay attention to what your dog says. Once you start listening, you will be amazed at the free flow of communication back and forth.

AUGUST

August 1

All dogs are created differently

What do you do when you get a dog who is so guidable, so honest, so sweet, and so willing that if she thinks she has done something wrong she is destroyed? Well, the obvious answer is to make it easier. But that is only partly right.

More importantly, we must teach those dogs that being wrong is part of life. You must dig deep and try again and again and again. There is nothing wrong with making an error, but you don't get to give up and stop. You must continue your efforts.

These dogs need to learn to be more robust. We need to bring out their cheeky side, find ways to empower them, make them prouder, and give them self-worth. My puppy Pippa now loves numerous games that would have initially made her shrivel up and hide forever. We box, where I pretend punch her in the face. She makes killer death sounds and gently knocks my hands away. If she has a soccer ball, I will gently kick it out of her mouth and do a victory lap with it until she disarms me of my toy. Her games are acknowledged, but she is required to be brave and put in effort for her rewards. If she is too slow wrangling the ball away, she simply doesn't get it. I will continue playing with it until she loses her mind and puts in that extra effort. She doesn't get handed things just because she is adorable. And weak.

I am also teaching her to be persistent, to not give up. I cheer my puppy up every time she tries hard, even if it's digging a disgusting rotten stick out of the pond. I tell her how clever she is, and clap while she parades her disgusting possession around, with her tail curled over her back. When she gives up on digging her stick out because it is too much work, I pester her, asking her where it is and pointing to the hole. My voice is a little bit frantic and urgent, which gets her back to her project. Giving up is not a solution—you must work hard for things of value, like revolting decaying sticks.

In her work, I occasionally deliberately allow her to be wrong so that I can teach her not to give up. I will help her through her issue, then bop her food reward so hard that it either pings off of part of her body (the bounce and movement will make her forget she was feeling sorry for herself), or I will fling it across the room so that she has to go and chase it. When she feels really down on herself, I will fling it against the wall, where it makes a perfect *thunk* sound that she cannot resist. (I have already gotten her wild with sounds, so it is the perfect way to snap her out of a moment.)

Dogs will make errors. If you are training them for sport, it is going to happen. They must learn not to stress but rather to try harder, and to forgive themselves.

Remember, dog training is not only a science but also an art. To teach exercises is science. To train the right emotions and personality is art.

August 2
How do I fix this?

The most common question I am asked is, "How do I fix this?" And the answer I most commonly give is "I have no idea."

I do have an idea. I have many ideas. Five could be horrendously bad ideas, four could be mediocre, and one might be bang on, depending on the dog. But until I see that dog and that owner on that day, I have no idea which one will work.

Dogs, like people, have dynamic personalities. Their needs change frequently. What is going on in the environment is going to affect them. They have feelings that might need to be built up, which they might need to learn how to control, or that might need to be catered to.

August 3

Toxic levels of stress and exercise

High levels of stress have been proven to actually shrink specific parts of the brain. This frightening process can, thankfully, be reversed with exercise. As outlined in the book *Spark* by John Ratey, MD, physical activity releases neurochemicals and other factors that can grow the brain—reducing anxiety and stress and actually increasing the ability to learn.

Reactive dogs who are exposed to toxic levels of stress and not given the opportunity to exercise are being done a huge disservice. As parts of their brains shrink, they are literally being held back from the ability to learn.

It is not until we can actually start to get their bodies moving that we can get positive neurochemicals and growth factors flowing back into their brains, which will bolster brain size, increase their ability to learn and retain information, and reduce stress. Exercising them is very difficult to do. But when you do, you will see those dogs transform in approximately two weeks.

The easiest way to exercise them safely and effectively is on a bicycle. While the thought just made you gasp in horror, if you try it, you will see a profound difference in your dog almost instantly and you too will become hooked.

If you have a stress-case of a dog, and exercising her is a nightmare, just try it. Let her pick the speed and follow her lead. Watching her gallop and seeing the joy it gives her will make you feel really good about dusting off your old bicycle.

August 4

Mental discipline: Force yourself to work on your weaknesses

Good trainers work hard at perfecting their strengths. They get out and train, even when they are feeling tired, and have great fun with their dog, continually improving on what they are already good at.

Excellent trainers work hard at perfecting their weaknesses. They get out there, even when they are feeling tired, and start with the exercises they dread and hate. This is the work that makes us better at what we do, and it takes great concentration to master.

You are moving forward in your training if some of the exercises really challenge you mentally and leave you fatigued after completion.

Brilliance isn't born by always having fun. Make sure you are more committed to training the exercises that you dislike and struggle with than the ones that you love and are already good at.

There is a component of mental discipline that separates the good from the great.

August 5

Keep a training journal

The key to being a successful trainer is to continually assess each element of behaviour that you are training, to make yourself aware of what is working and what is not. Reflecting on our training will keep us honest, which will prevent us from doing the same old, same old, while hoping for a different outcome.

Keeping a training journal can be the best way to do this. Reflect on your successes (we need to remember what we did right so that we can repeat it). Pose a question to yourself about any struggles that you have, but do not come up with the solution on paper. Only ask the question. I find whenever I do this, I always know the answer right away, because the simple act of writing the question down gets me processing. And always write down your short- and long-term goals, so that you remember where you should be a month from now and your ultimate goal.

Doing this will keep you from only training and remembering the things that you like to do, and will help you get better by working on your weaknesses.

August 6

Walk straight ahead

I was asked a great question by a client who was in the last stages of rehabilitating her reactive dog: if arcing, or curving, around is a calming signal for dogs, why am I going in a straight line when I pass a dog and not arcing around it?

Arcing away from a threat is dog language, and it's something a nice dog does when challenged by a jerk. Well, in this case, I'm the jerk.

Most dogs have fear-based aggression even if they've become really convincing in their display. This answer is for all of those dogs—not dogs with aggression that comes from place of confidence. I do handle those differently.

These fear-based dogs need to learn that I'm Mama Bear, and I have things covered. When I observe at the dog park and watch the dogs that get left alone, they walk in a straight line, staring as they approach, often with intent. And they tend to slow down. Most other dogs don't mess with them. I decided to copy them.

I don't want my rehabbed dogs to be friendly with strange dogs. I want them to learn to *ignore* other dogs, and keep their forward momentum. To teach momentum I need to focus on a destination.

If I am driving on ice and lose control, I need to keep my eyes on where I want to go. If I focus on the lamp post that I want to avoid, that is where I will end up. Instead, I keep my eyes on my lane.

If I'm running agility, I need to keep my body aligned with where I want my dog to go, both now and in the immediate future, not the path *I* am travelling. We use our body to show the right way. Your dog is going where your two hips and two shoulders tell him to go, which for me is straight ahead, past the approaching dogs.

Riding horses, you need to almost push your horse toward the outer edges of the arena to get perfectly straight lines and perfect circles. Our animals naturally want to move away from barriers, so if we want them to drive into a target, we need to focus our bodies and attention on that target. My fearful dogs want to avoid others, so I need to focus on driving into the oncoming dog.

So, by walking straight ahead with all my energy and momentum committed to my path, I can get almost any dog past anything. I am looking ahead, beyond the dog that I am approaching. If I focus on the dog immediately ahead of me, I will have a slow reaction time if something happens—just like driving on a highway. I am focused several cars ahead, to keep forward momentum and I keep my intention on where we are going, not on the distraction just presented to me. This tells my dog precisely where we are going, and that the people we are about to pass *are not* a detour along the way.

What I've seen happen thousands of times is that at that last critical moment the owner will flinch and side-step away, or pull their dog away, and that is all the permission the dogs needs to take over for them and get snarky at the passerby. If the handler can hold her line, resist the urge to tighten her hands and forearms, and deliberately let her muscles soften, it is a very rare dog who will misbehave. Some will, but very few. But for handlers, this is so counter-intuitive, and a challenging habit to break!

And this is why I do not arc!

August 7

Off-leash etiquette

When you use off-leash areas, make sure to also use etiquette. If a dog that you are approaching is on leash, do not allow your dog to approach him. Just take yours by the collar or snap him on leash and walk on past.

There are many reasons why that dog might be on leash. The dog could be sick. The dog could be injured. The dog might not like other dogs. He might be working, training, or . . . really, does it matter?

Regardless of the reason, if another dog is on leash, he is not there to play with your dog. So, please be polite and don't allow your dog to approach.

And please teach this to every person you meet at the park.

Happy walking!

August 8

Tips for reactive dogs

For all those teaching their reactive dogs to watch them, it rarely works. Teaching your dog to watch you in a distraction-free area won't likely transfer to your dog watching you when another dog walks past. Asking a dog whose reactivity is based in fear to give you his eyes, which means he can't look around to see where any danger might be, is asking *a lot*.

I have found a cheat.

Instead of asking for eyes, focus on loose-leash walking. It will get you your goal much quicker and easier. Giving you his eyes is challenging. However, moving forward is exponentially easier. Just work on your loose-leash walking and make sure you walk with momentum.

The hidden benefit is that now your dog will be exercising again, and learning self-regulation. And once he starts exercising, it all gets a whole lot easier.

Once you've mastered retraining your first reactive dog, it is unlikely you will get this type of dog again. While you will get challenging dogs, your handling will be so much better that their responses will be ones that you like.

August 9

How long does it take to train the perfect companion?

This one is for my fellow dog trainers.

There are many, many training methods that can get you from A to Z. One big difference is the length of time it takes to get there.

My pet clients pay by the hour and, for the most part, need results in a timely manner or about 20 percent of those dogs will need new homes. Their dog's role is to supplement their already busy lives, not to create a new life for them.

We owe it to our clients to give them methods that will give results, with effort, in a reasonable time frame. Normally we get two to three months to train a dog, and when we luck out, they will give us about five months.

Make that time count. Give them the essentials so that they have no reason to rehome their dog. Or if they are forced to, their dog can easily adapt into a new home and be a delightful dog to live with.

August 10

Holding our teeny, tiny predator puppies

Our puppies are predators. Teeny, tiny, biting predators with milk teeth.

When we cuddle them and hold them, those teeth are flying all over the place. Part of it is their need to chew because they are teething, but an even greater part is their need to chew on *us*.

I redirect them to toys as much as humanly possible when they are in my arms. But if we are cuddling, I want to relax and cuddle, and not be an ongoing toy-retrieving machine. When the toys get ditched for the eighth time, and my hands are the new replacement toys, I will not move my hands away like a fleeing rabbit. Rather I will tuck them back, casually, away from the puppy's mouth. I keep them at the top of the neck, flat, so flexible jaws cannot reach them.

If you move your hands away quickly, the game changes to, "Bite the hands and make them move." Quickly this game becomes what cuddle time is all about, and it isn't very fun. Well, it is very fun for your dog, but not for you.

The handler's job is to stay calm, kiss their puppy, and calmly, discretely, adjust chomped body parts so that they are no longer on the menu.

But the more you move them away, with speed, the more your puppy will want them. And in some dogs, this movement can actually begin to make them have nasty thoughts. Great, pushy dogs can learn very bad things just from the innocent act of you moving your hands away when they go to bite them.

And pray, forbid, if you ever stop cuddling because your puppy told you so. That is a perfect way to teach your puppy how to bite to get his way. Please don't ever do it!

August 11

Horse people make great dog trainers

I am yet to meet a horse person who is not an outstanding trainer, with just a small amount of coaching. In my eyes, this speaks volumes to the skill set, feel, and timing that horse people learn. They are masters at knowing when to push, how much to push, and how to reward the slightest try.

August 12

Progress is messy

There is no such thing as a bad training session, even though it might feel like there is. Don't be tempted to turn into a victim and feel sorry for yourself. Instead realize that you have been presented with an opportunity to work through your difficulties.

Progress can sometimes be messy. We don't just gain in one area without losing in another. Think of problems as progress in wolf's clothing. Your new challenges show you that you're moving ahead although it may not always feel like it.

Let's say, for example, that you've struggled to get your dog to lie down when she's at a distance and, finally, she gets it. But then you can't get her back up on her feet or she has no speed or she keeps anticipating downing. Or let's say you teach a brilliant down and your dog is so proud of doing it. And then, no matter what words come out of your mouth, your dog leaps into a down. These types of things normally happen when you really have to work on problem A. Problem A is then the only thing that you get!

A bad training session means you are moving forward. They are necessary, and they are gifts that give you a chance to work on the gaps in your training that you may not have known were there.

Don't be scared of the mess that you create. Just plug away, and know that you are indeed moving forward.

August 13

Do something

When an emergency moment is about to happen with your dog, don't sit there and watch the train derail. Do *something*. Anything. Doing the wrong thing is actually better than doing nothing.

Never watch a train derail. Intervene and try to put it back on track.

August 14

"See" like a dog

Different dogs see their world in different ways. The more intelligent the dog, the more they will see in their environment. How stable they are in their temperament will affect whether they see it and take it in, or need to respond to it.

Herding breeds typically see things that other dogs may not. They are more aware, as a general rule. Once, one of my dogs was scared to step on a gold zigzag pattern on a carpet in a hotel. Granted, he showed his great taste for good design.

Another one of my dogs, Reggie, noticed and alerted to a wee green box in a tree in the middle of the forest placed there by biologists to catch bugs. This is the forest we visit daily and my dog noted the change. Knowing how aware your dog is should affect your training of him. If he sees everything, you need to prepare him for everything.

We train in good light, poor light where shadows will affect what they see, and we constantly alter the area that we are training in. I know to add unexpected wee green boxes to my environment and ask my dogs to work through it.

At home, I do things as simple as move a crate six inches forward, or move a lamp to a new spot. When Reggie was a young teenager, just asking him to get into a different crate in the car would ruin his day. But it is also this part of Reggie that has made him such a great dog. He is so aware. He wants to know what to do, and he wants to do it right. This means I can teach him the slightest cues in his work, and he will pick up on them. His weakness is also his strength.

Be aware that many herding-type breeds who are a little unsure of people will always be triggered by a teenager in a hooded sweatshirt, people carrying boxes or bags, people walking with sticks, or people with stilted movements. Anyone out of the ordinary will affect them. And skateboards will trigger many young dogs in their eight-to-ten-month "fear period."

Celeste Meade, who is a master at understanding this stuff, taught me about the value of shopping in the party section at the dollar store. There, for cheap, you can purchase a plethora of different sensory challenges for your dog that you can hang up and manipulate in your home or training area.

Get creative and have fun setting stuff up.

August 15

Make them mind their manners

The first thirty seconds of getting your dog out of the car will set the tone for your entire walk. This is the moment that he can get out of the car and wait in a sit or down while you get your poo bags, get organized, and lock the car.

Then make sure he doesn't rip your shoulder off with his dragging. You should be able to hold his leash with a singular finger. If you feel the need for way more (unless of course your dog is dangerous, then please hold with more, but the same singular finger principal applies—you should be able to), then your training is not where it needs to be.

If your dog can wait while you get your stuff out of the car and, in that first thirty seconds, walk like a gentleman and keep his own leash loose, any issues that you might normally encounter on your walk will be minimal.

Make him put in the effort at the start. Set the tone for your walk, rather than waiting for his excitement and perhaps adrenaline to peak before attempting to school him (at which point he isn't going to give a darn what you say).

The first thirty seconds of your walk are the most important. Then you can enjoy harmony with your dog for the remainder of your time.

August 16

How lucky are we?

Next time you go walking and your dog rehearses how to look like a deranged beast when he sees another dog, or the next time you train and your dog's retrieves aren't so great, or the next time your dog totally screws up his weave poles, or the next time your dog steals your sandwich off your kitchen counter, rather than allowing yourself to feel deflated, find perspective.

No one died. No one will lose a home or a job. You are still as healthy as you were before the sin was committed. Through finding perspective, you can find gratitude and realize just how fortunate we are.

We live in a culture where we are able to focus huge quantities of resources on our dogs. They get our love, time, money, and energy. We educate ourselves, and we even fill our social needs via our dogs. Do you realize how lucky we are to be able to do this?

Some days, worrying about why our dog did something wrong is our biggest life problem. We are not worrying about our next meal, war, poverty, or homelessness, and the list goes on. If the biggest glitch in our day was the error that our dog made, it was a great day.

Try to find gratitude for the problems that we are able to fill our lives with. No one dies, starves, goes bankrupt, or loses a job when our dogs misbehave.

We are fortunate that we can fill our minds with such trivial problems. Life really is good.

August 17
Practice makes perfect

To be the best trainers that we can be, we are striving for an impossible goal—a goal that we will never achieve because as we get close, we simply set a higher goal. We set our first clear goal and aim for it, and as we begin learning and growing toward what we had our sights set on, our goal will no longer be good enough. Our eyes will have gotten trained to desire a more finite picture, one that we previously could not see.

This makes training dogs both impossibly hard and very alluring!

This is the frustration that I see in many people after they have successfully trained their first dog. My mentor says that training your first dog is like successfully completing your first 5,000-piece jigsaw puzzle. You can admire your hard work and skill, but in no way has it made the task easier, nor will it allow you to cut corners for your next 5,000-piece jigsaw puzzle. And maybe the second will be harder because generally our future dogs are more challenging, not less so.

There is nothing easy about getting good; it demands effort, grit, and deliberate practice in wind, rain, sleet, and snow, often with very little improvement from day to day. It is in these moments that our "work" of training our dogs slowly becomes a love and passion, as we get hooked on the details and nuances required for each and every dog.

Most often we get the dogs that we need, meaning that the skill required is just within our reach with effort and determination. Sometimes though, the work seems too hard for our skill level, the improvements non-existent despite our effort and commitment.

When stuck, we need to set up moments for ourselves where we can get our motivation back. This might be walking or training with friends, going to a weekly class to stay on track, journalling, or long peaceful walks to clear our heads and think.

Only our inner engagement will make us good trainers. We need to stay engaged and must be thinking about what we are doing.

There is nothing rote about training dogs. If you are just going out and doing, that is all that you will ever do. Reading this book, going to a seminar, or attending a weekly class will all have zero benefit if you don't process it, understand it, and reflect on it. All true masters of dogs have spent their 10,000 hours thinking. Not reading. Not learning. But thinking, practicing, thinking some more, and practicing again.

Don't get me wrong. Learning is needed. But learning will often be coming from your own mind, when you work out your problem and brainstorm for solutions. If you cannot find a solution, you can ask, but asking alone without first brainstorming won't teach you how to think. It is even useful to remember things that you did that got you the wrong result. That action that got you something, even though it was not wanted in that moment, might be right tomorrow when you need that result.

We must all learn to think. We must have the tenacity and inner grit to train our dogs even when we don't want to, and then we must process and think about what went right and what we need to change. Our practice must happen frequently enough that we remember this into our next session so that we can actually change.

Becoming good takes a long, long time, and probably three dogs before it becomes fluid. But it is worth it. The process with each dog is such an honour that we are all blessed to have.

August 18

Saving does not excuse failing in training

I hear stories daily about how people's dogs have been abused. This is often followed by a list of all the things their dog cannot do, should not be doing, and will not do. Then they explain that he was rescued. It's almost like the excuses start right up front to justify any failures that may or may not happen as training begins.

Saving a dog by bringing it into your home is a wonderful first step. It is the first step and only the first step. Now you must step up to the plate. Your Good Samaritan points don't excuse you from having to work as hard as everyone else. You will probably need to work harder.

Here's the thing. Very few dogs are abused. Some are, but they are the rarity. Most have been neglected, over- or under-socialized, uneducated, and perhaps have missed out on a quality relationship with a person. Or they just come with poor temperament, which is so often the case.

And even if your dog is one of the few who has been abused, the simple act of being sympathetic is not going to change anything. What will help him is a peaceful environment to start, then safety, exercise, clear expectations, education, and trust.

Rescuing your dog is the first step. Now you owe him a great life, where he can be the best dog that he can be. You need to teach him the skills he needs to fit into our world, to be comfortable within himself, to handle and recover from stressful moments, and to be a nice person.

August 19

Who's teaching who?

When we first get dogs, we can't wait to teach them a thing or two. When we get our next dogs, we wonder what thing or two they will teach us.

Our roles quickly change from considering ourselves a teacher to becoming a student.

August 20

Get real with aggression issues

Some of the safest dogs I work with are the ones I'm told in advance have aggression and issues.

These clients are aware of what they have, and I don't have to waste our lesson trying to point it out to them, or counselling them through the emotional heartbreak of the new reality they are being forced to see.

And because they know, and have accepted their struggle, they are aware enough to protect their dogs from their own potential.

This is the opposite of how I thought it would be as a newbie coming into this profession. I did not realize that the dogs coming in labelled as "aggressive" would be some of the safest and most gratifying to work with.

I really do feel blessed that I get to do what I do.

August 21

Keep it simple

Dog training somehow became really complex. It shouldn't be. Here, gleaned from some of the masters, are my simple rules to training a dog:

- Be as kind as possible and as firm as necessary.

- If it worked, it was right (if you followed rule number one).
- Leave something in it for the dog.

August 22

Decision-making paralysis

There is one all-important stage you must overcome in your growth as a trainer: indecisiveness.

Falling over is part of the learning process of dog training. As you learn to think on your feet and respond to the curve balls that your dog throws at you, you will make errors. Your errors are part of your growth as you move forward. Fear of making errors, and being paralyzed in a moment of indecisiveness, is something we all go through as trainers.

Learn to do *something*, and then decide if it was sheer genius, acceptable, or not clever. Reflect after the fact. Do not think in that moment, just do it. The rule of dog training is that if it works, it was right. Learning to think and do on your feet is a stepping-stone that we all must jump onto as we develop into trainers.

This is the biggest and scariest first step for all novices.

You can bounce back from an error. You can't bounce back from the paralysis of doing nothing—first you have to make that leap and do something before you can improve on what it is that you did!

August 23

How to build drive

Clueless pet owners always create the dogs with the most drive and fight. How?

When they cuddle their dog, they wait until the dog puts up the most fight, then they let him go. The fight worked.

When they put dog food down, they try and get a sit, but as the dog struggles and struggles, they just quickly feed him. The struggling worked.

When they play ball with their dog, they try and wrestle the ball out of their dog's mouth, building opposition reflex and creating a massive desire to hold onto the toy.

Really, they should be raising guide dogs or police dogs. They create fabulous working puppies that never give up their efforts until they get what they want.

August 24

The loose-leash secret

The loose-leash secret is to keep your arms moving. When you naturally swing your arms as you walk, your dog will no longer pull. And when your dog no longer pulls, almost all dog reactivity will disappear.

August 25

Praise and rewards

Some days I look at myself training my dog and shake my head. How can I make such dumb errors when I know better?

Take, for example, the other day when I was training a rather complex task. My goal was different to my dog's goal. While he was schooled in the task that was being asked, he was merrily adding his flare and twist, none of which were wanted.

The longer we struggled, the more I started praising ho-hum behaviour, things that weren't even related to the exercise at hand. I somehow thought this would help him. It was almost like I had a pre-allotted amount of "good boys" to dish out, and so I figured I'd better find something to praise him for.

To put it into human terms, my dog was there to present his PhD dissertation and it sucked. So instead I told him how clever he was for writing his name correctly on the top of the page.

I caught myself, bit my tongue, and enjoyed the silence until he bucked up his game. Then he got a half-hearted "good."

When I caught myself, I realized I had praised him more in that crap training session than my previous ten brilliant sessions.

The morals of this story are:

- Only praise when praise is due, or you remove the value of your words and the impact of the lesson.
- Praising mediocrity when the effort is not forthcoming in the hopes of creating success is flawed thinking.
- When in doubt, bite your tongue.

August 26

Feel, timing, and experience

A good dog trainer, in my opinion, has three key abilities: feel, timing, and experience.

Feel is knowing how much pressure to apply, or how to remove it (but not pressure as in corrections). This is about making your reward a reward, how to get the dog to do what you want, and how to stop him from doing something you don't want. Feel is about knowing how your body, mind, and hands are affecting the dog that you are working with.

In a split second, you need to understand if you should apply more or less pressure by adjusting the balance of your weight, releasing with a reward, and moving away from, or toward, a distraction. You might need to free their minds, let them move their bodies, or in some moments keep their bodies still in order to remove pressure—and that moment is about timing. You must have the feel of understanding what the dog needs, and the timing to be able to deliver or remove it in that exact moment.

Some dogs require minimal feel and timing and make us look brilliant. Others require the utmost feel and timing to make us look almost adequate—and by the time that we have gotten good with those dogs, we have become masters!

These dogs, the ruthless teachers who won't forgive any feel or timing errors, are the ones we all need to work with. These are the dogs that count toward our experience.

August 27

What's your intent?

When I'm irritated with a dog I might want to focus on the flaws of a particular trait, and not the benefits of this same trait. If I allow this, I give power to the flaws. I begin to focus on his flaws, which means that I see them more often as now I am looking for them.

I have taken what I love about the dog, flipped it, and turned it into a bad thing.

I believe we all get stuck in these ruts once in a while with our spouses, our jobs, our children, and yes, our beloved dogs. We decide where we direct our energy. It's much more beneficial if we put our energy into seeing the positive, and focusing on the positive aspects of a trait.

Those are the things that endeared us to the dog in the first place.

If I see a dog as argumentative, when I put my hands in his collar, even though I am doing the same thing that I have done a thousand times, the message that he is argumentative comes through my hands. You cannot lie to a dog. I can even smile as I do it, and still he will know that I believe he is argumentative. But if I smile as I put my hands on his collar and think of how I love his determination, which is really the same thing, I can instantly soften the dog. My hands will tell my thoughts.

Every emotion has a positive and a negative. It is our jobs as handlers, employees, and spouses to look for the positive in the emotion, and appreciate it for what it is.

Intention is the defining factor that determines the outcome of any action you do with your dog.

Dog training to me is not about teaching an exercise. It is about communicating with another species, and teaching them to be willing learners in a respectful environment. We cannot lie to them. So we better have ironclad control of our thoughts and feelings, or we won't be able to achieve our goals.

If you are struggling with your dog, and you're getting caught in arguing, work on your own thoughts. Change your thoughts and you'll see success. And yes, this is easier said than done, but easy is overrated. And for me, this is much easier to do with a dog than a person!

August 28

Own your space

A good dog trainer claims their space and has good posture in all of their dealings with dogs. Just like powerful leaders in business and politics, people naturally give them a wider berth.

August 29

Beware of the overly friendly puppy

When I got my goslings, I always joked that if they were German Shepherd puppies I would be in big trouble. But at the time, I didn't know how gosling temperament matured into adulthood, so I half-knowingly continued to joke.

They were, you see, overly friendly. They would take things from my hands, run to greet me, meander up and watch me teaching classes. They were charming and endearing, bold, curious, and—the biggest warning bell when combined with the other traits—very friendly.

The bold and curious stayed, the friendly not so much. The other day Gordon the Gander bit me in the shin. I pretended I was clueless of his intent and picked his ginormous downy body up and loved him to death as I carried him while I continued doing outside chores. He now keeps his distance for fear of a repeat hit to his dignity.

Now I have a bold and curious, very friendly puppy in a guarding breed that I'm not terribly familiar with. My instincts say that this is a repeat. When I see puppies that are pushy, forward, friendly (mega-friendly), obsessed with people and dogs—this is not friendliness. It is puppy aggression. It is what confident aggression looks like in a child. We are mostly only familiar with fear-based aggression, which looks completely different.

What concerns me in this puppy: she is overly friendly and adores all strangers, she is bold, curious, and a demon with her family. She loves strangers too much and with too much confidence. All of this could transfer into issues in puberty if this dog is allowed to keep mobbing strangers.

Mix bossy, bitchy, and strong with over-friendly and often it looks ugly later on in life. This doesn't mean it will inevitably go wrong, but I certainly won't wait to find out.

I have given her a few select people to mob and will encourage her to be indifferent to all others as she matures.

Right now I have a Boston Terrier in puppy class. He presents the same way. He is obsessed with other dogs. He wants to play more than he wants to eat. He cannot relax with other dogs around him. He *only* wants to play. He has puppy dog aggression, with confidence. To let him play with other puppies as much as he wants will be giving him the tools to fight better when he grows up. He needs to be hanging out with well-socialized older dogs who won't put up with his nonsense and will simmer him down. He should not be playing with puppies that he can manipulate or push around.

Remember, we must always cater our training to the dog in front of us because there are no set rules. While these rules would be detrimental to a fearful puppy, in these cases, it is what these puppies need to become well-balanced adults. With both of these dogs, teaching them to go forward and practice being rude is just giving them the skills to be scrappy later.

August 30

Dog park tip

When in a dog park, do not pick blackberries that are growing anywhere below waist height. This advice is along the same lines as not eating yellow snow.

August 31

Resource guarding in puppies

At the moment, I am working with three resource-guarding puppies; two are of breeds I might not expect to have this issue, and one is more typical. When we humans diligently raise puppies, following typical protocols for problems we do not yet have, especially if we have a good work ethic and are hard-working overachievers, we can end up being bullies and create the exact problem we are trying to prevent. Unless we possess good feel and timing.

I enjoy my glass of wine. If someone kept approaching me and adding more wine to my glass, I would appreciate that. Unless it happened too much, too often, like a painfully over-attentive waiter. Go away and let me enjoy what I have.

Now, if they wanted to poke and jab me as I drank to see if I would stiffen, I would. And if they did it every time I sat down to enjoy a glass of wine, I would start watching to see where they were, and would grumpily keep my eye on them. (When we get nervous and adrenalized, we lose our fine motor skills. Without realizing it, our touch becomes too firm, like a jab. If you are getting nervous wondering if your dog may try and bite you, your fingers will lose their feel and become hard pegs, and your touch may be uncomfortable enough to trigger a response.)

Some people are so focused on carefully watching their dog the entire time she is doing an activity, that this alone this could create an issue in the most normal of dogs . . . or people. If you don't believe me, start practicing tonight on your spouse!

I'm relieved I'm not a dog, or my wine intake would be limited because I'd be too problematic when it is available. I'd only be allowed it monthly, when locked in a crate. Then when given my monthly glass, I'd be even more determined to enjoy it, and even grumpier if I was being disturbed. Limiting my desired resource will make me want it way more.

Can you see how when training without feel and timing, we can become bullies and make a problem worse? Do your protocols, but read the dog. Know when they have graduated to a once-a-week rub while they eat, for a third of their meal, then leave them alone.

If they love toys so much that they want to go postal over them, put toys everywhere for an hour or two a day, play with them all, then pick them up. Don't control all the toys all the time, or you are just the mean kid who we need to get the toys away from so that we can have fun.

If they have issues with meaty bones, have a great abundance of them so they lose some value. Let them enjoy their bones. Maybe once ask for them to let you have it, and then give it back to them immediately, with less than a second delay. Leave.

This is not a guide to fixing resource guarding. This is a guide for why your protocols for resource guarding are not working. Or why your older puppy who previously had no issues has started to guard. At the end of the day, leave something in it for the dog. Remember, starving people will fight over a piece of stale bread. A baker's son will not.

SEPTEMBER

September 1

The pool noodle discovery

I made an interesting observation this week in Bravery Class.

As we did our regular ridiculous things to our dogs, which this week was jamming a pool noodle into their collars and getting them to walk around with it, there was an obvious trend among the dogs.

The dogs with the weakest temperaments were merrily trotting around bashing their pool noodle into people's legs. The dogs who had better temperaments were standing awkwardly still, like we had attached an anchor.

It was a proud moment. You know you have done some good dog training when the weakest dogs in class suddenly look the strongest.

Through training, we have built those dogs up, and taught them how to problem-solve, and how to be resilient with novel situations. The stronger dogs in class have never needed to learn this to the same extent, which, in this moment, showed.

Now granted, no dogs will need to be trained for the life experience of having pool noodles stuck in their collars—unless you have children around! Then you need to prepare them for every possibility.

September 2

Learn to read your puppy

Are you able to see a flash of inner turmoil in your puppy and know how to help her? Can you see when your puppy wants to fight, and is bringing on the fight, and yet raise her correctly?

Right now I have two puppies in my house who are polar opposites. One presents as a tough ass, and the other needs to be believed in and built up. With one dog I need to be tough. Nice, but with some physical toughness. I need to shove, tap, and torment. I need to engage this one in mini-battles. With the other, I need to be physically soft. I need to be mentally soft too, sweet and maternal.

So which is which? Am I physically and mentally tougher with the tough dog, or the soft dog?

My Border Collie puppy, Pippa, needs to be built. And I'm building her every single day by being a bit tough with her. At first, she would melt if I looked at her cross-eyed. Now I can tap her with my foot and she spins around questioning my audacity. She's learned that her opinions matter. She's learned that being bossy is fun. And as she overcomes all of the little challenges tossed her way, she is starting to believe that she stands 29 inches high and weighs 150 lbs. By being tougher with her, in the right way, I've given her some much-needed piss and vinegar. I've created a bitch. She's been told she is strong from day one, I've responded like she is strong, and I've slowly treated her like she is strong. Right now, she believes me when I tell her she is strong, but it could crumble in a single bad moment. But a year from now, she will believe unequivocally.

Then we have Mr. Tough Ass, Klaus the Rottweiler puppy, who is currently snoring on my lap. He came wearing a studded leather jacket, and he needs softness. He already believes he could rule the world. Hardness with him only brings out more hardness in him. If he wants to fight with another dog over a toy, correcting him would increase his toughness for next time. He will learn to strategize better, swallow it faster, and get nastier quicker. I give him a few little calm tickles and he instantly softens. Or I let him be with friends who simply sit on him when he tries to take their toys. Passiveness gets more with him than activity does. He needs to be held. To be carried. To be kissed, passed around, as though he is a little Chihuahua. He is only being exposed to dogs who are bigger and stronger, so that they keep reinforcing that he isn't really as cool as he thinks. Pippa is one of those dogs; she is older, needs building, and every day she continues to tell him that she is cooler than he is, and that every toy belongs to her, and she is benefitting from the interaction as much as he is.

Pippa gets to play with dogs that will let her be bossy and chippy. Baby Klaus Rottweiler's playmates have all been selected to be stronger and bossier. And the same is happening in their lives. He gets picked up and handed to people in their arms. She is encouraged to jump up on people.

No dog should feel scared during any of this. But he needs to come down a bit, and she needs to go up. Their lives are being adjusted so they can both get what they need.

Now there are still absolutes. Biting is forbidden, as it could get you euthanized, and all infractions will be communicated clearly!

But in the rest of their lives, I want to make my big softies tougher and my hard-asses softer (at least in this case I do, as he will be someone's beloved pet). And so I adjust my interactions with them, at least during their early months. As they change, I too will have to change.

September 3

Temperament does not hinder training

Somehow, many people came to believe that their dog's lack of ability to be trained is because of a temperament issue. No.

Your temperament issue is still showing because of your lack of ability to train your dog. We train dogs so that we can hide their weaknesses and increase their strengths.

Rather than excuse your dog's poor behaviour, increase her training and control. Tell her to walk nicely on a loose leash, to sit or down when asked, and to stand still for toenail trims and veterinary exams.

At some point in time, dog training suddenly became really confusing. It isn't, or at least it shouldn't be. Forget all of the words, and all of the terms. Instead, dig in your heels and make it happen.

For almost all dogs, it really is that simple—if you want it badly enough. If you have been diligently training and barely had success, it is time to divorce your training method, or trainer. Find someone else who can help you.

September 4

Let your puppy be a puppy

Your puppy should have confidence, be mischievous, and have the energy of a puppy. Your twelve-week-old or five-month-old should not have the energy of a ten-year-old dog. If they do, it probably means you have sucked the life out of them.

During all of your necessary training, and while you're busy being responsible, don't forget to keep your puppies young. They have their entire lives to act like adults, and puppyhood is such a short time in the scheme of things.

Enjoy it. Learn from them to be spontaneous and fun again. Have ridiculous games and enjoy their crazies, because soon they will be gone.

September 5

Beliefs, leadership, and intent

Dog training is not about teaching exercises. It is about creating a relationship with your dog using positive beliefs, good and honest intentions, and respectful, fair, and consistent leadership. This will create balance and harmony between you and your dog.

These three tenets of your relationship with your dog—beliefs, intent, and leadership—will determine how well you can train or retrain temperament issues. Retraining your dog by following someone else's recipe will fall short. You must tweak your program for your individual dog. To do this you must feel what your dogs are feeling, and operate from where they are at, without lowering expectations or criteria. Then guide them into how you need them to behave.

My *beliefs* about my dog will be based on the strengths that I choose to focus on. You get to choose your beliefs, and you can make them positive or negative. You can see a dog as fearful and weak, or you can see an inner strength that you need to bring out. I always choose to make my beliefs positive.

My *intentions* are what I expect to happen, although it is much more complex than that. My *intentions* are reflected in my energy, my body language, and that little voice in my mind. Intentions are what I turn my attention to and direct my body language toward. What I attend to will appear.

So with a fearful dog, I want to coach strength and bravery. My chin will be set high as we head out on our adventures. I *believe* my dog is brave despite the damage that has already been done, or the traits built into him or her. I see those tiny moments when she is brave, and I remember them. My *intention* is formed when I decide where to put my attention, and what I allow myself to see and think, and how I handle my body when a challenge is presented.

My *leadership* is based on the level of respect I have for my dog; who she currently is and who she still needs to become. My leadership is communicated by the way I act in her presence—how I stand, in my posture and gait, in the moments that my muscles tense and release. It is communicated in the way I think, and the way I don't allow anything to rattle me. My brain is steady, calm, and deliberate. As things speed up around me, my brain slows down and my muscles relax. I interact with challenges and obstacles that are presented to us along the way in a calm, focused manner. In short, there is a presence to me that tells the dog: don't mess with me. She knows I will coach her, and teach her to become a confident dog who is comfortable and safe in both her body and the world.

By training the temperament of who the dog needs to become, rather than looking at the individual issue in front of you, your dog will graduate to a confident and happy character who will do anything for you. Focus on temperament—it will put you so much further ahead, and you may only need minor tweaking to the training recipe that you have been given.

When you have a difficult dog and you finally feel perfect harmony, even if just for a few minutes—the feeling is so wonderful that you will continue training in the hopes of feeling it again.

September 6

Defining intention

Intention might be one of the hardest concepts to master, yet one of the most powerful tools that we have when training our dogs and living our lives. It is the one thing that separates the good trainers from the great trainers.

Intention is a field, invisible and formless, that affects everything. Your thoughts have power. What you think about, you can make happen, whether you intend to or not. While your mind thinks it, your body will speak it. What we think and focus on will affect who our dogs become. Intentions affect what we hear and see. Our body language effectively yells (loudly) to our dogs, and they will respond accordingly.

Choose to remember and regularly recall all the good things in your dog. Even if you don't think there is much good to see in your dog, find something positive and choose to see it. Once you find it, you will see it a lot more often. Smile, enjoy them, remember them, and you will see them a whole lot more. Don't remember flaws and weaknesses. See them and then let them go.

Train your dog, including his difficulties, but focus on the positive traits, not the bad. Set your chin in the right direction when you go training or encounter challenges. If you anticipate a war, you will get one. Your mind will think it, your body language will follow, your fingers will get hard when you touch your dog, and your dog will respond accordingly. But if you anticipate an effortful partner working beside you, your body language will reflect that. Even if you are presented with the same situation, you will handle it differently and so will your dog: you will get your effortful partner.

September 7

Leadership is not a dirty word

Somehow leadership became a dirty word. It shouldn't be. Leadership doesn't have to mean militancy. Yes, you should enjoy being with your dog, but your dog also needs to look to you for instructions about what he should do next.

I am always delivering the same message about respect and partnership. We must always follow through with our expectations, even if it takes ten minutes, or a thousand repetitions (except in the case of a Terrier where it might take thirty thousand repetitions). Our dogs can only be as consistent as we are.

I always act the same toward my dogs regardless of whether I am in a rush, if I am dressed for a wedding, or if I have all the time in the world. While this might explain why I am always dirty and late, it is why I am a very consistent and competent dog trainer!

Leadership is gained by quietly guiding your dog through life, giving help where help is needed, telling him to "knock it off," if needed, and acknowledging the many moments of success. Dogs must know what is expected and that we are here to help them. They must know not to cross the line in the sand.

Through your journey, you need to believe in your dog and understand his motivations and desires, and cater your response accordingly, but never sacrificing the goal.

Back in the good old days it was called dog training. Sometimes now I see it as dog-compromising with everyone worried about their dog's increasing anxiety levels. Let's change that by going back to being our dog's leaders. Let's make sure our dogs do not have to worry because expectations are clear. They know their job, and they know we have their backs.

September 8

Connecting with emotion

My friend's son struggled with reading, despite her fabulous parenting. Reading was difficult for him, and because picking up a book made him anxious, not happy, he had little motivation to practice.

We put him on a positive reinforcement schedule, where he earned a prize every time he read. It worked like a hot damn, and he turned into a reading machine. However, neither of us had anticipated this unfortunate consequence: he developed no love for reading. Instead, we had taught him to speed read in order to cash out. He was doing it only for the end result, the prize, and we had failed to teach him how to enjoy the book itself. We were trapped. As soon as we removed the prizes, he would stop reading. His behaviour was temporary and dependent on the reward.

This happens when we train our dogs too. My brilliant German dog-training friends realize this, and while they train with positive reinforcement, the emphasis is on the emotions expressed before the dog gets the reward when they do good work. If a dog works only for a prize, he won't develop a love for the work itself along the way. However, if we can build up the dog's emotions associated with the work, the work itself becomes the reward.

My friend and I quickly realized this too, and changed our approach. Before she gave her son any kind of reward she told him how clever he was, and she asked questions about his work that he was able to answer. His mother's excitement gave him a sense of pride. Her feedback about his reading was that he made her proud, and she believed him to be very clever. After that, it was easy for him to maintain the reading even without rewards. He continues to be an avid reader and now reads to his younger brother every day.

I frequently talk about the flaws of positive reinforcement. Everything in life has flaws. It doesn't mean the method is wrong. Positive reinforcement must be used to train dogs and is the best way to teach any behaviour. The good news is flaws can be worked around.

We can put pride and joy into our dogs' work simply by being happy with them, and telling them that. Make sure that when you tell them you are happy, you are speaking from your heart.

Many people have no idea how to talk to their dogs, and often the way we talk is demeaning to them. We tend to talk down to them as if they are weak. Or we get shrill and use an overexcited cheerleader voice, which also indicates we think they are weak. Pride and joy are not reflected by increased volume or pitch. Try using your voice to express different emotions, and see if your dog believes you. You will know by watching his tail rise and start to get higher and higher.

Increase your dog's work ethic by communicating emotions that make him proud of his work. While this is a fairly simple concept, it can be a challenge to execute. You have to learn to control your voice and your state of mind. Most people train using just one tone of voice, but this method will force you to come up with many. However, once you learn it, you will have unearthed a secret that will make every dog (and child) in your life adore you, and want to please you.

September 9

Master your craft

The method of dog training you choose does not make you great. Just like the brand of drill you use will never make you a good carpenter. The method you use is neither here nor there. It is your skill that counts, regardless of the method you choose.

Yet dog trainers continue to argue over dog-training methodology, and meanwhile, they stop learning. The method you choose is the first thing that you learn, and for many dog trainers who continue to debate this, energy goes into debating instead of growing.

Not until you start focusing on your technique, and how you apply your particular method, are you working on mastering your craft.

September 10

Be a parent first

I've been working with a rather unfriendly dog. She decided that I, and most others, look like a menu item. But I've never been one to turn away from a challenge, so she moved into my house.

Oddly, even after two days, I didn't like this dog. I could see redeeming qualities, which I forced myself to focus on, but we had no connection. And she did not like me. We didn't have fun together. We didn't have intimate moments. I taught her. She taught me. Then she went back home.

But an amazing thing happened. I just saw her again. In my absence, she decided that she is in love with me. My voice makes her wiggle from the inside out. If I leave she worries about where I went. If I ask her to try and to trust me, she gives me her greatest effort. All in all, she adores me.

I had to wonder what I gave her that made her fall so deeply for me. We did not start out as friends. I gave her very strict boundaries, rules, and expectations. My demands were high, though kind and fair, and my emotional availability was nil when we started; and yet she gave me her heart and soul.

It just happens. If they trust you, if they know you will keep them safe, and if they respect you, they will end up falling for you. It is just the way dogs work. I started with respect and ended up with a good relationship. Trust and respect naturally developed into love.

Training a dog is about a relationship and a blend of two personalities. The right blend must be earned. We can't always be their best friends; first we must be their parents. By being her parent, her fear was gone, her lunging was gone, her worries were gone, and her anxiety was gone. I now have a happy, confident, affectionate lug of a dog that smiles all day long. Now I can be her friend too.

I taught her the value of earning respect in an honest relationship. And in turn, she is going to make her owner better at things that she had no idea she needed to be better at. Funny the way that works.

September 11

A reason for every reward

I never reward my dogs with food without lots of emotional praise first and a valid concrete reason for delivering the prize. I believe that if it is good enough to feed, it is important enough to tell them so.

Making myself give valid reasons for every reward stopped me feeding them for breathing. My Pez dispensing stopped, and in turn, I started to make each reward a whole lot more valuable.

I love to feel good, and feeding my dogs treats does make me feel good. But that isn't a good enough reason to be a Pez dispenser.

Until you can become cognitive of your dispensing and build value to your praise, not only will your dog never be trained to a high level but your behaviours will only last as long as your food is there. And when your food is not there and your dog doesn't listen, you suddenly won't feel so good or positive anymore!

Raise your criteria by being very aware of when and why you are rewarding with food, and make sure praise always precedes your hand reaching into your pocket.

September 12

Journalling is key to training smarter

We need to be training daily, ideally several times a day for small chunks of time. Short quick sets give you a chance to continually work on the pieces that need work, and allow both you and your dog to progress quickly because your jobs are still fresh in your memory.

This means that you are processing what you are doing, and evaluating what is working and what is not working. Training is 80 percent mental and 20 percent doing, so for every five minutes spent training your dog, you should be thinking and pondering for about 20 minutes, trying to work out tweaks to perfect what you are trying to teach.

One of the easiest ways to do this—and to train your brain to think this way—is through a performance analysis journal (I use Lanny Bassham's). I find that this keeps me honest. It makes me remember what I did right, remember what my goal is and what my training should be getting me ready for, and it doesn't allow me to dwell on my errors.

Self-reflection is needed for you to grow into being a trainer from a handler. Handlers can perfectly follow instructions from their teacher, but are often unable to process and see what needs to be done. Trainers are able to process what they see, and think of solutions and tweaks that will get the goal they seek. Journalling will help you make this giant leap by teaching you how to reflect on your progress and goals.

September 13

Air hockey, cheeseballs, and self-esteem

Yesterday, one of my clients realized a very important lesson. She was supposed to be playing hockey against her dog by keeping a cheeseball moving forward with her leaf blower, and not allowing her dog to eat it. Instead of focusing on her goal of trying to keep the cheeseball away from her dog (and all the other dogs), she was focused on helping her dog succeed by praising her when she got close to the cheeseball.

There comes a point in time where helping your dog succeed actually stops her from succeeding. While help is a necessary piece in all learning, if done for too long it will actually inhibit progress. At some point, we need to let go and pray our training is enough to get them through the moment. We cannot hold their hands forever and have them be strong. We get one or the other.

I asked her to ignore her dog and just focus on keeping her cheeseball away from her dog. As soon as she focused on her job, which invoked an adrenaline rush in her, her dog suddenly committed to the game.

The dog no longer needed praise and encouragement. She needed fun. She needed excitement. She needed to see her mum squeal as she made her tricky moves and almost succeeded in stealing it. She needed to know that her efforts had real impact on her mum. And that she had the power to steal the cheeseball and actually win the game.

As dog trainers, we need to learn when to help, when to encourage, when to get out of a dog's way, and when to leave it the hell alone.

For those who are retraining dogs to be brave and bold, make sure to have fun with them and quit praising weakness. Instead, race them. Steal from them. Bring out their competitive spirit and watch them bloom. No one ever learned to stand on their own two feet by having their hand held. Handholding is a necessary step, but it will not get you to your end goal.

September 14
Swallow your pride

The dogs that teach us the most do it by making us look our worst, at least at times. With steely determination, real dog trainers find their way to get to where they need to go, without letting their pride compromise their goals or affect their focus.

September 15
Guard your puppy, kind of . . .

I love it when I get challenged. My students who question me force me to be a better teacher and writer. I was in puppy class, telling my students to be mother bears and not to allow anything bad to happen to their puppies, which is true. But not entirely, as they pointed out.

When I say, "guard your puppies," and, "be control freaks," I do not mean protect them from having a bad day or dealing with life.

Dealing with stress is a much-needed part of life and growing up. Without it, your dog will not be able to cope with life, and will end up weak and neurotic. However, the stress thrown at them needs to be manageable so that they can cope with it. So, while they need challenges, don't throw them into situations in which they cannot possibly succeed. However, life may throw that their way. If they do not yet have the tools to deal with it, be there to back them up, or help them develop the tools to deal with it.

Being the control freak that I am, I prefer to design my own challenges so that I know what we are getting into.

Be deliberate with what you throw at them, and only throw enough so that they can work through their stress and succeed. Don't allow uncontrolled situations to happen and then wonder why your puppy is weak and weird.

As my dear friend says, "through thick and thin, they need to know that we have their backs, and that we are in this world to tackle it together." As I say this, yesterday I did watch my foster dog fall off a plank into the water below, and I pretended not to notice him jump and scramble, and jump a wee bit more trying to get back onto the plank. If he had looked scared or panicked, or if he couldn't find his way out, I would have run and helped him. But he was he was doing just fine. I can't do everything for him, continually rescue him from stress, and expect him to get braver. By doing everything for him I actually undermine his self-confidence, telling him he is indeed useless. I let him think his way through his stress, and he did, all on his own like a big boy! Then we all got wet as he ran crazy circles around our legs to celebrate his success.

As mother bears our job is to school them. And I don't mean teaching them to sit. This includes teaching them confidence, resilience, robustness, how to think their way through stress, how to recover after something unfortunate has happened, how to be forgiving, and how to handle themselves to be functioning, thinking dogs. They must learn to stand on their own four feet, and make their own decisions to be our working partners.

As mother bears we need to raise bomb-proof dogs. That means controlling the environment so that they can learn the right lessons and not the wrong ones. Being terrified will not help my dog grow strong. But neither will being sheltered, smothered, and seeing nothing.

This doesn't mean keep your dog home. It means be ready to prevent the "He's friendly" asshole from attacking your puppy.

This is very different from letting them live in bubble wrap, in your arms, learning nothing. Your dog needs to see the world, and through his travels, good or bad, know that you are his partner and that you have his back.

September 16

Their weakness becomes their strength

I see this often in dogs who struggle with social issues. These are the dogs who make wonderful teachers for new dogs who are struggling.

My scrappy Irish Terrier had such patience when it came to schooling bratty youngsters! She became soft and sweet. Cranky, but with such incredible control that she would not bite. She is a perfect nanny for bratty puppies.

Hilda is one of my many project dogs who become the best dog to have social delinquents around. So, if you are working hard on a dog with social issues, remember, at the end when you master your goal, you will have a gift of a dog who can help many other dogs learn how to play nice in the sandbox.

September 17

Our part of the bargain (for competitors)

We all know how to train our dogs for our performances, but what about training ourselves? How many of you work on your own mental game when you're away from your challenge?

Do you journal? Do you work on visualizing perfect performances? Do you read techniques from sport psychology books and practice them? Do you work on your fitness so that when you do need to perform, you are not feeling fatigued and struggling to keep going?

If your training fails when you're under pressure, it might be time to work on you. Continue with your training, but take the time to also work on yourself. Let's face it—it is rarely the dog who is at fault.

September 18
What's in it for the dog?

Dog training is about learning to communicate. Through reading the dog's body language, we learn their motivators, triggers, and personality. For any message that we are trying to convey, there must be a reason for the dog to listen to what we are suggesting.

The reason must have value for the dog. Often, we tend to use things that have value for us. Sometimes that coincides with also having value for the dog, but not always.

We suggest what we want our dogs to do by using something that is important to them. The "important" thing can be context specific. Working out what your dog wants in each situation will help you find the training solutions that you seek. Here are some examples.

On walks the most important priority for many, many dogs is freedom. If you have a dog that has never been able to have it, because of aggression or another reason, giving it becomes a ginormous reward. Taking it away can also act as a punishment. (Your timing must be bang on for them to work it out.) Once schooled in behaviour around other dogs, use freedom as a motivator to get good behaviour.

For male black labs, the greatest joy can be to lick and pee obsessively where others have been. Use this as a reward for things well done. If you're struggling with desire for an exercise, ask them to perform it before you let them go and potty.

For my Terrier, calling her back off a squirrel shows great effort because I know how much she loves to chase squirrels. Her greatest reward is to send her back to get her squirrel. Her desire was to chase the squirrel. Her reward is that I allow it. Don't worry, there is no chance of her catching one.

When I was training my then-new starving, feral dog to not eat every object and dead thing, I went with his desire rather than fighting it. I knew if I forbid the eating of rotting dead fish, I would create a giant issue for him. So instead I encouraged it. I found every disgusting carcass that I could and pointed them out to him. When he carried them, I told him how clever he was for the first pace or two, then would offer him three cookies and without any words, steer his nose away as I was feeding him, and then just walk off. There were no commands. Within no time, his "finds" became much less interesting and he quit doing it.

This tactic also works well for puppies who like to eat gravel, or every woodchip that they see (a big thing for Bernese Mountain dogs and Labrador babies). Do not praise the eating; instead point out the gravel, then steer their nose away, feeding them their three cookies. Pretty soon they will look down at the gravel, then up at you for their cookie. They want something in their mouths, and we are meeting that need by giving them cookies. Pretty soon the habit will be broken. Unless you are Pippa the Border Collie, that is, then this method might make you want more gravel. In her case, I quickly realized the error and instead scolded her for eating gravel. She stopped.

Work out "what is in it for the dog" in the training situations they throw at you. Meet that need in a functional way, or find a reward with big value for your dog that you can use to get what you need.

September 19

The value of a coach or training partner

Practice is great, but you must be practicing the right thing. Practicing the wrong way with dedication isn't helpful, which is why you need a coach or a training partner.

Today information is everywhere. People are learning so much and trying to apply it to their training. Things might be going along swimmingly in their eyes, though their inexperience cannot see that the bolts are loosening right before the wheels fall off. A coach will know when an exercise or behaviour is derailing sometimes months before a student.

And you won't know what you are NOT doing right or what you need to add, simply because you don't know what you don't know!

Never underestimate the value of a coach or an outside set of eyes. Everyone needs one—no matter how good you are.

September 20

We are working on ourselves

Most of our dogs are born with endless potential. It is through our errors that mistakes are made and problems are created, or pivotal learning moments are missed. Carefully, as we get smarter, we give our dogs the right information, learn what we need to know, and sometimes fix the damage that was created.

However, the irony is that while we grow and change for the better, rarely are we able to see who was the problem. Our ego prevents us from seeing the obvious and persuades us that it was the dog who needed changing—rather than admitting the dog was the teacher who facilitated our change and growth.

We must never forget: we are not training dogs, we are working on ourselves. And our biggest hindrance is our own darned ego.

Whenever you struggle to achieve something with your dog, always look inward and explore how you might be stopping your dog from getting it.

September 21

Reinforcers

We do not get to choose our dogs' reinforcers. They get to choose what motivates them, what empowers them, and what they are willing to bust a gut for.

My new puppy has a rather unorthodox reward: her whip. The snap of a whip makes her forget every worry in the world and turns her into a crazy manic Border Collie. A loud noise does too. If I can thump a toy on the floor, or chuck a cookie at a wall and make a loud bang, she will go crazy.

If you are struggling with motivating your dog, it is time to think outside the box, and come up with your own unorthodox reward that makes them do back flips.

For my Italian Greyhound, it was always running. Genetically, she was bred to run. I used that in all of her obedience as her reward. If I fed her food, I threw it and made her chase it. Or I would simply chase her.

There are other things that I have used in the past: swimming, sniffing girl pee, cracking a whip, jumping, running full speed, chasing a lure, barking, tag (running away, then chasing them, then running away), and even sex (twice for lucky Basil). Don't judge the reward. Judge the dog. Judge her behaviour, her tail, her delight. Or, imagine this: don't judge at all!

We all have something that we will do anything for. Find out what that thing is for your dog.

September 22

"Listen" to body language, not words

Years ago, I abandoned questionnaires for my clients. If you are good at reading dogs, they will give you a much more accurate assessment of their people than the people will. In fact, they will tell you things that their people probably are not even conscious of. I'm guessing children also have this gift, though dogs don't express their assessment through words, but through actions. We must open ourselves to listening to these actions.

To start developing this skill, close your ears. Words confuse us. We naturally want to believe what we are told, so don't listen. Block out voices, both the words and tone. And instead, watch the interactions and body language.

A simple homework assignment to help you hone this skill is to start watching dog training videos on YouTube with no volume.

You cannot lie to a dog. And dogs do not lie.

September 23

Temperament first

There is nothing easy about raising a dog or a puppy. There are almost no rules that are absolute. What I will tell you to never, ever do with your breed, you will see me doing with my own dog of the same breed. Each dog must be raised as an individual, getting the freedom and rules in the split second that they need them. And what is totally right on Monday can be devastating on Tuesday.

Teaching a set behaviour like a sit is so much easier to do than creating a good solid temperament (personality). I often think this is why many group classes focus on behaviours and not personalities. For a dog like my Border Collie Pippa, this would have been devastating. She would have become, and wanted to become, a weak little robot, being told what to do every moment of every day. She would have become scared of so many things and not been able to deal with the big scary world.

I waited to train her in obedience until she was bolder, pushier, and more brazen. Then I slowly and carefully added her obedience. I didn't let her offer behaviours in our work. Shaping would not have been good for her, because she would have spent her entire days offering behaviours trying to find one that pleased me.

Instead, I needed her to learn to be happy within herself, and to stand on her own four feet.

Obedience is very important, and every dog needs it. They cannot become who we need them to be without it. But with puppies, we must train them for temperament first; obedience alone may be too confining for them.

September 24

Soul Dogs

Certain dogs we connect with on a whole different level. I love all of my dogs dearly, and I respect them all for the dogs they are. But certain dogs affect you differently than others. The connection is deeper, the understanding greater—some dogs are just very special little souls.

These are Soul Dogs. You will be lucky to have one Soul Dog in a lifetime, though some people have had several. And only someone who has had one will understand the bond and unique relationship that I am describing.

September 25

Enough already, just stop

It is very unusual to see a dog who walks nicely on a leash with behaviour problems.

If you are struggling with your dog—with reactivity or any other behavioural problem—don't try and train loose-leash. Just make it happen. Pulling is forbidden, so don't allow it, ever, past the age of about twelve weeks. Of course, there are exceptions with feral dogs, but the exceptions are rare. My twelve-week rule applies to pretty much everyone.

One of my mentors once said to me, "Why would you allow that to happen?" While the comment stung at the time, he could not have been more right. While I did not possess the solution to the problem, I lost all of my presence and belief in my own ability to stop it. My defeat, in turn, made the problem exponentially worse.

Sometimes I need to find my inner little girl, stomp my feet, and say, "Stop!" As a kid I had much more determination to not allow something I didn't want. Yet as an adult, defeat can sometimes overwhelm me. We all need to find that inner determination, which in turn gives us mental presence. We need to quit being victims, and quit allowing our dogs to do stuff to us. Rather, we need to be determined leaders, stand tall, and take control of the situation, even when we have no clue how to fix it!

While I am not advocating temper tantrums for everyone, there is a time and place. When you are feeling defeated and your dog has mashed all your self-esteem into the ground, then you may benefit from one. Find that inner child, and simply do not accept your dog dragging you anymore. You will be surprised at how easy it is to fix, once you simply refuse to allow it. *Ever. Again.*

And for everyone who reads this and thinks, "Yes, but, this is so much easier said than done," please reread this from the start. I wrote it for you.

September 26
Make and model matter

When I first started driving, my skills were questionable at best. But my first car was a Ford Escort, and because it would putt along at a snail's pace, I looked like an acceptable driver and I was able to somewhat hide my poor driving skills. When I got my second car, which had a bit more spunk, my driving weaknesses became more obvious. Had I been driving a Ferrari, I might not be here today writing this.

The breeds of dogs that we choose are the same. I think of the herding breeds as Ferraris, and also some of our strong working dogs. Within the breed choices, there are definitely starter dogs, and mid-skill level dogs.

While there are exceptions within every breed, we should be aware of the challenges or difficulties of certain breeds and then pick a dog to match our skill set. If you are brand new to dogs, a Kuvask, Chow Chow, or Dutch Shepherd probably shouldn't be on your list of breeds to consider. Instead I would suggest you get a Cavalier King Charles Spaniel, a Pug, or a Golden Retriever.

While you could end up with a really easy Kuvask, a very challenging Pug is still going to be exponentially easier than your very easy Kuvask. Pick the breeds that you know you can succeed with. Challenge yourself if you want to, but challenge yourself at a level that you know you can still succeed at.

September 27

Rewards versus training tools

Food and toys can be used to build the duration of a behaviour. By using them this way we are utilizing them as a training tool, and not as a reward. We are using them to keep our dog going, and not to acknowledge a job well done. However, often we are not aware of the difference.

We are unaware that our dog is continuing because of the placement of our next "reward." And that if that food or toy was not there, our dog's behaviour wouldn't be either.

This is something that we all must be aware of when training. I still use food and toys in this way, but am now very conscious of the difference.

If your "rewards" are predictable and expected, they are not functioning as rewards but as a training tool to keep your dog going.

September 28

Olympic dressage horses versus school ponies

Most pet dogs are reliable school ponies, but the dogs that I get to train are Olympic dressage horses. They will respond to every question, even the ones we do not know we are asking. By comparison, your school pony will barely respond to anything. The dressage horse dogs can cause grief in their homes because they will respond to anything; every breath that is different will get a response, and any tightened muscles will get a different response.

These animals force us to be aware of what we do, and then force us to be consistent with all that we do. By giving us such awareness and control, these animals are our teachers.

The school pony will barely respond to anything and, as such, will be a much easier animal to live with, or blunder along with. And deal with. However, all of his responses will be at a much more muted level. The word "brilliance" will never be paired with this animal, but they will be solid, reliable, and pleasant. And probably easier to love!

Most of the dogs coming into my reactive dog classes are Olympic horses, picking up on cues and then responding to cues that their owners are unaware they're sending out. They have great intelligence, which has gotten their more novice owners into trouble. All of the pointy-eared herding breeds fit into this group.

I do believe that we always get the dogs we need, though not necessarily the dogs we want. The perfect animal for us arrives when it is time for us to be working on a skill that we are lacking. To succeed with these animals, we must learn that skill. We are not training dogs—we are working on ourselves.

If you find yourself running into trouble, you probably got more dog than you bargained for. In addition to teaching obedience, your other solutions will be your own personal growth as you learn to be aware of the all cues that you are giving, which, in turn, will teach you to have complete control over what stresses you and how you choose to respond in those moments.

It's not always the most fun journey, but it is addictive. People who decide to dig deep and work through it with these dogs almost always end up hooked into a dog sport and doing very well.

We are so lucky that we get to play with dogs. And that our dogs make us better people.

September 29

The confidently dumb

"The problem with the world is that the fanatics are always so certain of themselves, while wise people are so full of doubts."—
Bertrand Russell

I've always known, but only recently found out, that there is a name for the confidently dumb. It is the Dunning-Kruger effect. Sadly, in the age of the internet, this has become a problem. Anyone with a keyboard and internet access can claim to be an expert by writing their own blog. As I type this, I pray irony has not made me one of the afflicted.

Our confidently dumb can and do have dog blogs, and use it as a teaching tool. When having a blog is the only criteria for expertise, these people are now educating the masses, without realizing how little they know.

This doesn't bother me. What does bother me is that we believe their answers as gospel. Just because you read it does not mean it is right.

What scares me even more is that very talented people are unaware that they are talented. Your experts will downplay their brilliance. They are aware of how complex problems can be, and how little they know in the scheme of things. While they are full of doubt, seeking more answers and education, your incompetents firmly believe they are the best. Researchers have recently coined this the "Lake Wobegon effect," in homage to the residents of Garrison Keillor's fictional town who all wrongfully believe their skills are above average.

These are the experts that people are faced with. Your true experts might give you a vague answer, explaining all possibilities, while your confidently dumb will give you an absolute for an answer. The latter is certainly more appealing if you are in need of guidance.

Please question everything you read. Make sure your "experts" have the credentials to give advice on specific topics. Don't learn dog manners from someone whose own dogs are unruly and don't listen.

Check that your expert truly is an expert. Don't let their confidence win you over. Let their credentials and experience win you over.

September 30

Are you good or great?

A good dog trainer can get a dog to do what she asks him to do. A great trainer can get a dog to want to do it.

OCTOBER

October 1

"He's friendly"

The phrase "He's friendly," is so incredibly bizarre.

To test my theory, I started announcing, "He's friendly," to people in the grocery store about my husband. It worked great! People smiled awkwardly, then retreated fast, and I got entire aisles to myself.

My husband really is friendly. Honest.

But by announcing something so unnecessary to strangers casually walking past, it made them all assume the opposite. Our out-of-context statements say so much about us, but what we communicate is the opposite of the words that we speak.

We communicate our fears, fears that forced us to speak the bizarre words in the first place.

So, if you hear the phrase "He's friendly," realize someone is saying it for a reason. Get your dog close to you, and be prepared to protect him. You may need to, because theirs is not friendly. You don't quite know what theirs is yet, only that seeing your dog scared them, and they felt a need to justify their own dog's behaviour before anything even happened.

October 2

Be cautious of your own behaviour change

If your dog makes you change your behaviour, realize it and put the necessary training in place so that you can go back to normal.

For example, if you have always cut your dog's toenails, and one day your dog challenges you and you give up, realize that you need to get help so that your dog trusts you to handle him again.

Or if you used to enjoy Saturday morning walks when everyone was out, but now you find yourself walking during the dinner hour or in the pouring rain so you can avoid other people, realize that your dog has made you change your pattern, and get the help that you need.

While adjusting our behaviour while we get help is often necessary, make sure that it is only temporary. You must remedy the issue. Otherwise, your dog is training you.

October 3

Keep at it

You know you are a true dog trainer when you train every day for minimal improvement, including the days you do not want to.

Keeping at it means aiming for greater purpose. The journey itself becomes the reward, rather than the goal at the end, so much so that sometimes when you meet your goal, you temporarily feel void of purpose.

To help you through the difficult times, make daily goals of bettering today's training session compared to yesterday's. In times of difficulty, daily goals will help you appreciate the minimal growth that you are making. This will give you the stamina to keep going until the end.

October 4

Beware of over-socializing

Once upon a time, puppies never left the house. Now puppies see the world, interact with the world, and are often overwhelmed by the world. Some puppies have busier schedules than children, with puppy classes, socialization classes, and obedience classes. What happened to letting them be children?

I'm continually warning people to be careful of doing this, but no one believes me until the damage is done. Now they have to spend the next eight to sixteen years living with their error, with a dog with shattered self-confidence and often dog aggression.

Recently I worked with two small toy dogs. Normally when toy dogs arrive they come with baggage, especially around fast-moving or larger dogs, and it can be a challenge to make them feel safe. With these two little toys, just one was uncertain of dogs, but within moments he was over it. It was surprising how quickly he forgot his fears and moved on.

When questioning his owners, I learned that because of unique circumstances and bad luck, these two dogs had never met other dogs, or left the house. They were completely unsocialized. And in this case, they were blank slates. No damage had been done for me to fix.

I didn't have to teach these little dogs that I would protect them from every person approaching and wanting to touch them. They were old enough and brave enough that they loved it.

I didn't have to fix a fear of getting trampled by big dogs. They did not know it was a possibility, and I just had to make sure that they continued believing this to be true.

For toy breeds, they were probably two of the easiest I've ever had to rehab, because I just had to show them the world was safe. There was no past baggage to fix.

Over-socialization is equally damaging, if not more so, than under-socializing. Once again, socializing, just like everything else, is all about balance. Not too much, not too little, but just the right amount for that puppy, on that day.

Make sure they leave every social encounter feeling braver than they did going in. Often, less is more.

October 5

The self-monitoring dog

When your dog is trained you will no longer need to constantly command her. She will start volunteering and monitoring herself.

I've worked with many dogs who have learned how to do this over the years, but I'll give you the example of a recent one. She doesn't like dogs that much, nor does she like people that much. We have taught her that rather than eating her victims, we want her to lie down. When in conflict and having bad thoughts, she has put herself into that position on her own, without us asking, on more than one occasion.

We are teaching her the right answer for her inner conflicts. And we know that when she has the desire to eat someone she shouldn't, we can still request a down and she will do it—even if she does not volunteer the behaviour on her own. That is mental control—an ability to over override her own desires.

And that is what dog training is all about. When you have it, you can take them anywhere, and let them live their lives to the fullest, regardless of their temperaments, because you know they can be safe.

October 6

Respect their needs

Today I have a third Border Collie. She has never bitten, but dislikes all strangers. She will bark at them and follow it up with an eerie growl. When I first touched her she gave me a hard stare, right in the eyes, and made it abundantly clear that if I dared to touch her again, she would make me regret it.

When she was young, she had to have emergency veterinary care. During her time at the veterinarian's, she learned that her body would be touched without her permission. She was a puppy, and it shouldn't have continued to be an issue, but for some reason she decided it was.

When I realized this, I asked her permission to touch her. I first touched her shoulder, then pulled my hand an inch away. She glared at me, then realized that I was waiting for her permission and shifted her weight so that her shoulder touched my fingers. I tickled her shoulder. Then I wiggled my fingers toward her cheek. She shifted her cheek into my fingers. It really was that easy.

She presented as a very challenging dog, yet once her needs were met, she got over all her issues. She needs other people to be respectful, and soon enough, she's going to let her issue go completely.

Sometimes training dogs is so simple.

October 7

Sleep with your puppy

If your young puppy won't sleep next to you, you have some work to do. Until she wants to be next to you, and chooses to cuddle with you even while she is out cold, she is unable to grow into the dog you need her to be.

Every single puppy who moves into my house sleeps on my bed. They do this for three nights, maybe more, and then they graduate to a crate next to me.

Through the years, I've had some puppies who have had very odd responses. One puppy woke up in the middle of the night ready to kill me when I touched him while I slept. Fortunately, he was just five weeks old, and we worked through it. But if I had not had him in my bed, and he did it to someone when he was eleven months old, he would now be dead.

When puppies move into my house, this is my measure of where we are on the path to success. It took a couple of days for the little puppy I have to seek me out to sleep next to me. At first, she was grumpy if anyone interrupted her while she was sleeping. Now when I move, she enjoys knowing that I am next to her, rather than being offended as she was at the beginning.

This is only something I do with teeny, tiny puppies, not dogs. But with this wee little youngster, I'm on the right path. Now let the progress begin.

October 8

Test the tone of your voice

Sit in your chair with your hands firmly secured under your bum and talk to your dog. Food is forbidden for this exercise.

Can you make him lose his mind and go completely wiggly, just with your voice? Don't cheat and use your body. You should be able to build intensity with your voice alone and then make him go wild.

If you are not able to do this, you have a homework assignment. Try using different tones of voice. And please realize that tone is not the same as volume!

October 9

Be realistic in your breed choice

Recently, I offended a dear client.

She had a dog of a very challenging giant breed that she struggled with for many, many years. The dog attacked dogs, bit people, and ran away from home, endangering anyone that she came across. She wouldn't allow her owner to groom her, and her coat was often neglected. One time I spent hours grooming her and realized she had fleas underneath her matted undercoat. I would trim her nails, which were more like eagle's talons, so she could use her feet properly again because her owner could not handle her feet. You get the general picture.

This dog was big. And could be dangerous. She was much too much dog for her owner and did not belong in that home.

After years of this, the dog somewhat mellowed with age, and the owner forgot all of these grief-filled years. Then her dog died.

The owner is now ten years older, and even less in the physical shape to handle a dog of this size and mental power. She sent me a very sweet message seeking my approval for her new puppy, who was from the same breeder. I didn't give it.

Her last dog did not live the life she deserved. It was a life filled with tension, and at times, even neglect. This dog was loved dearly, but love is not enough.

We must always honour the dogs. Just because you love a breed does not mean that you are right for them. If your last dog was filled with angst and heartbreak, don't get another one from the same breed.

October 10

Troubleshooting puppy problems

This week I've gotten to share my home with two precious puppies from puppy class. Both were struggling and needed more. It reminded me of two things: how things might appear to be may not be true. And never underestimate the value of a nap.

The first puppy had a rather furious temper. His temper improved during the course of the class, but remained far from acceptable. When this dog was in my household, he just morphed into one of my dogs. He looked and behaved just like the rest of my guys. His issue: his wonderful family felt bad about leaving him alone while they worked, so they kept him going from 3:30 p.m. until bed, at which point he was just exhausted. Because he was tired, he had no patience. Anything that irritated him was a reason for him to become unglued.

In addition to some minor changes at home, I think naptime was his key. After a walk, after a game, after hanging out, he always got a nap in his crate, in a private place where he felt safe yet included.

The dog he appeared to be in puppy class was not him. He was a darling, sweet wonderful puppy, who needed more rules, more frequent naptimes, and a wee bit more understanding. They got exactly the puppy they need for their lovely, busy family.

The second puppy is the kind of puppy that I am drawn to, meaning, the rest of the world will probably struggle with her. I keep rubbing her forehead, in the hopes that her horns can sprout. She is a vixen. Smart. Busy. Conniving. Cunning. Manipulative. Loving for fleeting flashes. In puppy class we all admired her, and then gladly waved farewell.

I always let every puppy sleep in my bed when they first arrive. Last night my dogs all hated me for my decision. I hated me too.

Everything described in class was exactly as it appeared, yet worse. Only very rarely do you see dogs with this level of drive, tenacity, and determination in pet homes. She was a gleeful beast. With a smile, crawling in on her belly pretending to be so submissive, she annoyed all of us for two hours. We got kicked, licked, licked with teeth, then just teeth without the licks. We got jumped on, pounced on, then we had her little body hurled at us. At one point, she mistook my head and Pippa's ribcage for a flyball box.

You get the picture. No wonder her family is struggling! I think the fact that they are all still talking is a testament to their relationship!

Through these two hours I was busy guiding her—and failing. Coaching her and failing. Training her and failing. Making her settle and failing. Giving her rules and watching her say, "You don't want me to do THIS . . ." as she did it with six times the enthusiasm.

Given my complete lack of success last night, I think I'm cheating tonight with beef chewies. If I can get her engrossed in a bone, or chew, I can consider that success! Though I am prepared that the bone might be thrown at my head.

Anyhow, my long-winded answer is that if you asked me in puppy class which of the puppies was more challenging, it would have been the first, by far. And while I was seeing the second one in class, and knew that her horns would sprout soon, her level of glee at her wickedness was more than I expected.

When clients are struggling, and you know they are doing their homework, sometimes you just have to live with the dog for a day to find their solutions for them. Things may not be as they appear, as was the case with both puppies. And never forget the value of naptime, which little vixen is getting LOTS OF.

Wish me luck. Wish her family even more luck!

October 11

What we see changes

When I look back through my old dog training videos of Reggie and myself, I can see all of my current problems right when they were beginning. Though back then I didn't have these eyes and this knowledge. Even though I have watched those videos numerous times, my eyes were unable to see what is so painfully obvious now.

And I had been told. My wonderful mentors told me every single week, but I couldn't grasp what they were saying. I heard them, or at least tried to, but the lesson was so over my head. If only I had not let the subtle problem start. If only I had schooled him differently, because now when I look at the videos, I believe I actually taught him my issues.

If only I had these eyes then!

It is an amazing journey that our dogs take us on as they teach us. I now have the eyes to see this problem so I will not allow it to begin in another dog. I wonder what new problems I will see when I look back on videos of my youngest dog, Pippa, three years from now.

I love that I am in a hobby where we never stop growing and learning . . . our eyes change because we have grown and continued in our learning. And the things that experience teaches us to see, we never become blind to ever again.

October 12
Don't be a control freak

The purpose of rules is to give freedom. And the reason we teach control to our dogs is so that we no longer have to use it. By teaching control, in theory, our dogs learn to self-monitor and become nicer people. Once you have the ability to control your dog, it means that the frequency with which you need to exert that control will exponentially decrease. Of course, each dog is an individual and we can all come up with hundreds of exceptions, but for most dogs, this is true.

Rules with absolutely no purpose are degrading. Proud dogs will ignore them, or stop coming to you to avoid them. By this I mean rules such as making your dog sit before giving them affection. Why? If every time I went to someone they controlled me first, it would not take long before I stopped going to them. If I am requested to do something redundant, for no reason, I'm probably not going to do it well.

We need rules. We need control. But there must be a reason behind them. Just like with a parent who continually controls a child for no good reason, or an employer that micromanages, resentment may develop in the one being controlled.

Don't degrade dogs in the name of training. Remember they have pride, feelings, and a whole lot of other complex emotions. They are not robots.

Marc Goldberg, co-author of *Let Dogs Be Dogs*, says that "somewhere between indulging crappy dog behavior and squishing his free will lies the relationship you both crave." He is so right. Find your balance, which will be different with every dog. And enjoy them for who they are.

October 13

Help them be the best they can be

Through training, we must make our dogs' weaknesses invisible and build their strengths. Your fearful dog should become silently proud. Your pushy thug should become a guidable gentleman. Training isn't just about training behaviours: it is about helping them to grow up to be proud and functioning members of your household.

To get this you must learn to stroke their ego and make them believe what you tell them when you give praise. You want their tails up over their backs and their skin loose over their bodies and rib cage when you talk to them. And they must have an evil glint in their eye (a trademark for me that I seem to put into every dog I work with).

Learn to develop all these traits in your dog with just your voice, your body language, and your facial expressions. Positive reinforcement is the method of choice for dog training, but its value is minimal compared to the value of your relationship.

The personality traits you see in your dog are the traits you will create and build. Your voice, expressions, body language, thoughts and views, and, ultimately, your relationship have more power than any cookie. Learn how to use all of these things, rather than just relying on a cookie or a toy. Once you are able to do this, you can begin to make your dog the absolute best he can be.

October 14

Does your dog make you move?

Our dogs are predators, meaning they chase and catch things. They will always respond to being able to make something move. It is instinct for them. Now think of your dog trying to get a toy from you, or a puppy biting at your hands. Or the biggest one, your dog continually cutting in front of you when you are out on a walk.

The more you keep moving the desired object away from them, the more they will want to get it. And, in the case of a puppy biting your hands during teething, if you keep moving your hands away because it hurts, after a time you will change the way your puppy thinks. You could turn your very nice puppy into a not-so-nice puppy.

Always be aware of how much your dog makes you move. Be aware of where your hands and feet are, and if your dog does things to make you move them.

October 15

The line in the sand

When training a dog, we must be aware of the line in the sand. Are we aware of when we should help? When we should make it easier, when we must reward more, when we need to get out of their way and let them work it out? And are we prepared to step over to the other side and tell them to smarten up?

The problem with the line in the sand is that it moves; it's never in the same spot from day to day. What helped yesterday may be way too much or not enough for today.

And this is what defines a trainer, parent, or anyone else working with a complex, dynamic, thinking being. Do you know when to say, "yes," and when to say, "no," versus when to say, "YES" and when to say, "NO"? Do you know when to say nothing?

Any and all responses are right once, and maybe a thousand times, but you had better know *when* to shift and *when* to move as your dog changes, or your communication will be very flawed.

October 16
The reason for my leash

Your dog's social etiquette is none of my business; we are complete strangers. My dog is on leash. Therefore, take the cue, and keep yours away.

There are many reasons why my dog might be wearing a leash. He might be injured, under the weather, having a really bad day, or he's simply enjoying nature with me and doesn't care whether your dog is friendly or not. It might not be my dog, or it might be a brand-new dog and I don't know how he will behave. However, we are total strangers, and other than a polite "hello," l do not owe you an explanation. Simply take the cue of my dog being on a leash and keep yours away.

I have met many a sweet, nice, well-mannered dog, and I have never been told they are friendly. I only hear this phrase along with the ones with their tails curled up high over their backs and hackles up who are standing as tall as they can (or stalking like a cat), and rushing forward to their victims.

If you feel yourself wanting to call out, "He's friendly!" as you see your dog galloping away from you and toward his victim, please do some soul searching.

Your adult dog should not be this interested in another adult dog. It is weird and is an insult to you; your dog thinks random strangers are more fun than you. Take this as motivation to really enjoy your dog on your walks.

Use this time to connect and enjoy watching him be a dog. And please put the time into training him so that not only can you and your dog enjoy your off-leash time, but so can everyone else who might not want to engage with you.

Sometimes the things we blurt out in a moment of pressure are our most honest dreams and prayers. It is what we wish was true.

"He is friendly."

I shall say no more—other than, "He isn't."

October 17

Be careful what you teach

There are certain commands I don't teach pet dogs, and one of those is to look in my eyes.

There are two reasons. I thought there was only one, but I just recently came across a second.

If I talk to you, I expect that you will look at me. I expect the same of my dogs. A command is only to be done when commanded. But I expect eye contact whenever I say their names.

My new reason: I just worked with a dog that scared me. Her eyes would lock onto a dog, then with no words, turn to me and have a hard stare into my eyes. One time she then dropped her eyes to my knees. In my experience, she was letting me know her next move: the location she planned on biting me.

I did wonder if this dog had been taught to look at a dog, then look at her human. But everyone forgot to consider her emotional state. They taught her to redirect on people. She was staring in my eyes, then went rigid in her body and mind, and locked on with a hard stare that made the hair on the back of my neck stand up.

I appreciate how my sheep must feel with my Border Collies . . . and I've suddenly developed a huge appreciation for a soft eye.

Be careful what you teach. And always consider your dog's mental state when she's learning.

October 18

Attentiveness works both ways

When working with our dogs we expect them to pay attention. You cannot communicate with someone who is not listening to you, so attention between team members is a fundamental starting point.

My ultimate pet peeve is when the dog is staring adoringly at his human, who just walks away, or starts in a conversation with another person without ever telling the dog. Their poor dogs continue to stare adoringly, not wanting to be rude and break the attention.

If you expect your dog to be attentive, you must lead by example. Walking away on them is incredibly rude. Forgetting they exist while you are in a conversation with someone else is not allowed.

Lead by example, and demonstrate what active attention looks like. Through example, show your dog how to keep his attention under distractions by keeping your attention on him when other people chat to you.

October 19

Unlock the block

Before you can teach a dog to sit, or down, or any of those "things" that we deem necessary, first you must have a willing student who is trying to understand the lesson that you are teaching. Until you have a willing student, it is all for naught.

If your student is unwilling, you must find out why. Is she too scared? Too on-edge to give you her focus? Too independent? Maybe she doesn't trust you? Or she has no connection to you yet? Or maybe she just doesn't care what you think?

Once you have established which of these is your block, work on it.

By unlocking the block, you will have fixed your relationship. Once your dog listens to what you are trying to say, you will be off to the races.

October 20

Train in black and white, not grey

How do we know when we're training in black and white? There is an absence of nagging.

So many trainers I see spend their time training in dark grey, though if you were to ask them, they would swear they are training in pure white. They nag. Then nag a bit more. They don't want their dogs to fail, so they inhibit them all day long, every day, nag after nag. Through attempting to be kind, day after day, they suck the life out of their dogs just a wee bit more.

And sometimes, when their dogs don't behave, owners are unhappy, even though they try and pretend they are not. Our dogs are not stupid and know when we are disappointed. Nothing can quash a dog quicker than our emotional baggage.

Try and make your dog's world clearer. Showing right and wrong is more humane than attempting to be really kind and involuntarily nagging as you try to keep control, which also comes with an emotional side of disappointment.

October 21

The forgotten art of domestics

My Pet Manners class blew me away this week. Everyone's control was outstanding with their pet dogs, so I decided to put my Competition Obedience classes through the same exercises. I know their dogs have beautiful heelwork and retrieves, but wondered if they would "lie-down" when told as their handlers were vacuuming?

Why? Because domestics are often forgotten. It doesn't matter how well your dog can do a retrieve or heel if he is a pain in the ass to live with. And first we have to live with our dogs.

We all create our own monsters, and I admire that. I don't care if your dog steals a sandwich off your coffee table every day, because he can still be a nice dog and steal, and stealing sandwiches won't risk his life. I'm only draconian about behaviours that make your dog a not-so-nice person and make everyone unsafe.

Regardless of what behaviours you've chosen to live with, "down" must mean *down until released*, and "come" must mean *come*. My students had to ask their dogs to down as they vacuumed, and also while my students moved two giant objects around the room (meaning both arms were full so they could not adjust their body language). They also had to ask their dogs to come, both off leash inside and outside of my training building, as their dogs were going through doorways, and even as they were about to go and pee. Each class had about eight off-leash dogs, with vacuums going, chairs being moved, the doors open, and general mayhem. I am pleased to say that after a tiny bit of tweaking, all the classes nailed it.

I'm totally against always controlling dogs who have no self-esteem. The purpose of rules is to give freedom: I want my dogs mentally free, with a tiny bit of cheekiness and naughtiness thrown in. But they still have commands that they must follow, without being reminded.

Obviously, my classroom exercises can't compete with a rabbit running across a trail, and our dogs are not going to have this level of control in higher-drive moments until we specifically teach it. But if they know all of their basics very well, perhaps today is the day to teach it? My classes are ready for the next step.

Our end goals are:

- You shall not pull on a leash.
- You shall lie down when told.
- You shall come back when called.
- You shall not bite when being handled or when your toenails are cut, even when you don't want them to be done.

If you have these four things, first in low-drive while you train medium-drive, then in medium-drive while you train high-drive, and then in high-drive, you will want for nothing more. Your dog will be a delight to live with, will be easy for your veterinarian to examine, and will be safe in almost all worldly situations.

Never forget the power of domestics. We all create our own monsters and that is fine, providing you have these four basics.

October 22

Honouring rescue dogs

Don't treat rescue dogs any differently than a regular dog. Making excuses and lowering your standards for past abuses and baggage will only limit them in their future successes. This will ultimately affect their happiness.

Have the same expectations for them as you do any other dog, and behave as though they are normal when you are with them; then they can become normal. They will rise to the occasion and you will accelerate their progress.

You will have to adjust your training with them, as you will with any other dog. While we must always train the dog that we are training, lowering our criteria means that we believe they are not capable. No one gets power from being a victim; it is our job to help them become capable.

If you truly love your rescue dog, give him a life by treating him like he is normal, with normal expectations. It is the kindest thing you can do for them.

October 23

What you say and do, your brain must think

Reggie is the most amazing dog I have ever met, but amazing doesn't mean easy. The biggest lesson I've learned from him over the last year has been about emotions, and the importance of feeling the words I speak.

I recently spent two weeks in Germany, and I don't speak a word of conversational German. When I was among a group of people, all I could do was watch. After a few days of people watching, I started to get an idea of what their conversations were about by watching the emotions of the group. Gestures and faces tell a full story! I knew when someone was happy, concerned, serious, or when someone had just said something really naughty. Our words are directly connected to our emotions. We feel what we say, although sometimes we censor ourselves, and this shows in our bodies and faces. Our bodies do not lie. They tell the full story.

Now, watch people training their dogs. Their commands and praise lack true emotion. People training their dogs are usually either happy, sucky, or look really bored! What we should see are emotions coming through our minds and body language. We have relationships with our dogs, and just like watching the people interact in their group, the owner/dog relationship should show happiness, concern, concentration and effort, thoughtfulness, seriousness when something is unacceptable and absolute joy when it is perfect.

If I coo, "No," while biting my tongue trying not to laugh at his latest prank that was wickedly naughty and clever, my "No" will not match my emotions and I will be lying to him. In my human mind, "No," conveys my stand on the matter. But my dog does not speak English. To him, everything in my body language told him I thought his behaviour was really funny. Reggie the prankster always tries to amuse me, so for him that feedback means to repeat. A Reggie prank, once approved by me, always tends to end with me being bruised, so these matters do need to be treated seriously. I must honestly convey to him what I want repeated, and what I do not want repeated, regardless of his creativity and energy.

Reggie forces me to match my words to my emotions. If I don't like it, I cannot even giggle in my head. "No" to a mischievous prank is now "Don't do that again or I will become unhappy with you." "Good boy" is now felt by me as a warming of pride. "Excellent" gets me excited at his brilliance. When I want him to be still and calm, I am still and calm. And when I want him to go wild, my mind goes wild. My body and mind now mirror how I want him to think and feel. Externally I might look the same, but Reggie is teaching me ironclad mind control. He is a very good, if unforgiving, teacher!

Pairing true meanings to words is the hardest training challenge that I have had in years. My tone has indicated the right message, as have my hands and body. My holdouts were my feelings and mind when I had to be serious or calm. Reggie is too smart to be lied to and would not forgive me this error. Now my feelings and mind are also on board, completing the message.

October 24

How do you feel about your dog?

What defines us as trainers is our relationship with our dog. Much of this is determined by your beliefs about your dog.

How do you feel about your dog? Please don't use a broad emotion, such as, "I love him." How do you really feel? Is he able to push your buttons? Does he do little things that make you want to throttle him? These are the emotions that your dog feels every single time that you pick up that leash.

Right now I am struggling with a dog, as many of you probably are. I struggle with controlling my thoughts, which will predetermine my outcome. I can get stuck in "this is hard work" or "he is so challenging." Really, we must all be grateful that we get to have dogs, that we have homes, and food on our tables. These are first-world problems that we are blessed to have.

Sometimes we simply need some perspective. Or a break. We need to build back up to a place of harmony, let go of all the negative associations that we have built and are clinging to in our brains, and simply be grateful that we have these wonderful dogs to share our lives with.

It is up to us to decide what we would like to focus on—be it past failures and flaws or strengths and future successes! Don't get stuck in negative thought patterns that will harm both your future success and your relationship with your dog. Focus your beliefs on all of their positive traits, so they can become that again.

October 25

The plight of a good dog trainer

Today I lost another great student. The problem with my job is that when I do what I am paid for, I lose my hard-working students.

The people I adore—the ones who do their homework, learn to think on their toes, and who always honour their dogs, even when stressed—disappear.

It is a double-edged sword. I help them achieve their goals, and in the process, I work myself out of a job and their company.

October 26

So much is right

I am blessed with my household of dogs. Yet I often let the tiny imperfect details get to me.

Yes, our dogs can be annoying. Yes, they can get into trouble, and sometimes lots of it. But we choose what to focus on: these tiny details or their strengths.

Remove the negativity and what you see will change. If you continue to only focus on your dogs' flaws, you will begin to dislike your dog.

If we have created issues in our dogs, we need to let go of our guilt and go and fix the issue. We need to forgive ourselves for our past errors so that we can move forward and give our dogs what they need. Don't waste energy on feeling guilty. Rather, put that energy into fixing the issue.

Your mindset is yours to create. You can be positive or negative. Neither will change your actual situation, but it sure will change how you handle your situation. Being grateful for all that is right is so much better than allowing the tiny bits of wrong to ruin your day.

October 27

Pay attention to weird moments

Perfect Pippa got her nickname because she wasn't. We must envision what we want our dogs to become and I wanted her to be perfect, which she now is. When she was a child she was odd, very odd. Now as an adult she is easy and delightful.

Back when Pippa was six months old, she suddenly decided she had to spend the night sleeping on my head. Then the next day she was weird, really weird. She growled at two people, hid in my car, and behaved abnormally in other scenarios. Was this unusual for her? No, but her weird moments were becoming further and further apart, were getting less severe, and I had learned how to deal with her better.

But this time I knew why she reverted back.

That night while I was sleeping, before a Border Collie curled up on my head, a piece of paper fell off our window. It was soundless, and would have wafted down from up high.

The following night she spent all her time in bed, continually looking up to the place it would have fallen from.

This one "thing" made her behave oddly for 24 hours.

Now, why do I write this? Think about leaving your dog in your backyard while you are at work and later coming home to an odd dog. You have no idea what happened during their day that could influence how they act. For Pippa, a branch falling from a tree could ruin her day and dramatically change her behaviour, just like the piece of paper. But what if a delivery person came in and pushed at her when she jumped on them? That is the type of thing that she might never recover from.

Because I work with odd behaviour problems, rarely do I work with dumb dogs. I only work with the dogs that see something fall off a wall and are affected by it. Pippa is also extremely clever and after showing her something once or twice it is locked into her brain, making her a joy to teach. But experiencing the wrong thing once or twice also locks it into her brain and it might never be gone.

Please be mother bears with your young dogs. Be control freaks and control their bubbles. Guard them from bad experiences. Guard them from paper that falls down from a windowsill on a wafting wind (I am joking). Know what happens to them every minute of every day when they are wee little whippersnappers. When you are unable to attend to them, put them away so that nothing bad can affect them.

There comes a time when they need to know there is bad in the world and have the skill set to deal with it. In the case of Pippa, she got carefully planned "bad lessons," such as the first dog that chased her. I waited until I knew she could deal with it, and set it up so that she had an opportunity to feel powerful coming out of it, or it would have been a disaster. The bubble wrap must eventually be ripped off, as they learn that bad things happen. And hopefully they can find their own inner strength to deal with it, which will make them stronger. But this stuff all takes time, patience, and maturity, and must not happen when they are wee and weak.

On those unexpected bad days, ruined by something falling off a window, take that moment to be their coach. When you see odd responses to things, guide them through how normal dogs should behave. The following day when Pippa was mega-weird, she got schooled in how to behave when scary people are walking toward her, what to do if a dog approaches, how to sit in the car, and other lessons that might not have presented if something hadn't fallen off my window!

October 28

Be determined, not disappointed

Find determination, rather than disappointment, when your dog screws up. Be determined for the two of you, as a team, to get it right.

Nothing can destroy a dog quicker than your disappointment. And nothing will destroy your confidence quicker than your disappointment. Be kind and forgive yourself when you make an error.

October 29

Aggression in the small breeds

When I work with big, strong dogs with aggression, their owners have almost always tried other trainers, done their homework, committed fully to retraining, and just need some final "icing on the cake," if you will. I get to offer the final key ingredients for success when a lot of the foundation work is already in place.

Now when it comes to the toy breeds, there is frequently an entirely different psychology at work. Not always but often.

Rather than taking the aggression problem seriously, almost all of their owners found it funny at first, and inadvertently rewarded it because it was entertaining and they wanted to see it again. Or, they denied and enabled it because their dog was scared. They strategically taught these little dogs that their teeth could get them what they wanted.

After so much time and success, these little dogs actually believe that they are invincible. Once they are at that point, there is almost no turning back. At least not without crushing the core of their existence.

Owners of small dogs sometimes have a different mentality. They actually build bad behaviour up because it *is* funny; we can all admit that. Seeing a little Chihuahua gallop as fast as he can to attack your shin really is funny, even in the moment. I have to bite my tongue so I don't burst out laughing. But the behaviour is still dangerous and does need to be taken seriously.

Continue to enjoy your wee bad dog, if you have one. But as you force the tongue biting, please do take the behaviour seriously. If your dog has success after success going after people, he will reach a point where he truly is invincible, and almost nothing is going to turn him back to being a nice, happy dog again.

You will make your once happy, spunky dog become angry, distrustful, and unhappy. You owe him better than that, especially when you allowed his behaviour solely for the purpose of having a laugh and didn't take it seriously.

Respect your dogs. Respect them if they are big and give them training to keep them safe. And respect them if they are small, so that they can stay happy, spunky, and fun-loving.

October 30

Growing beyond "no"

Pippa used to struggle immensely with being told, "No." She would disappear and become a shadow for forty-eight hours. However, "no" is still a necessary word in her life. She cannot be a powerful bitch when someone disagreeing with her sends her on a forty-eight-hour sobbing fest. To teach her how to grow beyond this disapproval-induced shut down, I strategically set up a series of lessons to put her under pressure, then let her win.

Last week was one of her stress lessons. It was, "sit means sit even if you don't want to." As she leapt out of her position with glee, she got put back where she needed to be. While this lesson was based on the "sit," that was just the ingredient used to teach her to be a nicer and braver person. The lesson is meant to build mental toughness, determination, and strength. By fixing her sit she underwent the same emotions as losing a soccer game, and she learned to work through them.

She would not have learned the same lesson if she got a cookie simply for taking part. Life doesn't work that way.

October 31

Beware of well-meaning advice

Facebook is a great place to watch people offer up free advice. Some advice is brilliant, and it comes from people who really know what they're doing. Some advice is not so brilliant. In fact, if someone follows that advice it could take thousands of dollars to fix. But what leaves me awestruck is when people who have so clearly failed with their own dogs believe they have something valid to offer.

On one thread, two people, both of whom have dogs that show dangerous behaviour and are out of control, were advising someone else on how to remedy a serious problem. So, if you follow their advice all that you could hope for is that you too might have a dog that behaves dangerously.

The part that befuddles me is *how* people who failed with their own dogs see themselves as experts. I wonder if in part these people lack insight into themselves? Which would explain how they got into such trouble with their dogs in the first place.

It happened again last night. A client who was on the right path decided to listen to someone who is failing miserably with their own dog. But the person who is failing speaks so confidently that people believe she is an expert. In just one week the first client was able to make their dog almost as muddled up as the dog belonging to the advice giver. And what else would you expect?

So please think before you follow advice. Does your expert know what they are doing? Are they succeeding with their own dog? If not, don't listen. Thank them for their kindness and run for the hills.

And please remember, for any ill advice that you choose to follow, your dog will always pay. I wish it weren't so, but it is.

NOVEMBER

November 1

How we cause dog aggression

No matter how much we try and hide our fears from our dogs, it is almost impossible. Our body language gives us away. How?

We start whispering in his ear, telling him what a good boy he is, as we hastily exit the trail and hide in bushes. Our bodies get small, and we crouch down like we are talking to a three-year-old child. And then right before the lunge, we start praising, "Good boy, Benji! Isn't he a nice dog? Be a good boy, Benji." And we start fidgeting, as we hold his leash with a death grip.

It's our behaviour that often causes the meltdown.

Sometimes the easiest way to retrain aggressive dogs is to stop your nervous chatter. Be silent. Stand up straight. Loosen your muscles. Breathe. Communication with your dog must be calm, slow, and clean. Hold your leash with no tension, yet short enough that your dog cannot get into trouble.

If you don't believe me, I challenge you to get onto a horse. Go for a nice trail ride, then when you see something that might scare your horse, lower your posture, tighten all your muscles, start talking in a frantic manner, and fidget in your seat with your tight muscles, as you urge your horse on. At the last minute get a death grip on your reins. Your horse will respond the same as your dog.

Retraining temperament problems like reactivity has nothing to do with training dogs or horses, but rather learning to be better poker players! Once we can act like people who have normal dogs, we will have normal dogs. Training ourselves is at least 75 percent of the puzzle. Training the dogs through reactivity is 25 percent at most. This is mostly a lesson for us, and not so much for them.

November 2

My black-and-white weirdos

We get easy dogs. We get challenging dogs. And sometimes our dogs are just weird—it seems like they were born with different wiring in their brains. (And more often than not these dogs are black and white, have pointy ears, and belong in the herding group.)

Let me be clear that I am not talking about badly behaved dogs. Badly behaved dogs are very common. And even more prolific than badly behaved dogs are owners who put little effort into their training, or who have poor communication with their dogs.

These weirdos force us to train them by making the wrong thing hard and the right thing easy. Or by training them from where they are at. Successive approximations get broken down into even smaller chunks: they learn that "mental give" for a split second will earn them the control that they seek.

Or we can use their need for obsessive control, that moment where their mind is fixated on their object, to teach them to get over their fear of touch, sound, or any other stimuli that they cannot handle. We use their desire to control to teach a completely unrelated lesson. We must think completely outside of the box, and search deep within ourselves, to come up with answers for these dogs.

We can only retrain these guys when we know what is important to them, understand what they see and feel, and work within the confines of what they give us. These are the dogs that we can never belittle or suppress.

Often one of the most important pieces in their retraining is removing their mental tension. And getting them to partner up with you.

The diagnosable black and whites, or pointy-eared members of the herding group, are the ones that force us to be better trainers. They are gifts to work with and live with. Though never easy, they are the most brilliant of all with their intelligence and perceptiveness.

These delightful dogs force me to question my beliefs, force me to think like a dog (with a psychiatric disorder), and make me a much better trainer. Yesterday I worked with one, and unravelled her problem in minutes, easing her mental tension. There is nothing more gratifying.

November 3

Training versus controlling

The Buddhist scriptures say that the purpose of rules is to give freedom. We do not teach control so that we can control. At least, we should not.

Start counting how many times you command your dog on an hour-long walk, versus how many times he commands himself without you having to say a thing. This will let you know if you are training him, or just controlling him.

Aim for the latter. Aim to get to a place where your dog is commanding himself and you don't have to say a thing. Teach rules, so that they may have freedom—mental freedom from us. This is the secret to having a happier, more confident dog.

November 4

Watch your weak moments

Right now I have a dog here who is so brilliantly behaved for me and such a turd for his mum. He belongs to a saint of a lady, who provides a home that any dog would be blessed to live in and outwardly her handling is perfect. Yet she fights flickers of doubt when confronted with a difficulty, or even just shows mental exhaustion, and then he acts like an ungrateful turd.

Why? Well, he is the type of dog who would have tormented substitute teachers in high school. He will behave only as well as he knows is required. And if you have a weak moment, you can bank on him taking full advantage of it. He has a mean streak to him that I do not like; yet I see it in many of the strong hound dogs who don't have a leader made of steel.

In my hands he is happy and mentally free, and he behaves well. In the hands of my apprentice, who is a less-experienced handler than me, he is the same. Yet in his mother's hands he lacks confidence and will take opportunistic cheap shots.

In his case I need to train the human, not the dog. However, somehow he needs to take some responsibility for his actions. I dislike that he takes advantage of his loved one being weak. This is not a nice trait in a dog or a person.

He needs to learn to mind his manners regardless of what his handler is thinking, fearing, or doing. They are supposed to be a team, when truthfully he is just waiting to take her down. He needs to stop looking for every opportunity to act out.

He behaves and is so strong when he is with me because of my strength and clarity; he knows that I mean what I say and say what I mean. To progress with his training I now need to become weak, a little tiny bit unclear in my body language, and teach him that the rules have not changed, and the onus is now on him to do his job regardless of my mental strength or weak body language. I will fake panic attacks in my brain as I walk past dogs, or as chaos happens around me. If he takes the opportunity to be a dink, I will school him through it, and I will be as unfair to him as he was to me. Unfair in that he will suddenly see my clarity and strength, when he was not expecting it.

His job is easy: mind your manners and be a nice person, regardless of what your handler is thinking or fearing in that moment.

My job is more of a mental game. To be effective for this dog, I need to dread walking him and start praying that I don't see anyone!

November 5

Don't mix and match

If you have committed to a dog trainer, stick with that trainer until they cannot help you. *Do not* mix and match dog trainers, or even advice. It does not work. All advice is right, yet all advice is wrong, depending on the foundation and other things that you are doing for *that* dog. So stick with your first unless you are not getting what you need. Then move on, but move on fully. Don't maintain both.

For example, I am a relationship-based trainer and I demand certain domestic obedience in dogs. All of my solutions and fixes will be based on your relationship with your dog, and I will go back to domestic obedience again and again. If you ask me advice, without me seeing your dog, I'm going to give you an answer assuming your relationship with your dog is strong. If it is not, my solution will not work for you and your dog and may actually make things worse. My solutions work with my way, based on my foundation. But you can't mix and match. Well you can, but there is no quicker way to ruin your dog than mixing and matching training styles and heeding advice from multiple sources.

November 6

He's never done that before

Pavlov conditioned a dog to salivate at the ring of a bell. I have been conditioned to respond to the phrase "He's friendly!" with full fear and adrenaline.

Every time I hear this phrase, a rude dog is quickly approaching me, and its owner is in denial. Their rose-coloured glasses are so rosy that they are obscuring their view, and I truly believe they have persuaded themselves that their dogs *are* friendly rather than facing the cold hard fact that they've allowed their dog to behave rudely. Generally, the phrase, "He's never done that before!" follows the encounter.

I now consider this phrase a warning about the impending encounter. If you hear these words, be prepared to guard your dog, and deal with their rude one.

November 7

Set your intention

How can two people pick up a leash seemingly in the same way, yet get such different results? It all boils down to your intention and the energy that you give off.

If you know he won't behave for you, you are right. Your energy will show your doubts.

If you know he will fight you, you are right, he will. Your touch on the leash will reveal your adrenaline-charged energy, and your energy reveals your thoughts.

If you know he will be scared, you are right. More often than not, just the eyes we put on them when we are fearful is enough to trigger a response. I learned this when I was trying to pull a prank on my poor friend Cass. I wanted to see her reaction when she sat on a chair that was wet. As I kept glancing in her direction to see if she was closer, she started to freak out. Her response taught me, and I got much better at succeeding with pranks by keeping my eyes and body language off of her.

Lightness aside, positive affirmations won't help your mental clarity as you pick up a leash either.

Hoping that he will be brilliant will not make him brilliant. Nor will "fake-knowing" he will be brave, pliable, willing, obedient, or any other positive trait that we need but rarely get. Somehow, you must *believe t*hat he will be what you need, but with plan B in your brain, ready to be executed if things fall apart.

Of course, if your dog never normally does something, believing he finally will is just foolish. It is denial masquerading as a positive affirmation, and it will always leave you disappointed shortly after the train wreck happens. Until you have a long history of success, picture in your mind's eye what you need, with plan B ready to remedy an error (should it occur). This plan B, a quick fix to a problem thrown your way, will give you the mental strength to make you believable. We cannot lie to a dog, but we can change our thoughts and become trustworthy leaders for them.

When I pick up a leash, my expectations are clear in my mind. My body language clearly communicates what I will accept. My feet move with very precise deliberation (as several clients can attest). I walk my path and set the speed. I hold the leash with a casual confidence that will make all but the naughtiest dogs behave. None of my muscles are tense for more than a split second at a time, giving instant feedback to the dog. I am aware that my body, hips, shoulders, and feet are in sync. I'm not so good with my voice and have learned the art of being silent when my voice might betray me.

I expect dogs to behave and not drag me. Every part of me gives off the confidence of someone who expects this. And almost always, I get what I expect.

November 8

Kids welcome

Kids are welcome in my group classes and always have been. The reason? I find they are generally far superior trainers than their parents. And, if they have been bitten by the bug, they have the time to train.

I have always believed that training a dog is learning to communicate with another species. You must be able to read them, to know what their next move will be. While words are not spoken, it is still a language.

Kids, before they hit puberty, can easily pick up diffferent languages. After puberty, many people are blinded to the communication and what is being said without words. Certain things can be pointed out, learned, practiced, and repeated, but this learning often lacks the ease and flow with which kids seem to be able to learn.

This is just my theory and I do not know if I am right, but I do know that I love working with kids. If a kid wants to learn to train dogs, the speed with which they progress is embarrassing when compared to my own progress! And I'm sure that all of you instructors out there can name at least five exceptional kids you have taught who just "got it."

November 9

Respectful ways to disagree

In today's world of social media, where every person has a platform for his or her opinion and voice, judgements abound everywhere. People are being judged for decisions they have made to train their dog, when in reality, at least they made a decision and did something, be it right or wrong . . .

The opinions received are judging training decisions that were made. Often strangers spout off superior knowledge and belittle the person who actually had the courage to go out and "do," and then share. Let's be gentle with our feedback. Even if someone was completely wrong, at least they thought and made a decision. And we all started somewhere.

So, before you knock the poor people who put themselves out there, first put yourself in their shoes. Withhold your judgement and see if you might actually learn something. Did their response work? If not, you could add a tip to help. Or be polite and bite your tongue, unless asked to help brainstorm a better solution.

To those who are picked on, I live my life by these two mottos: (a) Your opinion of me is none of my business, and (b) Only I know what it's like to walk a mile in my shoes with my clients or my own dogs. Let's all try to be nicer and more supportive.

November 10
Rehoming: Is it always bad?

If you have enough dogs, eventually you will find yourself with one who, while she may love you, doesn't necessarily like you.

I've had one. When she came home she instantly chose my husband. At four months we were still struggling to bond. With lots of effort, it did happen. But when all of that effort dwindled over the passing years, so did our relationship. She was difficult and grumpy. It wasn't until we went for a dental cleaning at the veterinarian, and she was clearly the office celebrity that I realized it was *me* who made her difficult and grumpy.

I'm older and wiser now, and I vow that the next time I get a headstrong dog who doesn't adore me, I will find her the right person. Keeping my dog was the easy thing to do. Sadly, it was not the right thing to do.

Someone just did the right thing for their difficult and grumpy girl and she is now my new project dog. After a tumultuous first few weeks, Kate decided she was mine. She gave me her heart, all of it, holding nothing back.

Pondering this thought the other day, I became anxious about the ginormous responsibility this girl has put on me. She loves me like she never has anyone before. Her love and commitment to me are fierce. I understand her and she is so grateful. When I leave, she sleeps with her head jammed against the glass door so that she can be the first to see me come home. She always knows where I am and is silently watching, waiting.

When I put her outside, she sets up residence underneath my van. This way I cannot leave without her.

Some dogs need us. Some dogs don't. Most of the dogs who don't need us love us with most of their heart, holding a small piece back. Few give their entire selves and when they do, it is a giant responsibility to be worthy of that much love, that much trust. My girl has decided she's all in, which for her was a huge sacrifice. Her feelings get hurt when she believes I'm not as deeply invested. If I were to rehome her now, I would crush her.

I recently experienced this with a board-and-train puppy. She came with extreme problems; she was her own little madam living in this big world. She did not trust at first but then allowed me in. She trusted me with her life. I begged her owners to let me keep her (it was an impossible match of a very clever herding breed with novice owners). However, she was their dog, and they wanted her back. She did come back to me a month later to be rehomed, but she never did trust me again. She liked me, but we remained only friends. I betrayed her trust when I gave her back the first time, and she would not give me a second chance. Orphan Annie refused to even let me rehab her a second time. I had to have another trainer work with her so she could get what she needed.

Most animals—and people—will not allow themselves to be this vulnerable and they will love you with most of their heart but not the entire thing. But when you are given the gift of their entire heart, with nothing held back, acknowledge it for what it is, and realize that it can be fraught with difficulties.

Then promise to do right by them. While it would be so much easier to rehome my problem child, she's staying. She gave me her heart. And in return, I made her a promise. This is her home, through sickness and health, through happy days and bitchy days!

November 11

From teacher to student

When we first get a dog, we can't wait to teach her a thing or two. On our second dog, we wonder what thing or two she will teach us. Our roles quickly change, and we go from considering ourselves a teacher to becoming a student.

November 12

Drive: Learn from other's errors

The most boring and unaware dog owners often have the dogs with the most piss and vinegar, yet these people are just looking for a nice pet that will lie at their feet. Dog sport people would love to build the same drive in our dogs, but often fail. Why?

Watch them. Their dog begs and begs for attention, and they ignore it. Finally, the dog barks at them so they give in and scratch his head. Or the dog brings the ball to their feet. They ignore him. The dog picks it up and places it in their lap. The ball gets brushed away. The dog picks it up and jams it in the owner's crotch, at which point they pick it up and throw it.

These dogs have learned to activate their owners. The dog is actively trying to get his owner to notice him. Pay heed, competition folks—their dogs have more drive and focus than yours, and they can teach you!

In my competition classes, people beg their dogs (from high-drive bloodlines) to take a toy. The dog makes the most minute effort and gets flooded with praise. By constantly rewarding the most minor efforts and giving them all they want for the tiniest of exertions, these dogs are almost taught how *not* to play and want food.

We dog sport people have a lot to learn by sitting back and watching the Doodles, Pugs, and Boston Terriers at the dog park, who will tug and retrieve until they pass out.

If you want a working dog, stop activating him. Get him to activate you. At least do this in the moments when you want to build drive in your dog and have him pester you—as is needed for training sports!

And if you want a dog with very little drive, celebrate them picking up a toy like they just won a Nobel Peace Prize. Reward the game when they are at their weakest. You will get a dog that is happy to lie at your feet.

November 13
Look for inspiration

Sometimes our dogs have such unique needs that none of our standard tried-and-true dog training tools seem to work. However, we still must train these dogs. But how do we do that when all the tools in our toolbox have not worked?

I look outside of dog training. What tools have helped autistic children with a similar struggle? What would an occupational therapist do if a child in the classroom was exhibiting these behaviours? What has helped horse riders in similar situations with the same type of animal?

This is how I started using weighted vests, balls in mouths, and squishing, just to name a few, many, many years ago.

Learn how to colour outside of the lines. And some dogs require us to colour so far out that we forget the lines are even there.

November 14
Are we creating dog reactivity?

I think dog culture in North America has set us up for dog issues.

We have been taught that dogs need friends, and that they need to be *socialized*, a term that has been misunderstood and misinterpreted to mean greeting every random stranger. When you take your dog over to greet every dog you see, you are teaching them to be dog obsessed. Instead of walking, you're just looking for dog after dog to say "hi" to.

If these dogs have a moment where they feel unsure, or cheeky, or if they're unaware of how they should act because they have been taught to always move forward to dogs, they only have one course of action: aggression.

I believe that *if* we teach our dogs to be less focused on other dogs most social issues will disappear, or be substantially reduced.

Dogs benefit from having dog friends. But having dog friends is very different than expecting them to hug every dog stranger they pass.

Try and make your dog less dog-focused, *especially* if you are seeing social issues in her when she is young.

November 15

Show some spirit

Humans are inherently lazy. When we train with food, we allow food to do all of our work for us. It works really well on days that I'm too tired to train. But quickly it can become a habit, one that is very hard to remove.

When you train with food, do you still use proper praise before you feed your dog? Do your dog's eyes light up when you tell them how clever they are?

Are you just a boring Pez dispenser monosyllabically muttering "good"? Or do your words have emotional value and meaning?

Is your body showing that you are happy? Or are your shoulders hung low, making you look like you just got a repair bill for a thousand dollars?

Do you just drop your food into your dog's mouth, or do you let them chase it, jump up and catch it, or even throw it at them? Make your food fun. Don't just pop it into their sleepy mouth. Lazy begets lazy. Put some energy into your food delivery and then you will start to get some energy into your work.

So yes, I like to cheat on lazy days and just use food. But it will be a cold day in hell before you catch me muttering monosyllabic, boring words as I mindlessly stuff food into my dog's mouth.

November 16

Trainers need humility and courage

Be careful of the critical things that you think and say about other people and their dogs. Judge not lest you be judged!

Doggie karma will put you in that same position one day. When we become critical of others, we lose our courage to take our dogs to the opportunities where we were previously critical, unless we know they will be perfect. And whenever my dogs are perfect for a set amount of time, I am experienced enough to know that I am about to be humbled.

Our perfect dogs will knock our ego to the ground when we need it. When you judge others, you will lose your courage to put yourself out there, in case that moment of ego knocking happens.

Dog trainers need humility and courage. If you spend your time judging others, you will lose both. (This lesson is courtesy of my Italian Greyhound.)

November 17

Respect for dogs

We get our first dog because *we love dogs*. We want to love them and have fun with them. But we have no idea who dogs are, or what their potential is. When we get our first dog, we are usually wearing a fabulous pair of rose-coloured glasses.

But then somewhere along the way we come across the dark side of dogs, the side that people never discuss or mention, and our rose-coloured glasses are yanked off our faces. We now have to deal with a new reality, one that we had no idea existed.

Know what your dog is bred for. Know what your breed is capable of. And protect them from themselves.

Dogs do attack people. They do kill other dogs, cats, and very occasionally, babies or children. Know who your dog is so that you can protect him from himself with training and knowledge, and avoid counselling for the remainder of your days.

Respect your dog for who he is. By doing that, you can keep him safe from his genetics.

November 18

Breeds have their own challenges

Trainers with Golden Retrievers and Border Collies tend to say that all dogs learn the same. For those of us who share our homes with alternate breeds, we beg to differ.

Teaching my Italian Greyhound to lie down anywhere, anytime, took me two years. Yes, you heard that right. Fortunately, I was more determined to teach her than she was to not comply! It took two years of hard work to get the consistency and results I needed.

People not experienced with snooty little sighthounds would never believe this to be true. They would judge the training that went into the dog. Those of you with sighthounds have all nodded your heads in sympathy reading my challenge! Teaching my Terrier to come back when she had seen a rabbit was an equal feat.

Each group of dogs has its own quirks, motivators, and strengths. It is up to the trainer to bring out the best in each dog—and to know what that is! If you haven't had to work and live with a breed that just won't do things that regular dogs do, it is hard to wrap your head around the struggles that your client may be having.

November 19

You are mother bear

To socialize your young puppy well, you must make sure that no other dog ever bullies him. You are teaching him that he never has to use his teeth because he doesn't have to—you have his back.

True play between puppies can sound horrendous. Human children play tag, and puppies play "prey and hunter." The hunter is supposed to sound savage. The only way to tell if the game is a good one is to watch the tail and body language of the dog underneath. He should be having as much fun as the puppy on top. Also, the two puppies should keep switching roles of prey and predator. Every ten seconds or so, call your puppy back to you, give him a cookie, and instantly send him back into his game.

If one puppy develops hackles at the base of his tail, or the base of the tail and shoulders, just walk in, and feed three cookies, one by one. This provides a wee mental break, and simmers the energy down to a more tolerable level.

Never allow two puppies to "work things out." Your job is to be a mother bear and let your puppy know that you have his back. It is you and your puppy against the world through all of your adventures together as he grows up. If ever you are advised to let your dog "work it out" in a class, grab your puppy and run for the hills!

And ultimately in puppy play, your goal is to be more interesting than the other dogs. A perfect puppy play session is when all of the little gaffers would rather chase their people than the other dogs. It should look more like a recall game amid puppy chaos, where you cannot lose your little dog.

November 20

Dog lingo translated

Here are a few common phrases that well-meaning dog owners utter all the time:

- **He's friendly.** We want him to be friendly, so we keep testing him and hoping he will be.
- **He's never done that before.** In this specific, precise moment, that is. The last person he bit had red shoes, not green, or the last person he peed on was wearing a skirt, not trousers.

- **Can my dog say "hi"?** This is a question they are really asking themselves . . . because they have never seen him say "hi." He goes straight to biting.

November 21
Retraining fear

When training a fearful dog, you will make improvements, and hopefully get to the point that you think the fear has gone away. Sadly, improvements with fear only last as long as you are willing to train. As soon as you stop training you will see all of your old problems creep back in.

Remember this and don't over-dog yourself or your household. Make sure you always have training time for your dog, even when he is twelve.

November 22
What makes a good dog handler?

Many of us do well when everything is going right. But who can think on their feet when everything is going wrong—and then turn it around?

Can you let go of the error you just made and focus on the new challenge directly in front of you? Does that last mistake make you determined to master the next hurdle, or does it leave lingering doubt in your head about your own abilities? Will you willingly go back out again with some great ideas, determined to start anew, without rehearsing how it all fell apart last time? What we think is what we will do. Staying in the moment, determined to do your job, is key. Remember what you need to do to succeed. Forget what you did wrong.

Remember to stay in the moment as you progress in your training. Let the last challenge be gone from your head, and be determined to master what is directly in front of you. When you master it, you get to jump forward a level. So dig deep, stay in the moment, remove all negative doubts from your head, find your inner determination to nail it this time, remember your jobs, and go and learn your lessons with your dog.

November 23
Book smarts versus street smarts

Too much theoretical knowledge seems to hinder, not help. Now don't get me wrong, we all need theoretical knowledge, but there must be a balance of reading hours to hands-on dog hours. When there is an imbalance, you gain book smarts instead of street smarts. If there is more reading than training, feel and timing seem to get lost, and people instead get stuck in their brains.

Getting stuck in our brains is already a problem for most novice trainers, who get paralyzed in the moment and are unable to make a decision about what they should do. The more well-read you are, the bigger this problem becomes.

We gain a powerful skill from experience—the ability to be able to act instinctively in the moment. This skill, however, can easily be disrupted. One of the most harmful disruptors is too much information. If we know too much background and history, we allow that information to override our judgement and it will work against us.

Please read great books and search dog-training forums online. But keep it in balance with hands-on hours with your dogs. Eliminate superfluous information, and build trust in your ability to be able to handle and act instinctively in the moment.

November 24

Don't think—do

Training people requires that I apply many of the same training skills as I do when working with dogs.

By this, I mean that we must start with the knowledge they come with and the toolbox they arrive with. As trust is earned, and as demand requires, both their knowledge and toolbox will change.

To be honest, it's the clients who do the wrong thing, in a dedicated way, that move ahead quicker in retraining because they learned to do *something*. Clients that sit back and watch the train derail struggle to get out of their brains and into the action. Many owners experience paralysis when what they really need to do is make a quick decision. They are too stuck in their heads and are thinking instead of doing.

No behaviour has ever been changed by prolonged thought, so my new students get full points for whatever they do, even if it was not the best thing, because at least they did something.

Don't wait until you know how to train a dog before you start doing it. Just begin. And learn en route, through trial and error.

The only thing that separates a master from a novice is that the master can see their error within a moment or two, while the novice might take a month to notice it.

You will make errors. Accept it. Embrace it. And enjoy the journey.

November 25

Dogs do as we've taught them

Dogs don't do things to spite us. They do things that they have been trained, or allowed, to do.

If they knew how to do it right, they would.

November 26

The Intuitive Dog struggle

To really understand some words, we must know their opposites; for example, you cannot understand "fast" without knowing "slow." The same goes of appreciating beauty, which has no value if you have never seen ugliness. And likewise, you cannot understand good without knowing bad.

Dog owners will experience different levels of bonding with their dogs. We have dogs who we love, then we have dogs who we connect with on a whole different level; they read our minds, they know our actions before we have even had more than a flicker of a thought of the action. They become a part of us. I call these our "Intuitive Dogs."

The Intuitive Dogs are almost always the "bad dogs" or the dogs who have been a struggle, or made us work way harder than we intended. By pushing us and making us dig deep to get them to become what we need them to be, they truly teach us what "good" means. And in the process of turning your monkey from a challenge into a good dog, you will develop a bond that people with more normal dogs won't comprehend. You must experience both opposites of a word to really appreciate what the power of that word means. Most of the Intuitive Dogs force that lesson upon us.

It is only through experiencing and understanding the bad that we can begin to appreciate the good. If you've only ever had good, you don't have a reference point to be able to fully appreciate exactly how great "good" can be, and the bonding involved in the journey to get there.

And when you do get to work through this with a dog, you will have a bond with a dog that only those who have walked in your shoes will be able to comprehend.

November 27

Forget he's a rescue

The biggest disservice that you can do your rescue dog is remembering that he is a rescue.

Our own minds and hearts cannot give them strength, and what they deserve, when we remember their past. Instead we pity them, and this weakness gets communicated every time that we look at them.

Embrace them as your new dog. Gradually show them the ropes of how dogs behave in your life and home. And work with them so that they can become that dog.

Your first four months are always a honeymoon period when you are getting to know each other. Show them your expectations and needs, and then enjoy the remainder of your lives together.

November 28

Love is not a training tool

I have worked with dogs in the past who I haven't loved. Eventually you find your way to "be" with them. One of these characters is here right now and there is nothing to love. The dog hates people. Hates life. Hates the world. He wants to crawl into a hole forever—and poops if you won't let him. Poo, which I accidentally stuck my hand in tonight, is a minor job hazard.

There is an unwritten expectation that we must unconditionally love dogs. Am I a failure for not only denying this dog love but not even liking him?

If I hate the dog and see him as useless, then yes, I will keep him useless and fail him. But I've only just met him and see no traits that draw me to bond to him, or even like him. To give him unconditional love just because he is breathing seems peculiar. Why would I love someone who hates me? There are no past memories keeping us together. And our new memory of me sticking my hand in his poo certainly isn't helping any.

Love is earned and is not an automatic. I love my dogs. I also have attachments to many of my students' dogs. Some of the rescue dogs that have been in and out of my house before finding their people were loved as my own. But I don't automatically love every dog I meet, nor do I love every person I meet.

If this dog hates me and wants to run from me yet I love him with my whole heart, what does that say about me? Am I worthy of then gaining his love? If someone dislikes me and wants nothing to do with me yet I love them so very much, I come across as weak. Desperate. Lonely. When I have those people in my life, I cautiously avoid them rather than stick around to develop a bond. I'm guessing this dog feels the same.

Let's not confuse love with kindness and respect. I might not like a dog when I first work with him, but I do respect him. And I am kind with him. I gain his trust. Then we move forward on our journey: you find a way to be with him, then you find things that you admire about him and personality traits you can build. And as you do this, suddenly you both like each other a lot. You share mutual growth, respect, and admiration.

But beginning the journey with love when the dog clearly dislikes you is odd. It says more about your own journey of needing personal growth, your weaknesses and failings.

Tonight, my journey began after a long stalemate. The dog hates me a wee bit less. Tonight, we shared emotions other than fear. There was a tiny bit of trust. I saw a look of bewildered amazement at my audacity. I saw a curiosity as he decided to keep an eye on me, the tricky bitch. And twice, for short moments in time, he looked in my eyes.

November 29

Leadership under pressure

When you are feeling pressured, don't confuse your desperation delivered with anger as leadership. While many think it is, it is not. Leaders are always mentally calm and under control.

Leadership is finding your inner calm when under pressure, while learning to concentrate, control your attitude, control your energy and become slower and calmer, all as you manage the pressure of the impending challenge with full commitment and steely determination.

Find your inner power by doing these things. When you live your stressful encounters in slow motion, you will become acutely aware of everything that you are doing, and find that every sense is finely tuned—all while you have full mental focus and calm. This is when you understand leadership under pressure.

If your training is in place, finding the right inner environment is the next step to attaining your goals with your dog.

November 30

Dogs are great people trainers

Dogs are such good teachers, they can train people to do the most bizarre things. And in turn, people make up the most bizarre reasons for what their dogs have trained them to do.

I've heard of dogs who can't travel in the car, can't lie flat, can't have their feet wiped, or can't wear a certain piece of equipment. I have heard of dogs who don't like it when their people hug each other . . . the list goes on.

Our dogs have trained us well. They have taught us that they will not cooperate if _____ (fill in the blank). But really, this has nothing to do with that particular moment. It has to do with our dogs not being willing to take our suggestions. In other words, your dog does not believe you. Or probably more to the point, your dog won't take your suggestion because she doesn't have to listen to what you ask. This all starts with you.

You must be willing to change in order to get a dog that cares what you think. If you don't follow through, all of your wishes and dreams about having a happy, cooperative dog are for naught. They will not be happy and cooperative if you are not willing to change and become worthy of respect.

DECEMBER

December 1

The corporate lawyers of the dog world

Pointy-eared bitches (mostly from the herding breeds) are smart, determined, and have a desire to be in control. They know the ways of the world and how to get around them to get what they need. They enjoy hard work, dislike stupidity, are intolerant of nonsense, have a desire to persuade others for the sheer sake of persuasion itself, and are faithfully devoted to those who are worthy.

These are my favourite dogs of all. They require the most talent to train, and working with them is very gratifying. I love them for their strong ideas and personalities. They are born with strong opinions that they share freely—they truly are the corporate lawyers of the dog world. They are not easy or forgiving. But they are wonderful.

December 2

A tale of two dogs

There is an old fable that tells of two dogs. Both walk into the same room at separate times. One comes out wagging his tail, while the other comes out growling. A woman watching goes into the room to see what could possibly make one dog so happy and the other so mad. To her surprise, she finds a room filled with mirrors. The happy dog found a thousand happy dogs looking back at him, while the angry dog saw only angry dogs growling back at him.

What you see in the world around you is a reflection of who you are.

December 3

Communicate your way to a stress-free dog

Communication of boundaries and expectations will give you a stress-free dog. The word "No" is the key to being kind, and will give your dog happiness in knowing his place rather than having to guess. If you honour your dog with the kindness of rules and fair communication, you can quickly turn your stressed or fearful dog into a functioning and happy member of society.

December 4

Our difficulties define our journey

Our greatest dogs, or at least the dogs who make us look great, are not necessarily our best teachers. The best teachers are normally the ones who make us look bad. They expose every weakness, every hole, but they require us to rise to the occasion.

So, for all of the trainers out there who know plenty, remember that they have learned this from their struggles and difficulties, not from their successes. If you are struggling right now with your dog, seize the opportunity to learn. The dog in front of you has a myriad of lessons to teach you, which apparently you need to learn. And know that you are not on your own in your struggles with your dog. All great trainers have struggled, and it was only by working through their problems that they found greatness.

Rarely do we get more dog than we can handle. Normally, we get just enough dog to completely shove us outside of our comfort zone, make us dig deep, and then find success.

It is important that we all remember this, when confronted with our next difficult dog! Rather than feel defeat after a horrendous walk or training session, take it as a challenge; a chance to learn more and to get better educated.

It is why we all stay hooked year after year, dog after dog. Once you get used to being humbled, the learning becomes addictive.

December 5

The best trainers have mastered acting

Watching the world's best dog trainers at work is a joy. Seeing them become the person their dog needs at precisely the right moment is like watching an actor morph into character. Their emotions change as if at the flip of a switch. Their dogs respond perfectly to the changed emotions, believing every emotion presented to them.

None of this is accomplished through words. It is facial expressions, sounds, and body movements. It is muscle tightening and breathing patterns. It is all the attributes that make a great actor a great actor.

Once you can make your dog feel how you need him to feel, you have become a trainer.

With the exception of a handful of trainers in the world who have this skill mastered, the rest of us will be on a life quest to achieve this. I hope you all enjoy the journey as much as I do!

December 6

Great teachers share the same traits

In high school, I had teachers who told me how great I was and their classes were really fun. I loved those classes . . . but I couldn't tell you what I learned.

Then I got Mr. Fleetwood for math. He never told me how great I was. He was stern, funny, tough, demanding, always grounded, and always calm (except for once when we went too far). He was always willing to help if you put in the effort, but didn't put up with any crap or nonsense—of which I tried to deliver plenty.

I remember one semester watching him transform three kids in his class, me being one of them. I think what started out as detention became voluntary "math camp" every lunch hour, and we wouldn't go away. I've no idea why we were so sensible for this man in our delinquent teen years, but we went voluntarily, learned, struggled, and stayed. Again and again, every lunch hour.

We all knew his intentions and responded accordingly. He never gave false accolades. While he could be fun, his demands far outweighed any levity that came with them. His expectations were high. But he valued each of us, and as he continually pushed us forward, he always showed us respect.

He was a great teacher. He would have been a great dog trainer. Thank you, Mr. Fleetwood.

December 7

Denial won't help you fix it

You cannot train a problem away until you are honest about the likelihood of it happening. You must anticipate and expect for it to happen. As soon as you are at the point of expecting it, you are in the right mental space and physical position to prevent it, or deal with it.

More often than not, my clients test their dogs to see how they will behave, rather than coaching them through the situation. But they attach an expectation to the test; they are expecting their dog to be good and are inevitably surprised when they are bad, and totally unprepared to deal with the aftermath.

If I had a wish it would be that we would always expect our dogs to need help. This bit of reverse psychology puts us in the position to educate our dogs. Expecting it will also make us kinder people to our dogs, as we will realize they are *not* unpredictable or acting out. Our denial was preventing us from seeing the predictable.

When we expect that our dogs will need help, we loosen up, give the correct information to our dogs, and the issue will go away. If you expect the issue to happen, you will always be pleasantly surprised and proud of your dog when he excels and doesn't do it.

If your denial expects for the issue not to happen and it does, again, your relationship will be riddled with disappointment and missed training opportunities.

If your dog has done something twice, expect it a third time in all equivalent scenarios, and be ready so that you can school him through the situation *before* he does it wrong again. By being prepared and expecting it to happen, you will have impeccable timing. And your communication with your dog will be clear and fair.

So always expect, then you can be prepared. Taking our denial-tinged rose-coloured glasses off is sometimes hard to do, but as soon as they are off, you can see situations for what they are, and be ready to train your dog before the problem presents.

December 8
Dogs who don't like their people

Some dogs do not like their people. It is heartbreaking to see, and I feel terrible for the owners though, in reality, most are clueless and have no idea. When I see this, the first thing I force myself to remember is that bad people do not come to me. They are not doing something terrible behind closed doors, even though the dog might be indicating as much. Well, they are. But terrible to their dog does not equal terrible in my world. They are in some way committing a sin toward their dog that is not being forgiven, but more often than not it is an innocent sin, being committed from love and good intentions, as they relate to their dog wrongly.

This is where I fault the internet and TV dog trainers. We can all turn on the TV, watch a show, and go practice the technique that we just saw demonstrated. But—and this is a very big BUT—that technique was designed for that dog, in that moment, with that owner's skill level, on that day. It might be useless a week from now. Or, it could make the dog worse a week from now.

There is nothing wrong with the technique. There might be everything wrong with you applying that technique to your own dog.

Often it can be broken down simply. Are you, as a handler, mentally strong or weak in your relationship to your dog? I am not asking if you can yell loudly enough in a piercing pitch to shatter glass. If you can, that probably means you are weak. More what I mean is, when presented with a problem, can you think calmly through it and never doubt you will get your way? Or do you get flustered and want to run for the hills, even though you make yourself get through it?

Then the other half of that equation is your dog. Is your dog mentally strong or mentally weak? And if he is strong, just how strong? Strong enough that we don't poke the tiger, but rather gently bend him to our way of thinking? Or strong in that we tell him to knock it off, and he leaves happier for the moment? If your dog is weak, first we need to build him up, and probably make him a little bit naughtier as we slowly increase our control. If we only put control on a weak dog, we can create a pressure cooker waiting to explode, and we fail to deal with the conflict he feels that causes him to make his poor choices. In no way have we dealt with his complex emotions, and that is the bigger problem.

Just like raising kids, there are ten thousand ways to teach something. The teaching process itself will work on almost everyone with tweaking needed here or there. But to stop a behaviour that you do not like requires knowing the kid that you are working with, under-standing the motivation that caused him to do what he is doing, and helping with that, in addition to modifying the behaviour.

The moral of this long-winded story: be careful with what you read, hear, or see. If you don't have enough experience to know how to apply it, you might do more damage than good. And take a careful look in the mirror. Are you a strong or weak handler? Is your dog strong or weak? Train him, and yourself, accordingly.

December 9

Find the right trainer for you

Very rarely do I refuse to work with a dog. It has happened, but only once or twice in my 25-plus years of dog training. More often, it's that I refuse to work with the dog's human.

When rehabbing problematic dogs, the bond between trainer and client is complex, and it must be filled with trust (which is earned). The clients need results. And they are relying on the trainer to produce those results. We must incorporate their level of desperation, work ethic, skill, and balance with how long we have until the dog needs a new home or a permanent veterinary appointment. And then we must determine a plan of attack.

When we are getting into this type of heart-wrenching stuff, you must trust your client, and they must trust you. And if they don't, there will be another trainer who has a more suitable personality type for them, so refer out.

There is a trainer for everyone. But we cannot be that trainer for everyone. When a client doesn't fit, send them to the place where they will. Not only will you as a trainer save yourself grief, but you are also helping that client get the help and support they need.

December 10

The deepest bond

We do not bond equally with all dogs. We have dogs that we love, then we have dogs that we connect with on a whole different level: they read our minds, they know our actions before we have even fully thought of them—they become part of us. They are much more intuitive than most dogs and know us better than we know ourselves. We often fail miserably when training these dogs until we get to know ourselves as well as they know us. Really, these dogs are our teachers.

These intuitive characters are almost always the "bad dogs" because we failed them in our training. They are dogs that have been a struggle, or made us work way harder than we ever thought we would have to. By pushing us and making us dig deep within ourselves to keep them "orderly," they teach us to know ourselves better. And in the process of turning these dogs from a challenging monkey to a well-behaved dog, you will develop a bond that most other people won't comprehend—until they get a Soul Dog of their own.

December 11

Rehabilitating reactive dogs

I get asked lots of great questions. This one was from someone seeking advice on how we should handle advanced reactive dogs who are in the final stages of being rehabilitated, and are learning to be semi-free in public: why do I ask them to slow down while going past other dogs when forward momentum helps them?

There are several reasons why I do this. Certain dogs are very quick to excite, to speed up, or to become aroused. These dogs need everything toned down just a smidge. Slowing your momentum just a tiny bit will keep them cognitive.

However, more often, these dogs come with owners who are in a rush. When I was a kid, I used to hold my breath when we were driving through tunnels, hoping the other side was coming soon because I was running out of air. Most of my clients act the same way when they're passing another dog. They want to rush through in a big hurry, hoping they make it to the other side. When I make them slow down, it can help keep the handler cognitive so that they can give the right information to their dogs. It's as if the handler's brain is going at the same speed as their feet. When you slow down your speed, your brain slows down too and it can think.

And finally, I will never go past another dog while the one that I am training is misbehaving. Most (not all) have fear-based aggression. They really don't want to deal with the other dog. They just want to sound very cool, and look the part, as they utter threats. Slow down, be very gentle with your hands, and show them what is right.

If the dog displays good behaviour, they can continue on, and they get the point quickly. If they utter death threats, they have to stay longer until they calm themselves and can stand with neutral weight (balance on all four feet). They can't lean toward the dog. They must stand on their own, still, on the spot.

December 12

Make your food a toy

If you use food in your training, and primarily use food, start making your training a little more fun. Use it like a toy. Fling it at your dog, make her move to get it, and generally make the dispensing of it a whole lot more interesting.

Some of the things that we ask our dogs to do are challenging. We need to give them movement where they can release any mental pressure. Just by tweaking how you dispense your food, you might be able to release that pressure, make it a whole lot more fun, and still get the rewards that food training gives.

And please, please, never place food on your dog's tongue. If you want a dog that gives you effort, at least make them stretch their neck forward to get their cookie!

December 13

Puppies must follow

Following, which turns into coming back when called, is the most valuable thing we can teach our puppies.

If you don't trust them off leash at eight weeks old when you can literally outrun them, then you don't stand a chance when they turn into fast adolescents. Puppies need to be free from the start, so they can explore their world with us as their backup when needed. Where we live in the Pacific Northwest it is safe to do this, and we get to live a glorious free life with our dogs, providing they are trained.

Raising a puppy is a delicate balance between being a protective mother bear, and giving them freedom to make their own choices. (Choices that we know the outcome of in advance and are fully sure will give our puppies the information *they* need for success.)

We need to know when to pick them up and make them safe, and then know when to put them on the ground and help them through an interaction, or when to leave them be, with no commands at all, so that they can work it out on their own, and then have fun chasing us as we run away. This delicate balance seems very challenging for people to grasp.

We need to school our wee babies on the ways of the world and be ready to help and protect when needed. However, we must fight the urge to micro-control, and we must force ourselves to give them freedom (in safe places with distractions of safe people and dogs, where we know we can control the outcome). If we don't ever take off their leashes and allow them the freedom to make the right choices with distractions, they will never have a chance to become the great dogs that they can be.

Having your dog off-leash means that they need to be under your control. When they are tiny, they may not be. But you can outrun them and catch them if needed. Or let them drag a long-line in case they are too fast!

Freedom is the hardest piece to get owners to do. People are too scared to let their babies have freedom going past a neutral person with a neutral dog. If you always call them back, clip them on leash, and march through, you are telling your dog that you have an issue with people and their dogs. This will turn into fear or aggression in many puppies as they age—when really they are just following your lead. They are doing as you have demonstrated through your example.

Instead, coach your wee baby through these moments so that the experience is good for them, and so that they are left knowing that you are still the coolest person in the world.

My clients are showing me that this might be one of the hardest things to learn, but I suppose something as valuable as giving your dog freedom, for a lifetime of enjoyable walks, shouldn't be easy to teach.

December 14
Ready to hear the message

Sometimes it isn't that we don't want to learn, it's that we are not able to hear what is being said.

Just recently I have finally heard what two great trainers have been telling me for several years. I heard them back then. I understood them back then. But the message was so against the grain of my education that, even though I heard and understood, I could not fully buy in.

Then suddenly the light went on.

I see this so often with my students. I can tell them something twenty times, twenty different ways, and a seminar speaker comes in and says the same thing, and they are able to hear.

Being able to pick up the message being given will only happen when you are at that point in your own personal learning. Or trusting your mentors enough to do as they advise, even if it goes against the grain of what you know to be true.

December 15

We don't want robots

The purpose of training is not to create a robot. Training is not designed to take the joy out of your dog, but if you get too strict and demanding with rules, it will.

This is where it comes down to balance. Alternate strict sessions, where you aim for control, with easy days—days when the dog gets to show you how clever she is. In these sessions, the training is set up for her to leave feeling really good about herself. I request less of my dog on these days. At the end of the day, she needs to believe she is the best and strongest Collie in the world.

If I only ever chip away at her self-esteem with rules, control, and, even worse, nagging, eventually there will be nothing left. With this kind of training, over time, the strongest dog can become sad and weak.

Our softer, young, green dogs should still look young and green, while giving us their ears when we ask for them. They should not have the refinement and polish of a trained dog—otherwise, after a few years of training, there will be no dog left. You will have created a sad, deflated pressure cooker.

Don't forget to leave something in it for the dog. The purpose of rules is to give freedom.

December 16

Say what you mean, and mean what you say

There are two parts to this. First, we must be consistent in our requests. If you ask for a sit, don't compromise. If you said your dog's name, expect an ear flick or a look. If we want to be valued in our dogs' lives, then our words must have value for both them and us. Make sure that your requests are actually important enough that you will follow through. And if it isn't important enough—we tend to call that nagging—no one appreciates or needs it, so don't do it.

If it is not important enough to follow up on, don't say it at all.

Second, your spoken words need to be spoken in a manner that your dog can feel what they mean. When you say, "good dog," would a non-English speaking person know that you were happy and proud? Your words need to have emotional value.

Our dogs might not understand English, but they do understand our intent. They know if we want it, and if we believe it.

December 17

Energy: Are you the leader, or are you the follower?

When your dog makes an error, you can respond in a variety of ways with a myriad of different training tools. What matters the most is the energy with which you respond to that action.

Mark Rashid, an American horse trainer, gives us a simple way to think of energy. You and your dog together as a team have a value of ten points. When I am in balance with my dog, he has five points and I have five points. Let's consider five points to be when I have normal-level energy. Now if my dog were to get mega-excited, his energy would go up to a seven. To remain balanced with my dog, in those moments my energy needs to drop to a three. Together, we still have a total of ten points to keep us both in harmony. In no way do I become passive, but I need to soften and calm.

If my animal escalates, I de-escalate. I slow my breathing, loosen my muscles, and physically slow down. I lead the dog by controlling the energy that I lead with. Whichever methodology you choose to train, you respond to your dog's error with this level of energy. As dog trainers, we create the energy balance for our dogs.

Or likewise, if my dog is feeling flat and mouse-like, with an energy level of three points, then I need to pick my energy up to a seven, bringing us to a ten.

When I am retraining reactive dogs, my job is teaching people to not be as reactive as their dogs. If their dog becomes a nine, then I need to guide them to become a one, rather than a nine.

In competition obedience, if a dog is a polite slug, then I need to change its handler's calm, laid-back energy into excitable, fire-breathing energy.

As handlers, we all come with a number for our energy default. My default is a seven out of ten on the energy scale. Training dogs, I must always remind myself to bring my energy down. When unchecked, I can make a hot dog snort fire. What is your default? This is something important to know, because when you run into trouble with your dog, this is probably the first thing that you need to alter to change your problem.

Where some people struggle is they think lowering their energy means becoming a doormat, or raising it means becoming a cheerleading rabbit. It does not. Just by walking a straight line, change your energy from a level two to a five and then an eight. No words are allowed. You need to change your muscles, your eyes, your breathing. Or can you sit in a chair and look at your dog with a two, a five, and an eight?

Can you pick up a book with a two, a five, and an eight?

This balance of energy is something that we must learn to control when things don't go as planned. And the sooner we can respond to our dog's energy change, the easier it is to get her back in balance.

December 18
As you thinketh

What you see in your dog will dictate how you act and behave with your dog.

If you see your dog as weak, you will make him weak. If you see him as timid, you will keep him timid. But if you choose to see him as strong with a blip in the road, you will indeed make him strong. Your dog will become what you see him as, because what you see and believe will dictate how you act and behave.

December 19
Prioritize your relationship

We often attend seminars and learn fabulous new ideas, then go home just to have it all tragically fall apart. Why?

The ideas are great, and more often than not they are correct, but they are also based on the assumption that you have a correct foundation: your relationship with your dog. If your relationship is faulty, no change will be able to last until the bigger problem is fixed.

At the end of the day the only thing that counts is your relationship with your dog. Does he care what you think? Do your own actions and thoughts honour and deserve his devotion? In his eyes, are you the best person in his world? And most importantly, are you fair? If you answered "no" to any of the above, you need to change these key elements before your other solutions can be effective.

Once you have done that, clinicians will be able to help you and the changes will last longer than a week after the seminar is over.

December 20

Goals and dreams

Rather than seeing your goals with your dog as such a big obstacle, you must change your way of thinking. In your heart, you need to know that you will achieve your goal. The dedication and commitment that you are putting in are the necessary steps for you to get to your goal.

When I'm hiking I never wonder if I will get there. Rather I wonder when I will get there. I have the same way of thinking when it comes to my goals. My goals will all be reached—I only negotiate on the "when."

Often the only thing preventing us from achieving our goals is our self-belief: that we ourselves don't believe we can do it. Our biggest hindrance in our training is our way of thinking.

But we all know that we are not training dogs—we are working on ourselves.

December 21

Focus determines destination

Dogs, for the most part, will go where we tell them.

Just like in a car accident, if you skid out on ice and focus on the lamp post that you want to avoid, you will hit it. The object that you focus on is where you will end up. If you look at the dog that you don't want him to eat, you are telling him to go to the dog. Or, if you bend back to look at him because his fears made him balk, your shoulders as they turn are telling him to stay back.

So point your two shoulders and two hip bones and LOOK where you want your dog to go. Don't look where he is going. Look where he "should" go.

More often than not, when our dogs get into trouble, they just went where our bodies were telling them to go. Once we are aware of what our bodies are saying, it is really easy to fix it and to send them where we intend.

December 22

Comfort inhibits growth

As I look around at the kids' soccer games where no team wins, I wonder what these kids will look like as adults. Then I realize I know.

The stress that comes with losing is what builds character. This stress is what gives us strength, determination, a desire to work harder, and a mental toughness. And, as I raise the most perfect Border Collie ever born and continue to enjoy coasting in mediocrity, one of my mentors forces me to remember this.

My dog could not handle hearing the word "no" and having me disapprove of her. Instead of pussyfooting around telling her when she is wrong, I must teach her mental resilience, so that things like this do not bother her. She must learn how to cope with being wrong and care much less than she does now.

This is such a difficult concept to put into words, but I think parents with well-adjusted children will know what I mean. Putting a dog in bubble wrap is a necessary step in raising a young dog, or child. But at some point the bubble wrap must come off, and we must teach them to deal with the stresses of life. If we do not do this, we keep them mentally weak. We must allow them to be exposed to bad moments to build character and to cope.

A mentally weak dog is going to suffer with anxiety, and lack the ability to problem-solve. His only solution to uncomfortable questions will be to use his teeth or to run away. And, he won't be a happy dog in adulthood.

So please prepare your dog for the high school bully, for getting turned down for a job he desperately wants, for being picked last for a team, and for bouncing back when he gets laid-off from his job. Teach your dog mental resilience. Raising a wimp is the easy, feel-good road. But it doesn't feel good for him, he needs to know how to problem-solve.

And ribbons (or cookies!) for participation are helping no one. They don't teach you to work harder, to dig deep, to give it all you have got. Be aware of what you are rewarding. If you reward mediocrity, you will get more of that in the future!

Ultimately dog training is all about honouring the dog. We have to dole out consequences, even when we would rather not, in order to give a dog the mental resilience to have a happy, functional adulthood. You owe it to your dog to prepare him for the trials and tribulations of life.

December 23

Reactivity: Careful of the words you choose

Reactivity is an overused word. I do believe some dogs have reactive aggression. Normally these dogs don't like a nose jammed up their bum and will say as much. They are not looking for trouble, but they won't tolerate their space invaded, nor will they tolerate rudeness. They react to these slights.

But now all dogs that lunge on their leash are being called reactive. What are they reacting to? This relatively new label has taken the onus of behaviour away from dogs. It is not their fault that they are reacting to something that offended them, such as a dog meandering down the street with his owner two blocks away. They could not help it because they are reactive.

Our watered-down terms are not helping dogs any. Let's call it for what it is. *Many* of the aggressive dogs that I work with are just poorly behaved with great temperaments. We still need to coach and guide them, reward them for what we do want and then expect some effort from them.

When retraining your aggressive dog, you should see vast improvement in eight-to-twelve weeks, while the remainder might take a year or more to get.

And some of the truly "aggressive" dogs, once they have realized how fun fighting and reacting can be, will never change and can only be taught to mind their manners. They are defined as "projects," and not "pets."

December 24

When the family doesn't fit

I've been in dogs long enough to know that I know nothing. But it still takes me by surprise when my lack of knowledge hits me upside the head.

I had one of my board-and-trains come in. These are dogs that stay with me Monday to Thursday, and go home on the weekends. This dog had a fantastic, amazing family. There was nothing untoward happening behind closed doors at home.

On the first weekend his family came to pick him up, he was uncomfortable. He was the most tense I'd seen him all week. Week two, I saw more aggression toward them. Week three, he showed evil growling. Week four, he barked at his dad.

This is the sweetest, easiest dog who, for whatever reason, does not like his family. I saw it at the start and then it got worse.

It finally dawned on me. He is a dog off the streets of Mexico, in a foreign country he is the equivalent of a tamed fox. He is a wild dog born into a human family. His dear sweet family wanted a normal dog, as we all do. But they are a young, busy family, trying to get kids to school on time, homework done, dog exercised, and dinners cooked, and he hated the busyness of this life. But it was all he knew—until he came to me. I showed him a different way. And he didn't want to leave.

I've only ever had a handful of Mexican board-and-trains at my place, and they have all ended up loving my place either more or as much as home. I give them clear boundaries, I don't harp on them, I put them "out to pasture" so to speak, as in I do not nag. But they are still kennel dogs. They do not live in my house. And they are not my dogs. Because of this finite line, my training dogs love me, but normally cannot wait to go back home. They want their creature comforts back, and their people who they can boss around, albeit less and less each week.

With this little guy, his family did right. They allowed their dog the divorce he was requesting. He now lives with another client of mine and is happy. Really, really happy.

December 25

New learning from new dogs

Not all dog minds are created equally. I have a brilliant dog with a complex little mind who I want to train for competition obedience. She is a sweet, darling little soul who forces me to think outside the box and question what I know to be true. Here's what we have learned so far:

- Independent inhibited bitches will retreat inward even more when crated. The solution is simple: let them be with you whenever possible.
- Teach overly polite puppies that they can demand things of you.
- The effort and energy needed to compete with an older dog can affect how a sensitive, polite young soul feels about herself. My puppy realized that Reggie, my older German Shepherd, was really important and assumed that she was not.
- Always remember the breed and work diligently at turning them into that, regardless of what you see. Genetics are a powerful thing, and her inner Border Collie was always there waiting to come out.
- In her case, being a Border Collie, the key was to find her inner obsessive control freak and then put that into her work. For her, getting a reward is pleasant, but kind of ho-hum. But earning a reward and not being fast enough to acquire it woke her up.
- Every dog, everywhere, has something that will make him or her go wild. It wasn't food for my puppy, even though she loves food. It wasn't toys, though she loves her toys. It did become swimming. I am trying to make it barking. But what she chose, and what makes her go wilder than wild and willing to put her heart into her work, is the sound of a whip cracking.

I can only imagine what else she will teach me. So far, she has broken many of my "rules" of dog training. I can't wait to see what other twists and turns we encounter together.

December 26

Three reliable behaviours by puberty

By the time your young dog reaches puberty (eight to ten months), she needs to have at least three reliable behaviours, and they should no longer be dependent on a cookie or hand signal. If you are still relying on cookies to get simple behaviours during puberty, this is where you will find yourself in trouble with your adolescent. She's learned to work for the reward, not for you.

Your "down" in the kitchen, yard, and when on leash with no major distractions needs to be 100 percent reliable and you must no longer reward these with food unless it was truly spectacular. Your recall needs to be 95 percent, you should be able to run away yelling and screaming and call your dog off a rabbit, off a deer, or out of a playgroup (for this I make an exception and still allow food). And you should have a reliable settle, so that your dog can down while you talk to someone for at least one minute. It should be simple to walk beautifully with her on a leash, and she should let you cut her toenails.

These need to all be in place, without cookies or toys, by eight to ten months of age to give them the building blocks for adolescence.

Once you have these, continue your training. Ask for more difficult downs and recalls with less help from you, and ask for a down while you talk with craziness going on around you. When your dog succeeds and does what she was already capable of, but it was still impressive, reward it. Then ask for more next time! Don't ever over-face your dog. Your challenges all need to be small and manageable.

December 27

Stress is valuable

I've moved from England to Canada, gotten married, graduated from university, started my own business, purchased a home, and competed with many, many dogs. These have all been incredibly stressful events that pushed me outside of my comfort zone. And these have also been the moments that taught me to be strong, taught me to think through stress, and taught me to go for what I want. They have made me who I am.

Stress is a valuable part of our lives. We do not achieve anything of worth without being stressed before we achieve it.

To deny your dog stress will prevent him from growing. Stress is needed as we graduate from each stage of life to the next.

Our dogs need stress to blossom—however, not too much. Do not overwhelm your dog or be unfair. But if you protect him from all moments of stress, you are also denying him a chance to grow up and become a man. You will keep your dog weak and needy.

Our dogs, like us, need to know that they overcame a problem and can then feel good about themselves for having done so. Dogs do have pride, and they know when they have accomplished something big. It might be as simple as a tiny dog leaping up onto the very high chair with no help, or the dog scared of water braving it to retrieve his ball.

Don't always be too quick to deny them their lessons. If the little bit of frustration and stress can be overcome, allow them to learn the lesson. And if they do need help, offer help but do not do the entire thing for them. For example, I would boost the little dog up two inches and still ask him to leap up on the chair. Or I would move the ball in the water two feet closer and wade out with my dog to go and retrieve it.

None of us became who we are by being spoon-fed. And your dog will never reach his potential until you allow him moments when he can show you how clever he is.

December 28

Your dog in three words

If you had to describe your dog in three words what would they be?

Basil is cheeky, naughty, and proud. Neville would be entertaining, honest, and hard-working. Pippa is adorable, funny, and manipulative. Reggie is funny, powerful, and kind. Ms. Kate, the new project Border Collie, is so very happy, fun, and endearing, with a side of angry.

Do the same for your dog. Are your words equally positive? Or do your words reflect annoyance or pity? Do you feel sorry for your dog? Or does he push your buttons? These words are your beliefs about your dog. These words are what you feel when you think of your dog.

You communicate your beliefs every single time you look into his eyes, kiss his little ears, and pick up his leash. Our energy and body give it away. Basil is my wonder dog, though he has never been easy. He challenged me on everything that I asked of him, still challenges every rule he has, and generally, he is a handful. If Basil might get away with something, he will try. If I were to compare Basil to his younger brother, Neville, Basil is a lot of work. It takes energy and strength to get him to cooperate. I don't compare my dogs, at least I try not to, but after a fabulous smooth-sailing training session with Neville, I can sometimes have begrudging thoughts as Basil adds his own flair and twist to the exercises that he can master with his eyes closed.

Once Basil and I fell into a rut. I started to focus on his very few flaws. This was accentuated by the fact that I was training Neville, who would die rather than be dishonest and tried his hardest, first. Neville gives all he has and wants to please me. Training Basil after my A-student accentuated his naughtiness. As soon as I realized this, I trained Basil first. Then I could enjoy him for the stallion that he is, and I could appreciate his tenacity and determination rather than be annoyed at him for it. When I didn't have the comparison of keener Neville, who would do a back flip simply because I suggested it, it became easy to admire Basil for his attributes.

As soon as you can admire someone, everything changes. Our training became really fun, unpredictable, and a tad wild! I learned to love the challenges that he threw at me. I can't say my Basil has ever changed due to my thoughts, but neither do I want Basil changed. He is perfect as he is. I simply had to train him before Neville to appreciate that.

Be aware of how you look at your dog. It is up to you to decide what you would like to focus on—you can define them as their flaws and previous failures, or as their strengths and thousands of successes. Focus on their positive traits and have positive beliefs about your dog.

December 29

Why does it look easy?

Why does dog training look so easy, even though it is incredibly hard to do?

Each year, for as long as I can remember, I challenge myself to learn something new, something outside of my comfort zone, so I remember how my clients feel. We are now herding sheep.

Recently I watched some great trainers, and I was able to see all of these smooth handlers' minor errors. Yet when I was out with my dog, not only was I not smooth but my errors were not minor.

So how can something be so easy to see, so easy to understand, yet so challenging to do?

There could be several reasons: lack of knowledge; lack of understanding of what to do in a particular moment; and, sadly, sometimes our own egos get in the way with unwanted and unhelpful emotions.

My own struggle was simple: my brain cannot move as fast as the events unfolding in front of me. While I am thinking, the moment has already changed three times. Or, if I push myself to not think and just do (which is the better of the choices), then my body says one thing, and my mouth contradicts it with the complete opposite.

Bless my dog. It is a miracle that she can take any instruction from me.

When I train my dogs, I always break the lesson down into smaller, more manageable pieces. Right now, I'm breaking the lesson down into pieces for me, not her. I'm altering the situation so that fewer variables can get thrown at me. I am trying to prepare myself in advance for expected scenarios so I can fumble through a few unknowns, or just watch in awe as she covers my ass again.

I can survive the first unknown well, and the second, and the third, but by about the fourth I lose my ability to stay in the present. I think each moment gets me a quarter of a second behind, so after a few of these, I'm too far behind and cannot recover. I need to stop her, get my brain into the present moment, then start again.

Soon this won't be happening. Right now, my training is reactive. I'm always reacting to her response, rather than being able to predict her response. Three things will happen in time:

1. I will know her potential responses as the scenario unfolds, so I will be in the moment, steering it where I want, rather than always being reactionary to the outcome.
2. My eye will see things sooner.
3. With experience, the whole event will start to slow down in my brain, and my responses will become more deliberate.

Until that time, I will continue to fumble—and love every moment of it.

December 30
Be honest with your dog

If your dog does something that can simply never happen again, then you need to let him know that or you are being dishonest with him.

So as a New Year's resolution, vow to be honest with your dog. In addition to telling him how perfect he is, be sure to tell him when his behaviour sucks and is life threatening. "No" is not a dirty word. It is one that might just keep him alive.

Being told he is right is mighty powerful. But it does not eliminate the need to clearly tell him when he is doing something dangerously wrong. He needs to hear it from you in a way that is crystal clear, so he doesn't repeat it in the near future.

Somewhere along the way, training got much too complex. It really shouldn't be. Our job is to frequently say, "that was right," and sporadically say, "that was wrong." We are not trying to get Nobel prizes here. We are only aiming for clear communication.

December 31

When did respect become a dirty word?

"Respect" has become a dirty word when it comes to our beloved dogs and it shouldn't be.

In my own life, I would never ask a person for advice if I did not respect them. I would never take guidance from a person if I did not respect them, and I would be cynical if any unsolicited guidance was given. If I do not respect a person, their opinion means nothing to me.

Respect is a beautiful word. You cannot value a person and hold them near and dear to you if you have no respect for them. I love my husband dearly, but equally as important, I respect him.

And I love my dogs and respect them. I respect who they are as dogs, I respect their genetics, their potential, and most of their personality traits. They do the same for me.

I work with many people who do not respect their dogs and many dogs who do not respect their people. Until there is respect, and the mutual flow of trust, a relationship has no value.

At least that is the way it is in my world and my own personal relationships with both animals and people.

INDEX